D1112416

PLANNING AND ORGANIZING
CAREER CURRICULA:

ARTICULATED EDUCATION

PLANNING AND ORGANIZING
CAREER CURRICULA:
ARTICULATED EDUCATION

LARRY J. KENNEKE

Division of Vocational, Adult, &
Community College Education
Oregon State University, Corvallis

DENNIS C. NYSTROM and
RONALD W. STADT

Department of Occupational Education
Southern Illinois University, Carbondale

HOWARD W. SAMS & CO., INC.
INDIANAPOLIS · KANSAS CITY · NEW YORK

FIRST EDITION

FIRST PRINTING — 1973

International Standard Book Number: 0-672-20947-0
Library of Congress Catalog Card Number: 72-92619

To:

Jon and Susan

Brant and Lori

Rory and Ronda

Contents

Foreword

There currently exists a strong emphasis at both the state and national levels to provide career education. Career education should and will allow significant options.

There has been more rhetoric than rational planning relative to career education. The definition of what career education is has been the main point of discussion and dissension. The authors of this book have started with a simple focus; namely, that the place to begin planning and organizing career curricula is around economic careers. This book does not claim that such focus is the only avenue—rather that this serves as a most effective beginning.

Managing Career Education Programs is the title of a previous thrust by members of the same team of writers. It is a practical how-to-do-it book on program management. Now the emphasis in this manuscript has shifted to the curriculum. It stresses articulation from "cradle to grave" for learners in organized educational programs.

Teachers, managers, facilitators, administrators, and other roles of change agents will find assistance in the following pages. It is recommended that readers examine the suggested ways of fusing the academic and the vocations. Such efforts will yield more than disputing the definitions of career education.

If curriculum development is a dynamic process; if curriculums must be rebuilt as we build new learners; if former disenfranchised learners must be included in such processes, then this book is helpful in defining the what, why, and how of relating people and programs. Evaluation of this book will help the readers decide what is best for themselves in the fusion process. The target for this aspect of the curriculum is to give students the ability to select and pursue a livelihood. This ability is possible for the majority of learners, whereas now only a minority have it.

HENRY A. TEN PAS
Director, Division of Adult, Community,
and Vocational Education
Oregon State University

xi

Preface

For more than a decade, there has been need for a curriculum book which is useful to teachers of other than academic or traditional subjects. The literature of curriculum has more or less kept pace with contemporary developments in mathematics, science, and social studies. But, hardback material for occupational and career education has remained in essentially the form it had in the forties—that is, several very similar treatments of trade analysis which are not useful to curriculum builders in new occupational areas or to educators who concentrate on other than grades ten to twelve.

This book takes cognizance of the breadth of offerings in modern educational systems, the trend toward articulated career education curricula along the educational ladder and from agency to agency, and the fact that not all curricula can be developed according to a single set of assumptions and procedures. The book has four sections which parallel the development process and are very closely related, even though they can be used to great advantage independent of one another.

Section one, Transition to Articulated Programs, sets the stage for modern curriculum building. Chapter one, "The Need for Change," underscores some of the very pointed, recent realizations that schooling is not satisfying anyone's goals. Chapter two, "Articulated Programs," defines terms and underscores the need for systematic approaches to curriculum building. If only to understand and consume some of the plethora of curriculum changes at various levels and in the many kinds of institutions, educators must use the systems approach to defining, examining, and adopting curricular components. Chapter three, "Developmental Process" defines an approach, beginning with assessing societal and community needs and ending with the management of resources. Each of five steps in the overall process is presented in detail with practical illustrations and examples.

Section two, Structuring Experiences, is the heart of the book. Four organizational schemes are presented in successive chapters. These are: (4) Occupational Cluster Curricula, (5) Technological Categories, (6) Business System Analyses, and (7) The Integrated Curriculum. Each of these is a relatively new approach to curriculum building. Each has advantages in certain situations and disadvantages in others. Unlike most, this book describes each in detail, giving underlying rational, analytic methods, and illustrations from practice. Local education agency professionals are charged to use approaches which are appropriate to their level, specialty, community, and other peculiarities. Each chapter in this and other sections includes lists of activities, discussion questions, and references. These are obviously useful in college classes but also can be used by individuals or groups who are building curricula in schools and colleges.

Section three, Developing Learning Experiences, deals with the second and third levels of detail, i.e., what learners will do and how professionals will facilitate learning. Chapter eight, "Planning for Instruction," describes how several kinds of professionals and others should be involved in the instructional planning, evaluation, and systems redesign process. The chapter is based on the premise that instructional planning at the second level of detail should respond to student and community needs while functioning in concert with larger curricular and program goals. Chapter nine, "Analysis Procedures," describes several ways, rather than one way, to view the world of work to arrive at learning experiences. These are traditional occupational, content, concept, job, trade, and task analysis. Many examples are used to show how professionals can use the results of one or more (appropriate) analysis procedures to do an instructional analysis, i. e., to organize material into sequential learning experiences for classrooms, laboratories, work sites, and homework. Chapten ten, "Organizing an Instructional Strategy," describes steps which facilitate learning. The five steps of instructional planning are described with examples which demonstrate how professionals who have used different kinds of analyses for selecting learning experiences can plan unit, weekly, and daily plans. Sample formats for units, weekly, and lesson plans are illustrated and evaluated, in light of varying purposes and requirements.

Section four, Assessing, Staffing, and Managing Career Programs, treats three critical aspects of contemporary professional work. Chapter eleven, "Assessment of the Program," introduces teachers to tasks which might otherwise confront them unexpectedly. Program element analyses which have been done by special commissions, professional associations, and other agencies are described so that professionals may be prepared to participate in similar studies. Accreditation as it affects career education and State agency-conducted evaluations of local career programs are illustrated. The professional is admonished to foresee and prepare for participation in several kinds of assessment in the age of accountability. Chapter twelve, "Staff Models for Occupational Programs," speaks for a differentiated staffing model in keeping with the social and technical characteristics of career education. The roles and functions of master teacher, staff teacher, associate teacher, and technical para professionals are defined. Advantages for recruiting, professional development, and other professional goals are made obvious. Chapter thirteen, "Establishing Classroom and Laboratory Managerial Policy," shows the professional how to "put it all together." Instructional data collection, student personnel services, safety programming, and facilities management are treated in keeping with principles developed in earlier chapters. Sample forms for assigning students to laboratory maintenance, for inventory, for budgeting, and other management tasks are shown. This final chapter exposes professionals to the "extra" skills which are essential to assuring that learners have the efficient and effective environment they deserve.

The class, curriculum committee, or individual which uses this book will be led to new understandings re the process of curriculums renewal. People will be at once awed by the magnitude of major dimensions of the problem and warmed by their ability to secure helpful resources and cope with professional problems.

Section One

Transition to Articulated Programs

The concept of career education holds great promise as a potential method of better meeting the developmental needs of youth and ill-fitted adults. To realize this vast potential, the educational planner must master several fundamental precepts. This section will serve to provide the learner with answers to such critical questions as:

1. What is the need for development of a completely articulated career education program?
2. What are the specific characteristics of a totally articulated career education program?
3. What procedures are required for the development and implementation of an articulated program?

These and other questions are treated in three chapters:

Chapter 1. The Need for Change

Chapter 2. Articulated Programs

Chapter 3. Developmental Process

Chapter One

The Need for Change

INTRODUCTION

This chapter makes a plea for change by answering three questions.

- What is wrong with traditional occupational education programs?
- What stance has been taken by various governmental agencies with regard to improving instructional programs?
- What changes have educational professionals proposed for traditional occupational education programs?

Several thousand articles, chapters, and books have been written about problems in contemporary education. Prescriptions for improving the educational enterprise range from improving instruction through the use of media, such as films, to revision of the basic educational process. Pucinski described the magnitude of recent concern quite appropriately when he said:

> Public education, for the most part, has been long on rhetoric and short on results. Many of the most stalwart, aggressive, inventive change agents have eventually found themselves "killed off" by the system—victims of bureaucratic freeze-outs . . . scorn and apathy from colleagues and superiors, opposition from the public, or sheer exhaustion from the magnitude of the task. Discouraged at expending so much energy with such disappointing results many have ended up modifying their dreams or retreating to other areas. This tragic trend must be halted; we must develop the courage to change.[1]

The educational process has remained virtually unchanged over many decades. Regardless of the reasons for the lack of innovation, something must be done. The *First Annual Report* of the National Advisory Council on Vocational Education stated:

---

[1] Roman C. Pucinski and Sharlene Pearlman Hirsh, eds., *The Courage to Change* (Englewood Cliffs, N.J.: Prentice-Hall, 1971), p. 3-4.

The violence that wracks our cities has its roots in unemployment and unequal opportunity. Those who have no jobs in an affluent community lash out in anger and frustration. Young men and women who cannot qualify for decent jobs distrust the society which reared them. Dissidents speak with the voice of rebellion; campus and inner-city revolt reaches into our schools. Our Nation seethes.

Racial unrest, violence and the unemployment of youth have their roots in inadequate education. Each year the ranks of the school drop-outs increase by three-quarters of a million young men and women. They enter the job market without the skills and attitudes employers require. They and the millions of others who are underemployed—among these the students who are graduates of our high schools but who are inadequately prepared for anything—are tragic evidence of the present inadequacy of our educational system.

The failure of our schools to educate to the level of adequate employability nearly 25% of the young men and women who turn 18 each year is a waste of money, as well as of human resources. The Nation supports a galaxy of remedial programs some of which have cost as much as $12,000 for every man or woman placed on a job. Those who remain unemployed may cost us $4,000 or more per year in welfare support for themselves and their children, who will repeat the dreary, costly cycle.

The costs, the blighted lives, the discontent, the violence, and the threat of revolution are needless. Schools can prepare young people to realize their potential. Each city in the country succeeds every year with some of its students, in even the most depressed parts of the city. Why is success not universal? Why is the failure rate so high?

The reasons are attitude, program and money.[2]

Attitude is largely a matter of national concern. The "everyone must go to college syndrome" must be alleviated. Dedicated efforts by all manner of education professionals, as well as the general citizenry, are essential to changing attitudes toward vocational education in a changing society.

Michael H. Moskow, Assistant Secretary of Labor, underscored the college student dilemma at the Southeast Los Angeles Conference on Management and Higher Education:

---

[2] National Advisory Council on Vocational Education, *Annual Report* (Washington, D.C.: National Advisory Council on Vocational Education, 1969), p. 1.

. . . the point I want to stress is that even a balancing of supply and demand represents a much gloomier picture for college graduates than in the earlier period.

Teaching is one occupation where the long run job outlook seems to be on a downtrend. Since the teaching profession has historically claimed a large portion of college graduates, the drying up of this source of demand will have major repercussions on overall job prospects for college graduates, especially for women.[3]

It is pointless to assume that college graduation is good in all instances. *Money* is largely a matter of political device. Only in response to constituent hew and cry can legislators support increased funding for vocational education. Constituent concern will be evidenced only as attitudes are changed.

Program is the one component of change over which the frontline teacher has immediate control. Vocational programs must be changed to meet the needs of the nation. With regard to program, the National Advisory Council has said:

Within high schools the student should have multiple choices. A separate vocational school or a distinct vocational track should be exceptions, not rules, in a technical and changing society. Communication and computation skills become relevant in a context that relates them to an employment objective. All students must be allowed to move into and out of vocational-technical programs and to select mixtures of vocational-technical and academic courses. Students should be released from school to acquire employment experience, and should then be taken back for further education. Students should be able to go to school the year around. It is inconceivable that we plan to continue to let our school plant lie idle three months of the year. Rural schools must give their students opportunities to train for urban jobs, since many of them are bound for the city.

Those who do not acquire a job skill before leaving the 12th grade must have access to a full range of post-high school programs to train them for employment at their highest potential. Vocational and technical programs should be readily available to most adults through adult high schools and community colleges. The rapidity with which Americans will change jobs in

---

[3] U.S. Department of Labor, "Moskow speaks on the Job Outlook for College Graduates," USDL 72-561, *News* (Washington, D.C.: Office of Information, August 15, 1972), p. 2.

their lifetimes must be matched by the variety and accessibility of training programs through which new skills and subject matter can be learned at any age in every locality.

Changes in the elementary curriculum are also needed. Exploration of the world of work should begin early. Respect for work and pride of workmanship are essential in a trillion-dollar economy. Direct job-related instruction, starting in the upper elementary grades, should be made available for some pupils.

We recommend that substantial Federal funds be allocated to support curriculum development, teacher training, and pilot programs in vocational education. No Federal investment will bring a higher return. We challenge State and Local governments to throw off old habits and take a hard, fresh look at what they are doing in vocational education. We urge the public to watch carefully, and to demand and support the innovations that work.[4]

Change of this magnitude will require full commitment on the part of faculty and administrators in public schools. The specific nature of this commitment has been clearly defined in *Vocational Education: The Bridge Between Man and His Work.*

The second step in the commitment involves the total faculty of the school community. This is to say that the sixth grade social studies teacher, the junior high school physical education teacher, the high school mathematics teacher, and the junior college physics teacher, and all other teachers have significant roles to play in the vocational development of an individual in addition to the teacher whose instructional responsibility is directly related to the skills and knowledges required in an occupational setting. This is not a new concept in education, but never before have the occupational goals of students been so totally dependent upon their total education.

This is a difficult task because all members of the educational family must give up some of their cherished patterns of instruction and work together as a team to achieve one of the immediate goals—an appropriate integration of subject matter.

The rationale concerning the integration of subject matter is less controversial than the methods and procedures of achieving the goal. It seems obvious that an approach to implementation requires that a number of changes occur in both the so-called general part of the curriculum and the vocational part. The nature of the resulting mix should have more of the characteristics

---

[4] National Advisory Council on Vocational Education, 1969, p. 2-3.

of a mechanical mixture rather than a chemical combination; the first retains the identity of the elements mixed, the latter produces a new substance with characteristics quite foreign to the original elements.

The desirable goal is a situation in which the total educational effort can contribute to the total vocational education of students, and at the same time leave enough room for the hardcore instruction in vocational education which leads to employment.

It is relatively easy to develop a program of studies that tends to provide liberalizing forces, which are the root of every student's learning experience. Similarly, it is relatively easy to organize a program of studies leading to employment in a single occupation or a cluster of occupations. The difficult task is to develop a program involving both of these essential aspects of education, and to get the right combination of these to meet the needs of each individual student.

This is not wild theory, it has already been carried out by some schools and with considerable success. The students like it because the flexibility of the system makes it possible for education to "fit" them rather than the necessity that they "fit" the system. Such a commitment negates the old description of the curriculum as a race to be run by the bright, the dull, the lame, and the blind, and those that finish on time are educated. Teachers like the system because it provides so many opportunities for teaching to become the exciting profession that it *should be*.[5]

It is up to individual professionals to promote needed changes in occupational curricula. The frontline teacher has not heretofore had the training and resources to do much more than replicate past practice.

Very little effort has been devoted in teacher education to developing professionals with competencies in the articulated career education area. Sidney P. Marland substantiates this contention.

Let me add a third basic component of the career strategy: teacher education. Perhaps we will come to this later, but we see a need for a very large effort in helping teachers at all levels increase their capabilities to relate their teaching to the career theme.[6]

---

[5] Advisory Council on Vocational Education, *Vocational Education:The Bridge Between Man and His Work* (Washington, D.C.: U.S. Government Printing Office, 1968), p. xxiii.

[6] "Marland on Career Education," reprinted from DHEW Publication No. (OE) 72-52, *American Education* (Washington, D.C.: Office of Education, November, 1971), p. 21.

In this book, the present authors have tried to provide preservice and inservice teachers with several curricular organization and development patterns. These patterns are based on a totally articulated curriculum with occupational education and career development as the central unifying theme. Only through an articulated effort may students systematically analyze career opportunities and exercise valid decision-making activities, leading to entry-level employability by the time of high school graduation.

The proponents of Career Education and many curriculum innovators have asserted the importance of an articulated approach to schooling. In many cases, proposals re articulated curricula have not been specifically verbalized as such. Fortunately, career education is offered up as an articulated curriculum vehicle. Moskow has stated that "Career Education, which is still in the development stage, would provide information on job alternatives at the very start of school and build basic subjects from grades 1 through 12 around career opportunities and requirements in the labor market."[7]

Marland also has stated:

> During the first six years of his schooling, the youngster would be made familiar with these various clusters of occupations and what is involved in entering them. In grades seven and eight, he would concentrate on learning more about those particular job clusters that interest him most. In grades nine and ten he would select a job cluster to explore in some depth, an experience that would include visiting places where this kind of work is going on, trying his own hand at certain basic skills, and in general getting practical experience in what that line of work involves. In grades 11 and 12, he would pursue his selected job area even more intensely, in terms of one of three options: acquiring skills that would enable him to take a job immediately upon leaving high school; taking a combination of academic and on-the-job courses in preparation for entering a post-secondary institution that would train him as a technician, for instance; or electing a somewhat similar combination of courses in preparation for a professional degree from a four year college and beyond.[8]

From these and many other segments of the literature, it is patently clear that a 1-through-12 career education curriculum assumes a high degree of articulation from grade level to grade level.

---

[7] U.S. Department of Labor, p. 3.
[8] "Marland on Career Education," p. 2.

Speaking to a "curriculum continuum," Harold G. Shane has said:

> For generations most education in the U.S. has been divided
> into arbitrary segments. It also has been given labels such as
> "the elementary school" and "the secondary school." A century
> or more ago, in view of what was then known about teaching and
> learning, and when the school population was expanding rapidly
> in urban centers, such grade-level divisions instituted for adminis-
> trative purposes made a great deal of sense. However, education
> now has reached a level of sophistication at which serious
> thought can and should be given to the development of a care-
> fully reasoned and well-designed continuum of experience for the
> learner, one which can replace the disjointed divisions of the
> past and the present.[9]

Sobol also described the need for articulated programs:

> The several current revolutions in American society make
> our time one of abrupt and polarizing discontinuities. The gaps
> in our perception and experience are so divisive and fragmenting
> that it is now an open question whether we can survive with our
> social health and sensibilities intact.
>
> As the revolutions continue, they produce fissures in the
> foundations of our public schools which demand a broader kind
> of articulation than schoolmen are used to considering.[10]

Agricultural educators at the post-secondary level have wrestled
at length with articulated curriculum articulation. Paul E. Hemp has
described the concerns of vocational agriculture professionals with regard to articulation.

> Community and junior colleges which offer vocational and
> technical education in agriculture have more than a passing con-
> cern with articulation problems. Since these institutions offer
> "transfer" courses in addition to career-oriented courses, they
> must develop an articulation program with four-year institutions.
> Equally important is the articulation that should be developed
> between post-secondary programs in agriculture and the voca-
> tional agriculture programs in secondary schools. No post-
> secondary program can survive the scrutiny of vocational edu-

---

9 Harold G. Shane, "A Curriculum Continuum: Possible Trends in the 70's," *Phi
Delta Kappan*, Vol. 51, No. 7 (March, 1970), p. 389.

10 Thomas Sobol, "The Broader Meaning of Articulation," *Phi Delta Kappan*, Vol.
53, No. 1 (September, 1971), p. 25.

cators and employers unless it is articulated with the demands and needs of the business world.[11]

From the foregoing it is clear that the concept of articulated curricula is not new. However, professional development for preservice and in-service people has not dealt in appreciable measure with articulated programming. The new concepts of career education, innovation for traditional occupational education programs, and all of formal education rely heavily on the articulated curriculum approach. If career education goals are to be achieved, educational personnel of all ilks must be thoroughly grounded in the theory and practice of articulated programming.

SUMMARY

If innovation is to be the vogue in occupational education programs throughout the United States, an essential ingredient of such change, i.e., articulation, must be understood by professionals. The intent of this chapter has been to emphasize the importance of articulated programming. The following questions have been answered:

1. What is wrong with traditional occupational education programs?

Changing societal needs and the changing nature of schooling have left most educational programs open at the midsection. In *Man, Education, and Manpower,* Grant Venn put the matter succinctly.

Education has been too successful in doing what society has expected it to do. Two centuries of success tend to keep pressure on the schools to do more and better what they are presently doing. When weaknesses appear, the response is to increase the resources, change the methodology, or increase the effort. The generally accepted belief is that more of the same will result in continued success.

Unfortunately the concept of what education is or what the school should do is the same for the most successful citizens as well as for the least successful. For example,

Most people believe that schools that are the most selective have the highest quality.

They believe that the percentage of graduates going on to college is a mark of a school's quality.

Most people prefer that the school their child attends contain mainly students that are like their own child.

---

[11] Paul E. Hemp, "Articulation: A Responsibility and a Challenge," The *Agricultural Education Magazine,* Vol. 43, No. 1 (July, 1970), p. 3.

They believe it is better that their child attend school without having to earn while he learns.

They want the schools to prepare their children for subsequent schooling.

Most people believe that schools that teach occupational skills are of low quality.

That fact is that our schools today do most of the things that people want them to do and do them quite well.

But the questions that become more pertinent everyday are: What must the schools be doing for the one-third of today's youth who are handicapped in finding employment and who encounter serious problems in making the transition from school to work? And what is the school's role in preparing the needed manpower in a society that by 1975 will find only 5 percent of the work force engaged in unskilled work?

The job the schools must do in a new society must be different than it has been in the past. Technology has created a new relationship between man, his education, and his work—a relationship that places education squarely between man and his work.[12]

2. What stance has been taken by various governmental agencies with regard to improving instructional programs?

Research and development activities are at all-time high levels in education. The USOE and various regional and state agencies are developing totally new approaches to education. However, effective change depends on classroom teachers who are afforded opportunity to innovate as student needs dictate and new approaches to education are developed.

Improvements in instructional programs can only come about as lay attitudes toward education are changed, as programs are redesigned, and as money is made available for development.

3. What changes have education professionals proposed for traditional occupational education programs?

The Vocational Education Act of 1963, the 1968 Vocational Education Amendments, and the 1972 Education Amendments emphasize development of relevant occupational education offerings. Many state departments of vocational education have been channeling resources in the curriculum and program development phases of occupational education.

---

[12] Grant Venn, *Man, Education and Manpower* (Washington, D.C.: The American Association of School Administrators, 1970), p. 11-12.

The career education concept has had greatest influence on occupational education in recent years. The concept of a K-through-12 or K-through-adult, articulated curriculum, based on career development as a central theme, has caused many frontline professionals to contemplate and initiate changes at the course and program levels.

Articulation is a significant characteristic of nearly all contemporary occupational education program innovation. Traditional programs are enhanced as the articulation function is improved. A major key to program quality, i.e., to student success, i.e., to entering and maintaining employment in various occupational establishments, is articulated curricula.

ACTIVITIES

1. Prepare an annotated bibliography of books, articles, and research reports related to the topic of articulation.
2. There has been much recent research and commentary in the area of innovation and change. Prepare a review of this literature. Analyze various change models that have been developed.
3. Develop and maintain an up-to-date file on current innovations in occupational and career education.

DISCUSSION QUESTIONS

1. What types of public relations programs can be developed by local occupational education personnel to apprise the local community of the need for career education programs? Who, at the local school level, should be responsible for the public relations function?
2. What is your understanding of career education as defined by Sidney P. Marland?
3. In what types of activities may teachers engage to assure a smooth articulated curriculum effort for career education?
4. What are some of the major reasons for developing articulated curriculum offerings?

BIBLIOGRAPHY

Gross, Ronald, and Gross, Beatrice, ed. *Radical School Reform.* New York: Simon & Schuster, 1969.

Havelock, Ronald G. *Planning for Innovation Through Dissemination and Utilization of Knowledge.* Ann Arbor, Michigan: Center for Research on Utilization of Scientific Knowledge, 1969.

Hoyt, Kenneth B., Evans, Rupert N., Mackin, Edward F., and Mangum, Garth L. *Career Education, "What It Is and How to Do It."* Utah: Olympus, 1972.

Law, Gordon F., ed. *Contemporary Concepts in Vocational Education.* Washington, D. C.: American Vocational Association, 1971.

Pucinski, Roman C., and Hirsch, Sharlene P. *The Courage to Change, "New Directions for Career Education."* New Jersey: Prentice-Hall, 1971.

Purpel, David E., and Belanger, Maurice. *Curriculum and the Cultural Revolution.* Berkeley, California: McCutchan, 1972.

Rogers, Everett M., and Shoemaker, F. Floyd. *Communication of Innovation.* New York: Macmillan, 1971.

Silberman, Charles E. *Crisis in the Classroom, "The Remaking of American Education."* New York: Random, 1970.

Taylor, Harold. *Students Without Teachers.* New York: Avon, 1970.

U. S. Department of Health, Education, and Welfare. *Annual Report of the U. S. Commissioner of Education, Fiscal Year 1971.* Washington, D. C.: Government Printing Office, 1972.

U. S. Department of Health, Education, and Welfare. *Education for a Changing World of Work.* Benjamin C. Willis, Chairman. Washington, D. C.: Government Printing Office, 1963.

U. S. Department of Health, Education, and Welfare. *Reports on the Implementation of the Vocational Education Amendments of 1968.* Carl D. Perkins, Chairman. Washington, D. C.: Government Printing Office, 1971.

U. S. Department of Health, Education, and Welfare. *Vocational Education, "The Bridge Between Man and His Work."* Martin W. Essex, Chairman. Washington, D. C.: Government Printing Office, 1968

Venn, Grant. *Man, Education, and Manpower.* Washington, D. C.: American Association of School Administrators, 1970.

Chapter Two

Articulated
Programs

INTRODUCTION

Those who would develop and manage articulated career education programs must have ready answers for the following questions.

- What is career education?
- What is occupational education?
- What are the specific characteristics of an articulated program?
- How can articulated programs be implemented?
- What implications do articulated programs hold for the planning of career-oriented educational experiences?

CAREER-OCCUPATIONAL EDUCATION DEFINED

Career education is an integral part of the preschool-through-life education of every man, woman, and child. It establishes a new marriage and balance of traditional vocational, general, and college preparatory curricular components in hopes of maximizing opportunities for self-actualization, forming desirable attitudes toward employment, and developing salable skills and knowledges. Overall career education goals include:

A. Development of varying levels of competence re performance and understanding of unique and specific job requirements.
B. Integration of work activities with individual life styles and patterns in order to enable learners to select future goals and assume occupational roles benefiting their interests, aspirations, and abilities.
C. Creation of desirable work habits and attitudes toward all manner of work and productive effort.

United States Commissioner of Education, Sidney P. Marland, put the matter succinctly when he stated that career education is designed to

31

"... give every youngster a genuine choice as well as the intellectual and occupational skills to back it up. Career education is not merely a substitute for "vocational education" or "general education," or "college-preparatory education." Rather it is a blending of all three into an entirely new curriculum. The fundamental concept for career education is that all educational experiences ... curriculum, instruction, and counseling ... should be geared to preparation for economic independence, personal fulfillment, and an appreciation for the dignity of work ... Thus career education will demand no permanent bondage to a single career goal. Rather it will reveal to students the great range of occupational options open to them and help them to develop positive attitudes toward work.[1]

Hence, career education is a kindergarten-through-life continuous process which seeks to create and maintain an informed and competent citizenry with wholesome attitudes toward, and successes in, work and other aspects of living.

The primary concern of this book is description of ways to develop integrated career education programs. If career education is to be realized, selected old and new curriculum components must be cast in new forms which will prepare youth and ill-fitted adults for "attache case professions as well as lunch box occupations."[2] Conventional vocational-technical and practical arts education components, such as agriculture, business, home economics, industrial arts, and trade and industrial, must be assessed to determine potential contribution to career education objectives and put together in new forms, together with curricular elements yet to be identified.

Existing components should be studied for their value in providing learners with experiences which lead toward realistic career goals and opportunities. Course offerings in each of the service areas should be evaluated for contribution to various levels of awareness and competence within the broad categories of:

Benchwork occupations
Clerical and sales occupations
Farm, fishery, and related occupations
Machine trades occupations
Processing occupations
Professional, technical, and managerial occupations

---

[1] Sidney Marland, "Career Education" (paper read at the 33rd session of the International Conference on Education, Sept. 1971).
[2] *Ibid.*

Service occupations
Structural occupations

If, in fact, current offerings do not lead toward career fields which encompass occupations with promising futures, they should be revised or deleted.

Upon completion of this task, attention should be directed toward elimination of traditional, artificial, pedagogical groupings which have led to fractionalization and subsequent departmentation. Such action would result in an integrated educational unit entitled occupational education. Herein conventional areas of agriculture, business, home economics, industrial arts, trade and industrial, etc. must put aside vested and divergent interests and strive collectively to achieve articulated program objectives. Occupational education is a composite of experiences leading to employability. It is one segment of a three-pronged program for maximizing self and occupation.

PROGRAM CHARACTERISTICS

An articulated program is concerned with life-role education which will reveal to young and old alike the multitude of career opportunities awaiting them. The kindergarten-through-life model (Fig. 2-1) pro-

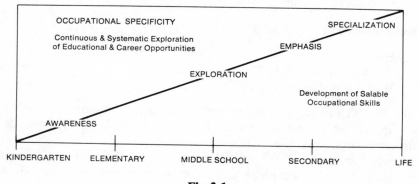

ARTICULATED OCCUPATIONAL CONTINUUM

OCCUPATIONAL SPECIFICITY

Continuous & Systematic Exploration of Educational & Career Opportunities

SPECIALIZATION

EMPHASIS

EXPLORATION

Development of Salable Occupational Skills

AWARENESS

KINDERGARTEN   ELEMENTARY   MIDDLE SCHOOL   SECONDARY   LIFE

Fig. 2-1

vides a graphic illustration of a continuum of experiences which enables learners to enter, exit, alter goals, and reenter programs wherever and whenever individual interests, aspirations, needs, and competencies dictate. The program serves the elementary school child, high-school graduate and/or dropout, veteran, the automation casualty, and/or the retiree seeking part-time employment. It is characterized by four inter-dependent occupational levels: (a) awareness, (b) exploration, (c) em-phasis, and (d) specialization. Progress through each level is accom-plished by completion of real and simulated work experience, carried out in a setting composed of classroom, laboratory, community, busi-ness, industrial, government, and home environs. Hence, program activity moves beyond the confines of the classroom to encompass the courthouses, railroad yards, financial institutions, retail establishments, and manufacturing complexes of the nation.

Central to program success is a concentrated and comprehensive guidance effort, designed to assess at all levels of occupational maturity, individual aptitudes, interests, and temperaments. Such action is carried out in concert with the day-to-day occupational, general and college preparatory instructional effort, not isolated from work-related activ-ities. Real and simulated experiences acquaint learners with broad cate-gories of occupations, as well as specific jobs. Coordinated effort at every level identifies and clarifies questions re unique and specific jobs and their related:

Earnings,
Employment location (geographic),
Preemployment and postemployment requisites,
Trends and opportunities, and
Working conditions.

Experiences also clarify work roles in terms of:

How it gets done,
What gets done, and
Why it gets done.

The breadth and depth to which work roles are investigated is dependent on individual differences. Certainly the third-grade child, and the itinerate farm worker demand systematic exposure to the realities of the work environment at a level different from that of a recent college graduate. It is this sensitivity and ability to meet varying needs which makes the articulated program work well.

Let us now examine, in turn, each of the four levels of the program model. Although each level will be presented and discussed separately, in practice, one level leads without division to the other. Note the lowest level, awareness, in the diagram in Fig. 2-1. Whereas this level has primary application for kindergarten to sixth-grade children, it is of equal importance to those individuals who, regardless of age, do not possess advanced levels of occupational awareness and expertise.

This level seeks to enable learners, regardless of age, to become aware of the impact and consequences of work in society. It further seeks to illuminate and emphasize their relationship to the world of work. Representative objectives of the occupational awareness level are:

1. To discover the interests of each learner and then demonstrate their relationship to the world of work.
2. To instill dignity of labor.
3. To start building a concept of self-worth and responsibility.

These objectives can be partially achieved through a cooperative instructional venture which includes the services of general and occupational education personnel, committed and informed parents, representative local employers, governmental representatives, and concerned citizens. Young and old alike are exposed to many work roles through contacts with real people, engaged in actual productive activities. Simulated work experiences are carried out in programs which link the three "R's" of general education to the life style of each individual. Both theoretical and practical knowledge are communicated through activities wherein learners:

A. Acquire knowledge of mathematics and related occupations through interaction with computer terminals and allied personnel.
B. Assume roles of consumers and sellers in a department store and bargain over the cost of goods.
C. Develop basic reading skills by studying elemental job descriptions.
D. Develop understandings of human, social relationships through visitation to many and varied work environs.
E. Play the role of filling-station operators, loan officers, heads of families, public officials, lawyers, etc.

Elementary, business, English, industrial arts, and social science teachers work collectively to organize role-playing activities, class visitations, videotapes, guest lecturers, library work, experiments, discussions, etc., so that learners might better understand themselves and the employability milieu.

The second level seeks to provide increased self-understanding through occupational exploration. It is a logical extension of the awareness stage and incorporates similar resources and personnel. Its major concern is for examination and evaluation of information about career opportunities and the clear and patent needs of a productive society. Through such experiences, learners are assisted in decision-making endeavors. Career education enables them to alter and plan futures in accordance with realistic personal goals and with the dynamics of changing employment requirements.

Assumptions of the rationale for this level, the junior high or developmental level, suggest that:

All students should have an opportunity to explore the broad spectrum of the world of work.

All students should have opportunity to develop self-concept.

All students should have experiences in meaningful decision making, and in accepting responsibility for their own decisions.

The junior high school years are a time of high potential for developing an awareness of relevant factors to be considered in decision making.

Career choice and its implementation is a developmental process.

A challenging experience-centered program that stimulates creative individualism is valid for junior high-age students in that they become more aware of both strength and weaknesses, and reflect more positive interests.

A program that provides opportunity for acquiring self-understanding and knowledge of the world of work, in combination, will contribute much toward helping youth and ill-fitted adults prepare for their place in a complex socioeconomic world of reality.

More adequate educational goals and tentative career choices may be established by students, as a result of the experiences provided through an organized pedagogical approach.[3]

Whereas this concept may well be applied to the middle-school grades, it is also appropriate for workers displaced by technological and/or economic change.

Sample objectives of the exploration level are:

1. To develop self-understanding.
2. To relate educational experiences to the planning of occupational goals.

---

[3] Oregon Board of Education, "Teachers Guide to SUTOE" (Salem, Oregon: The Board, 1969), Mimeographed.

3. To understand individual roles in the economic system.
4. To understand the relationships of data, people, and things to productive effort within the world of work.

Exploratory occupational experiences might involve a cooperative venture wherein learners participate in activities directly and indirectly related to the laying of a concrete foundation for a building. Pupils would engage in both preparation and on-site construction activities. The expertise of mathematics, physical science, social science, industrial arts, and business teachers, coupled with the competencies of a general contractor, ready-mix operator, form carpenter, and cement finisher provide for realistic interaction with elements of the real world. Guided by such personnel, learners participate in real and simulated activities which involve:

Calculation of required cement yardage	Rough carpentry
Cement finishing	Site selection
Excavation	Surveying
Finance	Wage and salary
Labor and management relations	determination

Whenever and wherever competencies and safety permit, learners participate side-by-side with all levels of personnel.

Through real and simulated exploratory experiences, learners make informed but tentative choices of occupational clusters. Learners begin to isolate families of related occupations which they feel might be in keeping with their own aspirations, temperaments, and abilities. At this level, individuals delimit their career interests at their own pace, through on-the-job observations and simulated occupational experiences. Career education must be a multidisciplinary endeavor. Appropriate specialists collect and organize all manner of resources for the express purpose of facilitating learner exploration of broad career fields.

A sample family of agricultural occupations might have the following key categories:[4]

Agric. Production	Agric. Supply & Service	Agric. Mechanics	Agric. Products	Ornamental Horticulture	Forestry
Livestock	Feed mixer	Mechanic	Processing fieldman	Greenhouse	Forestry
Dairy	Seed cleanerman	Setup man		Nursery	Forestry aide

[4] .... , *Agriculture: Occupational Cluster Guide* (Salem, Ore.: The Board, 1970), p. 11.

Agric. Production	Agric. Supply & Service	Agric. Mechanics	Agric. Products	Ornamental Horticulture	Forestry
Field crops	Seed fieldman	Parts man		Landscape	Forestry technician
Row crops	Feed fieldman	Salesman		Garden-center	
Fruit & nuts	Chemical fieldman			Golf course	
				Parks (Ore. Cluster Guide)	

The logical extension of the awareness and exploratory levels is development of skills and knowledges pertinent to families of occupations. At this level in an articulated program, occupations are systematically categorized according to similar manipulative competencies and intellectual abilities. Clusters may include the following occupations:

Agricultural   Graphic communication
Bookkeeping   Health-related
Clerical   Marketing
Construction   Metalworking
Electrical   Mechanical
Food service

A sample agricultural curriculum might include the following courses:

Agriculture business management   Leadership training
Agricultural mechanics   Plant science
Agriculture occupations   Soil science
Animal science

A structure of this nature facilitates (a) attainment of skills and knowledges which are essential to employment at an elemental occupational level and (b) pursuit of additional education or training in postsecondary institutions or within the business system.

Educational experiences at this level should focus on the common characteristics of occupations in the family. Activities should provide a wide range of competencies within a related cluster of employment opportunities. Many alternatives should exist for the learner. He should not be forced into a rather narrowly defined occupational role from which escape is difficult.

The capstone experience of articulated programs is specialization. After establishing a degree of self-understanding, exploring many facets of the world of work, and sampling experiences within families of related occupations, the learner may specialize in a particular area of work. For example, effort may be directed toward developing salable job competencies for the following:

Accountant	Lawyer
Agricultural economist	Machinist
Architect	Microbiologist
City planner	Nurse
Computer programmer	Pharmacist
Dental technician	Tool and diemaker
Electronic technician	University professor

Specialization may occur at any time and place in an individual's working lifetime, i.e., when career goals and employment patterns dictate. Occupational competencies may be obtained from one or a combination of unique and specific agencies, i.e., public schools, private schools, apprentice training, on-the-job training, full or part-time co-op training programs, universities, community colleges, military service, governmental agencies, employer training, or home study.

Articulated programs provide each citizen opportunities which facilitate full participation in society. Movement toward this end is facilitated through an integrated program consisting of general, college-preparatory, and occupational experiences which (a) create awareness of self and the world of work, (b) provide exploratory work-related experiences, (c) facilitate participation in broad occupational fields, and (d) develop specialized job competencies.

RESOURCE ANALYSIS

Initiation of programs which facilitate easy entry, progression, re-orientation, and easy exit at appropriate times is a formidable task for even the most experienced program planners. Planning, organization, coordination, and control of the many components of integrated programs can best be accomplished through established guidelines (Fig. 2-2). The broad strategy framework is: (a) establishment of educational direction, (b) identification and analysis of available resources, and (c) orientation of all concerned.

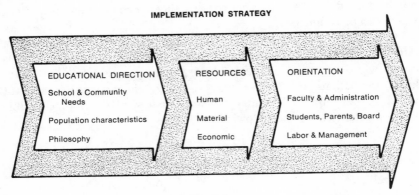

Fig. 2-2

Educational direction is best determined through analysis of school and community needs, population characteristics, and prevailing philosophy. To anticipate the needs of various learners in articulated programs, several kinds of data must be gathered and synthesized. The numbers and kinds of pupils expected to enroll at the preschool, elementary, middle-school, high school, and adult levels; current enrollments in general, occupational, and college preparatory curricula; and agency resources must be delineated. Such effort enables the planner to make assumptions regarding numbers and kinds of learners along the kindergarten-to-life continuum. Population statistics, measures of interests and achievement, information about dropouts, follow-up information on employed graduates, and forecasts of employment needs provide perspective for developing programs.

A comparative analysis of traditional and career-oriented educational philosophy should be conducted at the same time as data are gathered on population and employment. The objective should be to formulate a plan by which general, college preparatory, and occupational programs may be integrated into one kindergarten-to-life series of real and simulated experiences, which culminate in rewarding employment. This will entail such subtasks as development of cooperative education programs, organization of bodies of knowledge about occupations, and determination of evaluation procedures.

After program strategy is well established, effort should be directed toward review and synthesis of data re available human, material, and economic resources. Human resources which need be identified include: teachers, aides, technicians, administrators, businessmen, industrialists, representatives of organized labor, etc. The numbers and kinds of existing personnel and their qualifications must be recorded and viewed in light of the anticipated needs of the articulated program. Discrepancies between existing and projected resources must be noted so that plans for retraining old and securing new personnel may be laid judiciously.

Equipment and facilities must likewise be thoroughly examined in light of overall program goals. Vested interests which give rise to empire building and overequipped or duplicated shops, laboratories, and classrooms must be alleviated in the best interest of career pattern development of children, youth, and adults. Detailed study of existing physical resources must be made in light of articulated program objectives. Equipment and space allocation must come under close scrutiny. Some redistribution will undoubtedly be necessary to satisfy unified program objectives. Finally, existing facilities and equipment must be inventoried and compared to articulated program plant and equipment requirements. Deficiencies must be noted and recorded for subsequent planning, erection, and requisition.

Instructional materials constitute the second material resource consideration. A detailed inventory of available films, slides, film strips, audio tapes and videotapes, maps, charts, handbooks, guides, books, models, mock-ups, computer hardware and software, etc., should be taken. The inventory should be compared to the composite listing of materials required by an articulated program. Plans should then be developed for sharing existing and acquiring new learning resources.

The final consideration has to do with funding. Efficient and effective conduct of articulated programs depends on funding from a variety of sources. Current and predicted sources of revenue must be examined and reevaluated, if financial support is to be maximized. The potential of local, state, and Federal sources must be studied in detail. Particular attention must be paid to current Federal legislation. Funds are being made available for exemplary career and/or occupational program planning, development, and implementation. Additional economic support may be obtained from foundations, institutes, and societies. Agencies which support educational endeavors include a large number of trade associations and nonprofit foundations. Significant sources of financing must not be left untouched. Because the educational dollar is shrinking at the same time that the public's demand for more and better educational services is growing, the planner must seek ever wider sources of economic support.

Program success will, to a great extent, be dependent on favorable attitudes and support of faculty, administration, governing board, students, parents, labor, management, and the community at large. Without majority support, little can be accomplished to unify educational effort for the benefit of all. An overall public relations plan should be effected. It should reach all of the aforementioned in a manner eliciting positive action. The public relations campaign must assure frequent contacts with all concerned parties through regularly scheduled press releases, radio and television spots, public addresses, open houses, door-to-door surveys, etc. Staff and students should be recognized as change agents in the home, school, and community.

IMPLEMENTATION

It has been argued that successful implementation of total career education programs is dependent on analyses of conventional and contemporary thought, review and synthesis of existing and required resources, and continuous orientation of affected individuals and groups. Note the Developmental Checklist (Fig. 2-3) of items essential to overall program implementation and success.

IMPLICATIONS

To achieve desired results of articulated programs, the planner must be intimately familiar with antecedents in general, college preparatory, and occupational education. Understanding of and facility with the managerial, technical, and human characteristics of curriculum innovation also depends on (a) close cooperation between the business and industrial community and educational agencies, (b) a unified developmental effort, (c) flexible learner options, and (d) reorientation of personnel.

Close collaboration between the work community and educational agencies is of utmost significance to success of an articulated program. Real and simulated learning experiences will be conceived, designed, implemented, and evaluated in concert with qualified personnel in the productive sector of the community. In fact, much of a career development program may be carried out under the smokestacks, in the restaurants, on the farms, in the shipyards, and elsewhere. The school should facilitate unhindered movement of learners and resource people to and from the schoolhouse and all manner of work environs. For example, an English teacher and an automotive teacher might join forces and travel to an automotive dealership to provide needed learnings for mechanics. Biology, chemistry, and health occupations personnel might work cooperatively with surgeons, nurses, laboratory technicians, and aides in both classroom and clinics to further preservice and in-service training of health-related occupation personnel. Similarly, bank tellers, loan officers, and accountants might conduct simulated work experiences for economic classes. Such experiences will not be token one-day-a-month occurrences. Rather, they will be everyday planned and concentrated efforts to share the expertise of educators and workers for the benefit of various and sundry citizens.

Articulated programs can only evolve through cooperative efforts of experts from many fields and levels in general, college preparatory,

---

DEVELOPMENTAL CHECKLIST

Directions: Use this list as an aid in determining overall articulated program direction. Review and synthesis of data collected will assist you in efforts to conceptualize and develop rationale for a comprehensive career program.

I. Determine Educational Direction

	Current	Predicted
Enrollment		
Kindergarten		
1 to 5		
Middle-school		
Secondary		
Post-secondary		
Adult		
Employment opportunities		
Graduate employment		
Achievement ranges of learners		
Interests of learners		
Drop-out statistics		
Community & business system needs		

II. Resources

	Existing	Predicted Need
Human		
Material		
Economic		

III. Orientation
Is there an overall public relations plan in effect? If no, detail just such a plan.
What provisions exist for orientation of staff, adminstration, students, and parents? Detail a plan for orientation.

Fig. 2-3

and occupational education and from the community. Businessmen, teachers, laborers, students, curriculum specialists, parents, and school administrators must be involved. Participants should represent all segments of the educational and employment communities. The awareness, exploration, emphasis, and specialization phases of the program should be conceptualized, designed, implemented, and evaluated in terms of total program structure. Individual teachers should not develop courses without regard to what has been taught previously or to what is to follow. Learning experiences must be aligned with realistic individual and occupational needs. The conventional barriers which have isolated mathematics, science, industrial arts, agriculture, English, business, social science, and home economics must be eliminated. The result will be a composite of real and simulated activities centering on career orientation and preparation. All other endeavor will be periphery (Fig. 2-4). At the elementary level, basic skill development, reading, writing, and arithmetic will occur within a core of activities concerning career awareness. Advanced levels of mathematics, science, physical

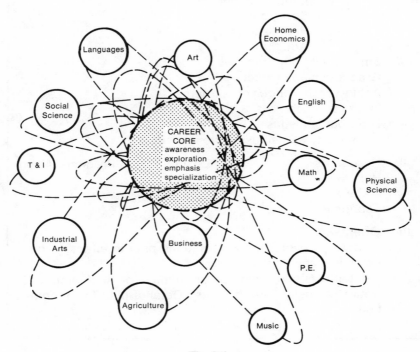

CAREER CORE SYSTEM

Fig. 2-4

education, home economics, etc., will occur in accordance with principles of occupational exploration, emphasis, and specialization. Put another way, what are now called general, college preparatory, and occupational experiences will be blended into career-oriented activities.

A variety of options will exist for learners with varying abilities,
interests, and levels of development. Both in-school and on-the-job
experiences will be designed to facilitate learner entry, progression, and
completion of requirements at rates commensurate with individual
characteristics. The system will permit reorientation, without penalty,
whenever individual and manpower needs dictate. Alternate experiences
will permit individuals to choose routes by which they may achieve
mental and manual skills which are required by various occupations.
For example, a learner might select an educational program comprised
of five half-days on the job, three half-days in apprenticeship training,
and three nights per week in general-related study. The learner will
select the combination, i.e., hours, days, weeks, which he and a career
counselor believe will assure mastery of required competencies in an
appropriate amount of time. Such decisions will be made with the
advice and counsel of instructional personnel. Courses organized around
rigid time blocks will give way to flexible learning options, comprised of
competency-based components.

Assessments of skill and knowledge achievement will occur when
the learner feels competent to demonstrate predetermined levels of
expertise. There will be no failures. Only successes will be "counted."
Learners will repeat experiences until mastery or select alternate experiences leading to other career goals. Within reason, this process may be
repeated a number of times until one finds himself and establishes
a pattern of successful career experiences.

In an articulated program, the teacher's role will change significantly.
He will no longer be the purveyor of information. Rather, he will be
a supervisor of learning options. His major responsibilities will be to
plan, organize, direct, coordinate, and control experiences of students
engaged in a number of learning alternatives. He will facilitate learner
advancement in the classroom, laboratory, stockroom, and work site.
The teacher will supervise paraprofessionals and material resources in
the interest of the individual—not in the interest of pre-established units
of subject matter. The emphasis will be on the *process* of career
development, not on *content*.

Articulated programs will demand reorganization and reorientation
of traditional subject matter. Bodies of knowledge must be available
to people with various purposes and time commitments. Flexibility will
be the prime requirement. Teachers will prescribe numerous learning

alternatives stating desired outcomes in terms of observable criteria. They will function as an integral part of differential staff machine systems, utilizing the latest in educational thought and technology.

SUMMARY

This chapter presented a general overview of an articulated career education model. The narrative answered the following questions:

1. What is career education?

Career education was said to include lifelong formal and informal experiences, kindergarten-to-old-age, which develop an intelligent populace engaged in self-satisfying and socially and economically sound work. Movement toward this end is facilitated through unified experiences which now exist separately as general, college preparatory, and occupational education. The system will assure ease of entry, progress at rates commensurate with ability, easy exit, and reentry at appropriate intervals.

2. What is occupational education?

Occupational education is one part of a three-phase, unified effort which is designed to facilitate attainment of knowledges and skills, leading toward eventual employment.

3. What are the specific characteristics of an articulated program?

Articulated programs deal with life-role education. Alert learners are oriented to and prepared for many and varied occupations through a process characterized by four interdependent phases: (a) awareness, (b) exploration, (c) emphasis, and (d) specialization. Career-oriented experiences are central in the system.

4. How can articulated programs be implemented?

Planning strategy must involve (a) establishment of educational direction, (b) review and synthesis of human, material, and economic resources, and (c) continuous and concentrated public relations efforts.

5. What implications do articulated programs hold for the planning of career-oriented education experiences?

Program success will, in large part, depend on: (a) utilization of business, industrial, and educational expertise, (b) a unified educational developmental effort, K-life, (c) a wide variety of learner options, and (d) retraining and orientation of personnel at all levels of education.

ACTIVITIES

1. Prepare a written set of general goals for an articulated career education program.

2. Interview several practicing vocational educators in your community and seek to determine their reactions to an across-the-board occupational program which eliminates the divisions of home economics, agriculture, business, and trade and industrial education. Report your findings in written form.

3. Interview a local school administrator and determine the extent to which he feels the general, college preparatory, and occupational areas can be successfully combined into a unified career-oriented program. Write your findings.

4. Secure vocational curriculum materials from a local school and determine the extent to which they facilitate learner awareness, exploration, emphasis, and specializations. Report your findings in writing.

5. Examine local elementary education career awareness materials and report in writing the extent to which role-playing activities are utilized.

6. Observe several different public school settings and levels and record the methods by which career and/or occupational information and/or skills are conveyed to learners.

7. Observe a cooperative work experience program and record the many and varied techniques employed to foster learner attainment of work-related skills.

8. Arrange to visit an operating career cluster program and note the manner in which pupils learn the skills and knowledge common to a family of occupations.

9. Observe an in-plant, on-the-job training situation and record the techniques and procedures employed in that particular learning environment.

10. Interview a businessman and an industrialist, and record their views regarding articulated K-life career education. Be sure to assess their views pertaining to field-based educational experiences in their business or industry.

11. Use the developmental checklist included in this chapter to secure information about a given community in terms of enrollment; opportunities; achievement ranges; interests; dropouts; community needs; human, material, and economic resources; and provisions for orientation. Synthesize the findings and state their impact on development of articulated programs.

12. Develop a plan by which a core of career experiences may become the nucleus of K-life learning experiences. Be specific. Detail real and simulated experiences for numerous learning options used in the plan.

DISCUSSION QUESTIONS

1. What problems do you anticipate in attempting to install career orientation as the nucleus with all other subject areas being peripheral in nature?
2. Compare and contrast the four levels of articulated programs.
3. To what extent can self-understanding and salable job skills be achieved in the same program?
4. What barriers hinder successful marriage of general, college preparatory, and occupational education?
5. Differentiate between the traditional role of a teacher and his role in an articulated career program.
6. What problems arise as learning experiences are shifted away from the classroom toward the productive sector of society?
7. Comment on the statement that career choice and its implementation is a developmental process.
8. How can the program planner provide experiences which will require learners to engage in meaningful career-related decision-making activities?
9. How might learners best be afforded the opportunity to gain understandings of the relationships of data, people, and things to productive effort?
10. Describe what you feel to be the greatest barriers to implementation of K-through-life career programs.
11. Discuss the pros and cons of a multidisciplinary approach to career education.

BIBLIOGRAPHY

Asbell, B. *Education and the Real World of Jobs*. Washington, D. C.: National Committee for Support of the Public Schools, 1968 (ED 029 990).

Ashmore, Freeman W. *Exploring Careers*. Anniston, Alabama: Anniston City Schools, 1967.

Bailey, Larry J. *Facilitating Career Development:* An Annotated Bibliography. Springfield, Illinois: Board of Vocational Education, 1970.

Bailey, Larry J. *Career Development for Children Project*. Carbondale, Illinois: Department of Occupational Education, February, 1969.

Bugener, V. E. *Basic Elements and Considerations in Planning and Developing Exemplary Programs*. Atlanta, Georgia: National Conference on Exemplary Programs and Projects, 1969.

Burchill, George W. *Work-Experience Educational Programs for Secondary Youth*. Atlanta, Georgia: National Conference on Exemplary Programs and Projects, 1969.

Career Education in Oregon. Salem, Oregon: Oregon Board of Education, 1970.

Crems, A. C. "Career-Oriented Curriculum: Cobb County Model," *American Vocational Journal*. 1969; 44, 17.

Devin, P. "Work Exploration at the Junior-High Level," *North Central Association Quarterly.* 1969; 44, 246-252.

Feldman, Marvin J. *Making Education Relevant.* New York, New York: Ford Foundation, Office of Reports, SR-21, no date, 14 pages.

Gysbers, Norman C. *Elements of a Model for Promoting Career Development in Elementary and Junior High Schools.* Atlanta, Georgia: National Conference on Exemplary Programs and Projects, 1969.

Krumboltz, John D. *Vocational Problem-Solving Experiences for Stimulating Career Exploration and Interest—Final Report.* Stanford University, August, 1967 (ED 015 517).

Maley, D. "Cluster Concept: Chance for Occupational Education," *American Vocational Journal.* 1967; 42, 22-23.

Marland, Sidney P., Jr. *Career Education Now,* Address given before the 33rd session of the International Conference on Education, September, 1971.

Marland, Sidney P., Jr. "Educating for the Real World," *Business Education Forum.* 1971; 11, 3-5.

Marland, Sidney P., Jr. "Career Education," *Today's Education.* 1971; 10, 22, 24, 25.

Occupational Cluster Guide: Agriculture. Salem, Oregon: Oregon Board of Education, 1970.

Parnell, Dale. "The Oregon Way: A State Plan for Applying Relevancy to Education," *American Vocational Journal.* 1969; 44 (9), 14-17.

Shirts, R. Garry. *Career Simulation for Sixth Grade Pupils.* San Diego, California: Department of Education, 1966 (ED 010076).

Teacher's Guide to Self Understanding Through Occupational Exploration (S. U. T. O. E.). Salem, Oregon: Oregon State Department of Education, 1968 (ED 024 965).

Tennyson, W. Welsey, and Klavrens, Mary. *Behavorial Objectives for Career Development.* University of Minnesota, 1968.

Washington County Intermediate Education Department. *Career Education in Washington County.* Pamphlet; Hillsboro, Oregon: Career Education Department, 1971.

Chapter Three

Developmental Process

INTRODUCTION

When a planner develops experiences which are appropriate for articulated career development programs, he must be aware of and understand information suggested by the following questions.

- What major components contribute to the successful conduct of an articulated career education program?
- What are the major steps in the planning process for development of articulated career education experiences?
- How does a program planner develop a long-range, master plan?
- How does a planner provide for implementation of articulated programs?

Articulated career education programs consist of numerous interdependent components (Fig. 3-1). Central to the total system are educational processes whereby learners and all manner of human and material resources interact. Supportive elements consist of preassessment and postassessment procedures, curriculum practices, methodology, resources, and facilities. These facilitate efficient interaction within the educational arena. This chapter clarifies the procedure by which such elements may be combined into effective and workable, articulated programs.

PLANNING PROCESS

Effective combination of program components is best accomplished through utilization of a developmental plan which consists of five basic procedures (Fig. 3-2). The five steps are:

1. Assess societal needs,
2. Formulate educational direction,

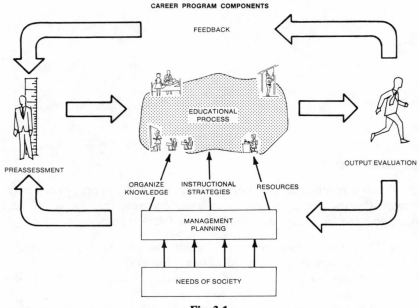

Fig. 3-1

3. Organize body of knowledge,
4. Develop instructional strategies, and
5. Manage resources.

Each step must be carried out in keeping with the kindergarten-through-life articulated program. Planners at respective levels, e.g., awareness, exploration, emphasis, or specialization, and in various occupational areas, e.g., health, police science, and industrial technology, must be aware of the impact of their contributions to the total program.

Example:

The planner developing an exploratory career program for the intermediate level must be cognizant of the impact these experiences will have on elementary, secondary, and adult career education efforts.

Hence, specific program objectives, content organization, instructional strategies, and resource management procedures need to be examined for compatibility with articulated program goals.

Step 1: Assessing Societal Needs

Valuable information about learner, home, school, community, and occupational needs can be acquired through a variety of means. Collec-

FIVE-STEP PROCESS

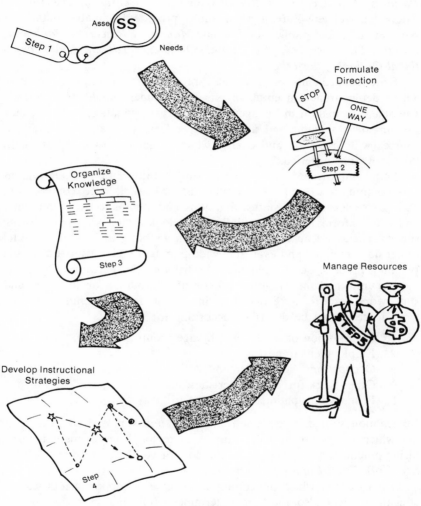

Assess Needs

Step 1

Formulate Direction

STOP

ONE WAY

Step 2

Organize Knowledge

Step 3

Manage Resources

STEP5

Develop Instructional Strategies

Step 4

Fig. 3-2

tion, review, and synthesis of such information will enable the planner to make intelligent decisions throughout the assessment process.

Nationwide data regarding population characteristics can be secured from the United States Census Bureau. Manpower statistics are readily available through publications of the United States Bureau of Labor Statistics, Department of Labor. Representative Census Bureau publications include *Statistical Abstract of the U.S., Statistical Atlas of the*

U.S., Statistical Profiles, Census of Manufacturers, Survey of Current Business, U.S. Census of Business, and *U.S. Census of Agriculture.* These and related Bureau publications provide invaluable data. Department of Labor publications include *Manpower Research, Manpower, Monthly Labor Review, Occupational Outlook Handbook,* and *Occupational Outlook Quarterly.*

State departments of labor also provide area manpower reviews. These depict trends in employment. The planner should not overlook valuable information in his agency's personnel, guidance, business, curriculum development, and administrative files. Utilization of such resources will save time and energy which might otherwise be spent in "rediscovering America."

State employment office studies supply information about regions and communities, e.g., (a) population, (b) work-force composition, and (c) socioeconomic status. Synthesis and summation of community and state information re population is a logical first step in assessing societal needs. Because of high geographic mobility, it is often essential to consider regional and even statewide population characteristics in the planning process. See Employment Distribution by Percent (Fig. 3-3).

Accurate and meaningful synthesis of information on the local and state work force is a second step in describing the community. The work force should be described according to:

1. Composition of work force by age groups,
2. Employment trends,
3. Occupational supply-demand,
4. Other work-force characteristics, and
5. Primary occupational families.

Information should be collected, analyzed, and summarized in a manner which points up the local, state, and regional employment picture, hiring practices, and occupational outlook for youth and retrained adults. See Work Force Survey (Fig. 3-4).

The extent to which the community is able to support a total career education effort also must be determined. Information regarding the socioeconomic composition of the area should include data concerning income in the following categories: farm, business, manufacturing, retail and wholesale trade, and services.

Information regarding the composition of the school population is likewise essential to the planning effort. Information which must be collected and synthesized includes:

A. Instructional data.
B. Student follow-up data,

Employment Distribution By Percent

For Primary Industrial & Occupational Work Groups (Statewide)

Primary Occupational Groups	Manufacturing		Construction		Public Utilities		Wholesale Trade		Retail Trade		Service		Government		Finance Insurance	
	No.	%	No.	%	No.	%	No.	%	No.	%	No.	%	No.	%	No.	%
Total Number Employed																
Unskilled																
Semiskilled																
Skilled																
Clerical																
Sales																
Managerial																
Professional																
Service																
Technical																
Other																

Fig. 3-3

WORK FORCE SURVEY

Work Force Totals	Age Ranges											
	Under 16		16-21		22-35		36-50		51-65		Over 65	
	M	F	M	F	M	F	M	F	M	F	M	F
State Totals 19____ 19____ 19____												
Community Totals 19____ 19____ 19____												

Fig. 3-4

C. Student interests, aptitudes, and achievement, and

D. Student population.

A first step in the analysis of school characteristics is determination of the number of students currently enrolled in the four levels of an ongoing career education program. In traditional programs, this would involve surveying enrollments in kindergarten-through-, *and* including, adult levels. Since enrollments vary from day to day, an average derived from adequate samples is sufficient. The number of learners, both current and predicted, should be determined by grade level, i.e., career development level, and sex.

Follow-up data on students who are terminated and/or graduated is likewise essential to the planning efforts at respective levels of the articulated career program continuum. Information regarding the reasons why pupils terminated their educational experiences with the system need to be compiled according to year, class, sex, and age. Effort should be made to ascertain reasons for exit, e.g., marriage, health, financial, opportunity for work, infraction of public laws, or relocation. Similar data should be collected about graduates. Developmental effort can be refined by collection, analysis, and synthesis of data regarding graduates subsequently enrolled in college, community college, trade schools, or apprenticeship courses. Such effort should be continuous and concentrated. It should provide information regarding graduates of at least five years.

Identification of learner interests, capabilities, educational achievement, and employment experience is essential. The interests of learners are best ascertained by published interest inventories such as the Kuder Preference Record—Personal and/or Vocational. Teacher-prepared assessment instruments are best utilized for determination of generalized interests reflecting course preferences, overall career goals, etc. Commercial instruments provide in-depth interest profiles derived from tested and validated techniques. A profile of district student aptitudes is also an aid to planning effort. Such a profile can be compiled with information from individual student scores on the General Aptitude Test Battery. A close working relationship with the state employment service will yield much helpful information regarding the aptitudes of potential students.

The program planner should also ascertain achievement ranges for the student population by synthesizing standardized testing program data. He should determine percentile or M scores for each of the grade or career levels, kindergarten-through-adult. Finally, he should secure a wide range of information regarding the instructional aspects of the ongoing program. This includes courses offered, enrollment, objectives, content, and staffing. The data collection instruments included at the end of this chapter illustrate how the several kinds of information can be secured.

It is important to remember that educational programs should be developed in keeping with real and perceived needs of the men, women, and children who comprise the community for which the school system was created. Information collection and synthesis are essential to this goal.

Step 2: Formulating Educational Direction

With awareness and understanding of the composition and characteristics of the population to be served, the planner may proceed to the second step of the developmental process. At this point, effort is directed toward development of an overall, articulated goal structure. With the aid of planning and advisory committees, statements re program direction may be written. The individual subject matter teacher or curriculum specialist cannot develop meaningful learning activities without guidance and assistance from external sources. Development of learning experiences should be a team effort to assure continuity and articulation.

The program planner, in concert with laymen and professionals, should define educational goals. He must synthesize input and state precisely the general and specific behavioral outcomes which are expected of learners at several levels on the educational continuum. A practical procedure for achieving this consists of a three-step process for goal formulation (Fig. 3-5) for (a) the entire kindergarten-through-life career program, (b) each of the four career levels of awareness, exploration, emphasis, and specialization, and (c) specific educational experiences or options at each career level.

FORMULATING EDUCATIONAL DIRECTION	
Step 1:	Determine total career program goals pre-school through life. A. B. C. D.
Question:	Do these objectives reflect the real life needs of the population to be served? If no, revise.
Step 2:	Formulate objectives for each of the career continuum levels. A. Career awareness objectives B. Career exploration objectives C. Career emphasis objectives D. Career specialization objectives
Question:	Are the objectives for each level compatible with total program objectives? If no, state why and revise. Are the objectives of each level compatible with those of the others? If no, state why and revise.
Step 3:	Formulate specific objectives for career experiences which fall under each of the four levels. <div align="center">learning option</div>A. Specific objectives at the career awareness level B. Specific learning option objectives at the exploratory level C. Specific learning option objectives at the emphasis level D. Specific learning option objectives at the specialization level
Question:	Are the specific objectives compatible with overall goals? Are specific objectives compatible with other goals at different career program levels? Are specific objectives compatible with other objectives within the same career level? If no, state why and revise.

Fig. 3-5

The first step of the three-phase process should involve all parties concerned. With the advice and counsel of appropriate groups and individuals in hand, the planner should prepare written, performance-based objectives which describe the conditions under which prescribed behavior is expected to occur. These should include performance standards. A representative performance-based objective for an overall career program follows:

Example:
The learner will demonstrate understanding of his personal capabilities and limitations by selecting from a given list of ten D. O. T. occupational descriptions those which meet the criteria of his general abilities profile, with no more than one error.

Overall program objectives should reflect the changing life needs of people who pursue worthwhile and productive careers. Career program goals must be continually compared with changing human and technological roles and revised accordingly. Failure to cull inappropriate goals causes misdirection and inefficiency within the articulated structure.

The second level of program specificity in the three-phase process requires formulation of goals for each of the four levels of career awareness, exploration, emphasis, and specialization. Again, performance-based objectives must point out the following for each career level: (a) who is to do the learning, (b) observable behavior resulting from the learning, (c) conditions under which behavior must occur, and (d) minimum performance levels. A performance-based objective which provides direction for exploratory career activity follows:

Example:
Given the opportunity to explore ten different career alternatives —a student will, with 90% accuracy, engage in experiences in career alternatives which are compatible with his GATB profile.

Similar objectives, appropriate to each of the other three career continuum levels, should be developed in written form. Objectives at each level should be tested for compatibility with total program objectives and revised accordingly. Furthermore, objectives should be articulated from level to level.

The third and final phase requires development of written performance-based objectives for all learning options within each career development level. Traditionally, these have been course objectives which represented a block of instruction measured in hours, quarters, semesters, or years. Articulated programs do not allow for inappropriate time limitations. Rather, learner interaction in the educational process occurs through learning options, not courses. A representative learning option objective for the career specialization level follows:

Example:
> Given a misaligned AM radio receiver, the student will align the receiver within ten minutes. Proper alignment will be judged through the actual use and via visual comparison of an oscilloscope waveform with prescribed maintenance manual specifications.

As in the case of previous objectives, objectives at this level must be tested for compatibility with total program goal, and revised accordingly. It is essential that objectives for every learning option and all four levels of career program be consistent with the overall goal structure of the career program.

Step 3: Organizing Content

Career development experiences are designed in keeping with the identified needs of the population to be served. Hence, subject matter and content are structured in a manner which will satisfy those needs. To achieve a practical framework for such activity, the planner must categorize and integrate relevant career activities.

When one categorizes entities, he seeks to classify or label them according to established groupings.

Example:
> Man's attempt to classify commodities results in the following ten general commodity categorizations:[1]

A. Animals and animal products (except wool and hair)
B. Chemicals and allied products
C. Commodities not elsewhere classified
D. Machinery and vehicles
E. Nonmetallic minerals
F. Ores, metals, and manufactures (except machinery, vehicles, etc.)
G. Textiles
H. Vegetable food products and beverages
I. Vegetable products, except food, fibers, and wood
J. Wood and paper

Many planners revise old groupings and/or devise new categories from old ones.

---

[1] National Bureau of Standards, *Supplement to National Directory of Commodity Specifications* (Washington, D.C.: U.S. Dept. of Commerce, 1947), p. 3.

Example:
Man has attempted to refine the above commodity classification to better meet his needs. Representative modifications include the following:

SCHEME A	SCHEME B	SCHEME C
Crude forest products	China	Animal products
Foods	Cosmetics	Mineral products
Fuels and power	Foods	Synthetic products
Metals and sulfurs	Gems	Vegetable products
Textile fibers	Glass	
	Gold, silver, platinum	
	Leather	
	Metals	
	Paints and varnishes	
	Paper	
	Petroleum	
	Rubber	
	Textiles	
	Wood	

One modification is no better than another. Only in specific instances and applications will one classification scheme be more appropriate than another. The perceived needs will, in most instances, dictate which categorization scheme is needed.

By the process of integration, the planner puts classes of things together again in manageable order. What the program planner systematically breaks down into distinct categories must be reassembled into meaningful wholes. An example illustrates this point.

Example:
When a planner seeks to categorize the entire world of work for educational purposes, he can choose from among a vast number of classification schemes. For example, all of man's activity can be classified according to (a) categories, (b) divisions, (c) groups, and (d) occupations. Each level, (a) through (d), represents a greater degree of specificity. The world of work is first classified according to categories representing professional, technical, and managerial; clerical and sales; service; farm, fishery, and forestry; processing; machine trades; benchwork; structural work; and miscellaneous occupations. Because categories are too broad for purposes of content organization, further

delimitation results in divisions of each category, e.g., eight for clerical and sales occupations. To more clearly define occupational divisions, one could designate groups within each division and finally arrive at discrete descriptions of specific occupations, i.e., court reporter (Fig. 3-6).

Integration of categories of learning experiences aids overall understanding and retention. The learner needs matrixes for storing knowledge.

Example:

A student who develops expertise as a stenotype operator must be aware of his or her impact on and relationship to the group and division of occupations which comprise the category clerical and sales occupations. Awareness and understanding of the role a stenotype operator plays in the entire world leads to complete integration.

Stadt summarizes this phenomenon:

"In most cases, categorization is not complete until integrations are made. When integration occurs, objects (or events) are no longer classed in isolation." (The stenotype operator is no longer just an isolated worker but rather a contributing member of the world of work.) "Put another way, classification is incomplete until spatial and/or temporal description are added, and these additions always involve integrations with other objects and/or events."

"Categorization may be defined as a simple beginning of description or identification, and integration may be defined as higher level, continuing description. But they are inseparable and convergent. Categorization establishes simple awareness which is concomitant with (or followed very closely by) the process of integration."[2]

If career education is to facilitate salable job competencies, self-fulfillment, and desirable work attitudes and if attainment of these ends depends on categorization and integration of learning experiences, the planner must understand the nature of categorical systems. The significant characteristics are: multiplicity, artificiality, mutability, and importance.

A foremost characteristic of categorical systems is multiplicity. Aspects of the world of work which occur with reasonable frequency

---

[2] Ronald W. Stadt, "Intelligence, Categorical Systems, and Content Organization," *Educational Theory* 15:123, April, 1965.

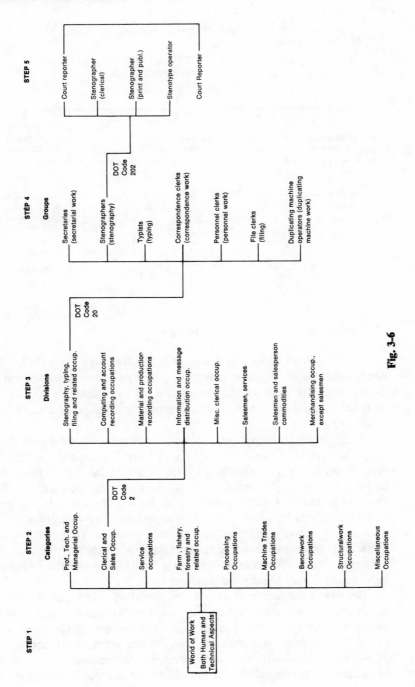

Fig. 3-6

CATEGORIZATION SCHEMES

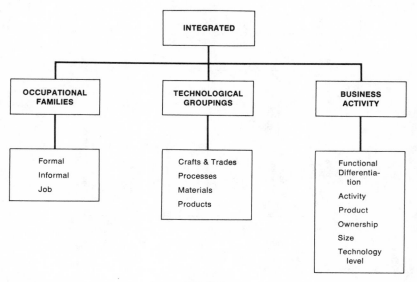

Fig. 3-7

can be categorized in a multitude of alternate ways (Fig. 3-7). Thus, curriculum planners may categorize the primary technological and human characteristics of the productive sector according to (a) occupational families, (b) technological groupings, or (c) business system activity.

A taxonomy (categorization) which describes occupational families might be further delimited according to formal, informal, and job families. Technological group categorizations might be even further delimited according to (a) crafts and trades, (b) processes, (c) materials, and (d) products. Categorization of business system activity might well be characterized by groupings which represent: (a) functional differentiation, (b) activity analysis, (c) product analysis, (d) ownership patterns, (e) organizational size, and (f) levels of technology. These are only representative of the infinite ways in which productive effort may be categorized for sundry purposes.

Because most components of the world of work can be classified in alternate ways, the purpose for which educational activities are designed will determine selection of a given taxonomy. If the purpose is to generate awareness and understanding of the impact and consequences of work in our society, categorical systems determined by several kinds of competent personnel should be utilized. If the stated goal is development of salable job skills, categorical systems should be devised by individuals and groups actively engaged in respective occupations.

Because categorical systems are man-made, they are artificial. Dichotomies and other discrete categories do not exist in nature. That is, natural occurrences do not lend themselves to mutually exclusive and exhaustive categorization. Elsewhere, Stadt used an account of the work of Karl Pearson to demonstrate that the various categorical systems are artificial.

> Pearson argued that many variables commonly thought to be dichotomous are actually continuous—even sex. He submitted that one consider the totality of sex characteristics rather than simple physiological equipment—the physiological sex boundary has been crossed by few individuals—one finds that most people display both masculine and feminine characteristics in nearly equal quantities, i.e., that most people fall near the midpoint of the composite sex variable, further that only a few people are so extremely masculine or feminine that they fall several standard deviations from the midpoint. In other words, one finds that sex is a normally distributed variable.[3]

Whereas man's attempt to categorize the world of work admittedly results in artificial systems, one should not abandon effort to arrive at mutually exclusive and exhaustive categories. Only through such activity can the planner improve educational process.

A third characteristic of categorical systems is mutability. Categories are not always compatible with human and technological interaction. This situation forces educationalists to devise new and/or revise old categorical systems. In other words, when a planner cannot clearly classify an industrial activity as either "primary" or "secondary," he establishes a "half-and-half" taxonomy. Such encounters force educational planners to recognize that categorical systems do not precisely describe all of the activities which constitute the world of work. Hence, through alteration of the existing systems, planners improve content categories which constitute the interaction of man and technology in efficient combination. This is accomplished when: (a) old beliefs and concepts are restructured, (b) new events require revision of old or creation of new systems, and/or (c) systems are deleted.

Categorical systems are significant because they enable educationists to structure and organize experiences for purposes of career development. It is imperative that planners continue to search for new and improved categorization systems which lend intelligibility to the vast array

---

[3] *Ibid.*, p. 125-126.

of variables which constitute the human and technological aspects of productive society.

In an effort to develop adequate categorizations along the many variables which describe the world of work, attention must be paid to the evaluation of such classifications. Each should be tested for adequacy by asking the following:

1. Does the classification scheme encompass all of the many variables of the phenomena under consideration?
2. Do the subcategorizations of the classification scheme represent mutually exclusive units?
3. May the scheme be applied to a learning situation?

Affirmative responses to the above open the way for subsequent development of career program components. Few, if any, classification schemes will meet all of the criteria because the world which they attempt to describe is everchanging. This is a fortunate situation, because it forces planners to continually examine and modify structures within which they propose to carry out educational endeavors.

Step 4: Developing Instructional Strategies

An instructional strategy is a plan to help learners achieve behaviors which enable successful interaction with many variables in their world. Strategy development is dependent upon identification of behaviors which individuals must possess in order to become participating and contributing citizens. Planning requires identification of pertinent behaviors and arranging them into logical sequences. These must be appropriate for learning experiences at respective career levels, i.e., awareness, exploration, emphasis, and specialization. A strategy must also identify bodies of information which facilitate achievement of stated program outcomes. Instructional strategies are derived from investigations and/or development of: (a) analysis procedures, (b) instructional units, and (c) evaluative procedures (Fig. 3-8).

The processes by which a planner organizes a body of content and structures content are regulated by career development level. The stated objectives of career awareness, exploration, emphasis, or specialization determine which one or combination of analysis techniques should be used. Short descriptions of representative analysis procedures are:

Systems Approach:
    This is an overall developmental process through which planners may effectively establish program goals, content sequence, and

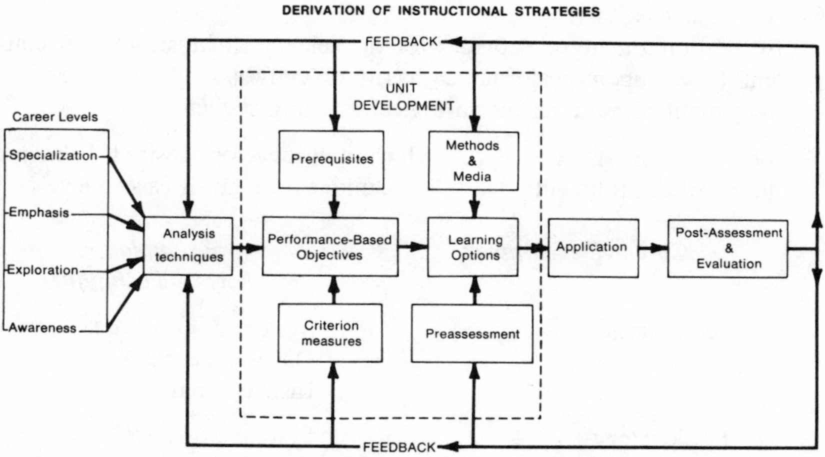

DERIVATION OF INSTRUCTIONAL STRATEGIES

Fig. 3-8

evaluation, using various alternate analysis techniques, i.e., developmental, occupational, job, trade, task, and instructional.

Developmental Analysis:

Developmental analysis is a process by which cultural variables, traits and factors, personality, and career task development are identified for varying levels of individual career development.

Occupational Analysis:

Occupational analysis is a method by which information about occupations and industries is obtained. It is, likewise, a first step in obtaining information about jobs, tasks, duties, positions, requirements, and environments.

Job Analysis:

Job analysis seeks to identify information about one segment of a cluster of available jobs. It emphasizes the characteristics of one specific job as a basis for derivation of learning experiences.

Trade Analysis:

Trade analysis is similar to job analysis, except that it is designed to synthesize a trade in order to determine content in terms of operations, tools, processes, and technical information.

Task Analysis:

Task analysis logically follows the aforementioned techniques and serves to delimit the entire occupation into its essential components; i.e., those aspects which should be taught.

Instructional Analysis:

Instructional analysis provides for the selection of instructional content based upon performance-based objectives, and facilitates arrangement of material into a logical learning sequence.

Identification of experiences which will develop desired behavior should entail the following analysis techniques for given career levels.

Career-Development Level	Exemplary Analysis Techniques
Awareness	System Developmental Instructional
Exploratory	System Developmental Occupational Instructional
Emphasis	System Developmental Occupational Job Instructional
Specialization	System Developmental Trade or job Task Instructional

Analyses identify elements of the world of work for instruction at the several levels of career development. There remains the task of organizing essential elements into units of instruction. Unit development depends upon identification of performance objectives, preassessment and postassessment criteria, guidance practices, skills and knowledges, activities, methods and media, equipment and facilities, bibliography, and evaluation procedures. Subsequent chapters will deal in depth with this process.

Step 5: Managing Resources

The last stage of the planning process deals with administrative tasks which coordinate and control all manner of resources. With increased emphasis on accountability, educational agencies have come under extreme and continuous pressure to account for staff time, supplies, equipment, and facilities in terms of the quality of program graduates. Requests for personnel and material resources are examined more and more in terms of observable institutional performance, i.e., whether or not program graduates exhibit behaviors consistent with the career development needs of individuals and the labor market.

Effort must be directed toward bringing about an effective combination of all manner of human and material resources. Maximizing the potential of all agency personnel is a high priority planning goal. Members of the educational team for whom planners must maximize opportunities for worthwhile contribution include learners; laymen; professional, technical, and clerical staff; and instructional aides. Of equal importance is planning for efficient deployment and utilization of supplies, equipment, and facilities.

Efficient utilization of resources begins with establishment of an information system through which data on all manner of contributing personnel, equipment, and facilities may be collected, analyzed, stored, and retrieved at will. Whereas expensive, sophisticated computerized information systems exist to provide reliable split-second information retrieval, the majority of educational agencies must rely on hand-gathering, posting, analysis, and retrieval techniques. Regardless of the level of technology employed, accountability will demand reliable up-to-date data on all aspects of educational activity.

Such a system is diagrammed in Fig. 3-9. Designed to process information regarding human and material characteristics, such systems provide invaluable data for management and coordination of overall personnel development, instructional activity, program development, and fiscal control. While presented categorically, such classifications are interdependent. Data from one category might very well have application and substance in others.

Data which is continuously and systematically collected and analyzed lends intelligibility and direction to instructional effort. System output assures that: (a) human effort is effectively coordinated, (b) instructional software, hardware, and facilities are effectively deployed and utilized, and (c) learner and teacher evaluation are continuous. Representative information which must be continuously gathered about human resources includes the following:

Learners	*Professionals, Aides, Resources*
Names	Names, addresses, sex, age
Address	Occupation

Social Security No.
Birth date
Developmental level
Race, Sex
Occupational classification
    code
Cooperative work experience
Interests
Achievement
Attendance

Education
Interests
Courses taught
Competencies
Availability
Place of employment

INFORMATION PROCESSING SYSTEM

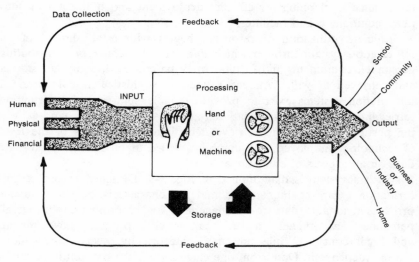

Fig. 3-9

Material resource data needed for effective program management
include:

Equipment and Supplies	*Facilities*
Student population	Student population
Program requisites	Career-level requirements
Kinds of resources	Available school bldgs.
Age of equipment	OJT & Coop. work sites
Condition of equipment	Maintenance provisions
Location	Age of facilities

Equipment and Supplies	*Facilities*
Safety provisions	Condition
Budget	Budget
Maintenance provisions	Use—hrs/day
Requisition procedures	
Use—hrs/day	

Thus, it is essential to continuously and systematically gather data of this nature, analyze it, and take action on the basis of system output to provide a framework within which to maximize the potential of all resources. An example of an ongoing information system which collects, analyzes, and disseminates pupil information follows:

Example:

The VERIFY information system (*V*ocational *E*ducation *Re*porting & *I*ndividual *F*ollowup by *Y*ear) of Scottsdale, Arizona provides participating institutions and states with computer printouts of data on pupils in career education programs. Data on pupil and teacher characteristics, institution, courses taught, and enrollment provide valuable information for program planning, coordination, organization, and evaluation.

LONG-RANGE PLANNING

Career development is best achieved through programs which have been and are continually being defined according to data derived from long-range planning effort. A long-range plan (Fig. 3-10) specifies factors, forces, effects, and relationships which enter into and are necessary to the conduct and modification of sound career development programs. Moving from the general to the specific, the process is facilitated through completion of long-range planning sheets, yearly schedules, and detailed task listings of yearly accomplishments.

Planning requires answers to:

1. What are the current and predicted five-year population needs and characteristics of the community to be served?
2. What should be the nature of career programs five years from now?
3. At what stage of development should programs be in one, two, three, and four years from now?

Program decisions, based on carefully predicted needs and well-defined plans, will do much to minimize confusion, error, and inefficiency. Suc-

LONG-RANGE PLAN

(Five-Year Cycle)

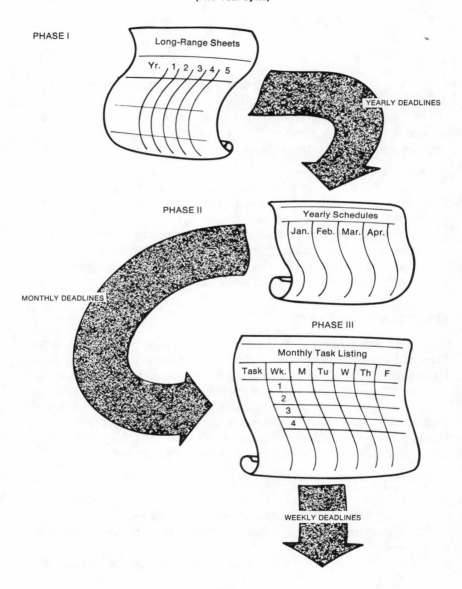

Fig. 3-10

cess of future activity is directly related to the thoroughness and extent of current planning practices. Good planning frees valuable professional talent from the mundane tasks of putting out "brush fires," and facilitates more effective use of all manner of human and material resources.

We shall deal, in turn, with each of the three planning levels. The first and most general level deals with long-term population characteristics and trends, overall program goals and content, general human and material resource requirements, and widespread orientation effort. Each aspect is described in general terms and categorized according to yearly deadlines for implementation. See Long-Range Planning Sheet (Fig. 3-11).

A first step entails description of the nature and composition of the populace to be served for the current year and at least four subsequent

LONG-RANGE PLANNING SHEET (Five-Year Cycle)							
Start Cycle, year 19_____ End Cycle year 19_____	Current Year	Year 1	Year 2	Year 3	Year 4	Year 5	
I. Student Population numbers characteristics							
II. Career Program overall goals specific career level objectives articulation & integration learning options evaluation							
III. Personnel instructional administration resource							
IV. Material Resources facilities equipment supplies finances							
V. Orientation in-house public relations							

Fig. 3-11

years. Predictions of changing population characteristics are based on analysis of available census and manpower statistics. For example, it is essential to record the number of pupils currently enrolled in career programs and predicted increases or decreases in enrollment over the planning period. Likewise, year-by-year predictions of changing employment patterns must be listed for the period in question.

Characteristics of the career development program which must be described for yearly intervals, include: goals, learning options, guidance practices, and evaluation procedures. The nature of current, overall program goals and specific continuum-level objectives should be entered in column one of the Long-Range Planning Sheet. Then, specific goal modifications and/or additions should be listed, according to established yearly implementation deadlines. Existing provisions for articulation and integration of career activities at all levels and in occupational areas should be entered on the planning sheet. This should be followed with yearly entries, pertaining to improved coordination of effort within and between all career continuum programs and levels.

Ongoing career development learning options should be listed in column one of the planning sheet with anticipated additions, revisions, or deletions designated according to the year in which they are to be implemented. The integrated teaching-guidance functions and activities at various program levels also must be recorded, according to present and predicted characteristics. Each must be described in terms of implementation datelines set within the planning period. Finally, current and anticipated evaluation procedures should be listed by year.

Current and predicted human and material resource requirements for the planning period must be listed. Present instructional, administrative, and ancillary staff needs, together with predicted personnel needs, must be listed. Specific personnel requirements should include numbers and kinds of teachers, technicians, aides, supervisors, counselors, clerical help, and resource people. Specific material resources which must be forecasted by yearly intervals include supplies, equipment, facilities, and finances. Lists of resources by type and quantity should reflect present and future program goals, articulation effort, learning options, and evaluative procedures.

Orientation techniques must likewise be recorded according to yearly datelines. These facilitate implementation of various program additions or modifications. At this stage, current and anticipated in-house orientation and public relations activities should be spelled out in general terms. Specification of yearly in-house orientation processes which aid and abet program implementation might include: preservice and inservice workshops or seminars, visitations, individualized instructions, mass meetings, staff handbooks, teacher's guides, instruction manuals, audiovisual aids, etc. Representative public relations activities include: open houses, student participation in information dissemination, addresses to community groups, informal citizen chats, and radio, television, and newspaper advertisements.

Concentrated and continuous planning efforts systematize the total career education program. Planning is a continuous process requiring regular attention and revision. As one planning year draws to a close, the planner must begin work on the sixth year which will soon become part of the five-year planning cycle (Fig. 3-12). The job never ends.

When a long-term planning cycle is well established, the planner must direct attention toward more adequate definition of entities which have been allotted to each year. Yearly schedules provide a framework

YEARLY SCHEDULE (Year .... of Five-Year Cycle)													
Item Description	Monthly Implementation Schedule												
	Ja.	Feb.	Ma.	Ap.	Ma	Ju.	Jul.	Au.	Sep.	Oc.	No.	De.
I. Student characteristics												
II. Career program												
III. Personnel												
IV. Material resources												
V. Orientation												

Fig. 3-12

for organizing and coordinating efforts. Each planning consideration, e.g., population, program, personnel, material resources, and orientation, must be developed in greater detail for each year, according to monthly deadlines. For example, the addition of three alternate learning options in the career emphasis level should be listed in the month of expected implementation (Fig. 3-13).

Year	Yearly Schedule						
Item	Monthly Implementation						
	Jan.	Feb.	Mar.	Apr.	May	June	July
Law enforcement I		X					
Ornamental horticulture			X				
Dental hygiene						X	

Fig. 3-13

To carry the example further, additional monthly data is required re: staff, facilities, equipment, finances, and orientation procedures needed to successfully implement each of the learning options in the months so designated. Hence, this procedure must be repeated for each year and month within the five-year planning cycle. Although this forces personnel to commit their plans to writing, it allows for redirection and change of purpose. As time progresses and needs and circumstances dictate, priorities can change and appropriate modifications can be made in the long-range and yearly schedule sheets.

A final phase of the planning cycle requires preparation of detailed task listings which describe monthly deadlines. Such listings are prepared for each task within a given month. They provide a day-to-day, advance planning guide whereby all manner of affected personnel can check progress and gauge movement toward immediate, intermediate, and long-term goals. Action based on such knowledge will do much to ensure maximum utilization of both human and material resources in the total career program. See the Monthly Task Listing Sheet (Fig. 3-14).

SUMMARY

This chapter was concerned with clarification of the overall process by which total career education programs might best be planned, developed, and implemented. The narrative provided answers to the following questions:

MONTHLY TASK LISTING SHEET						
Year __1__	Level					
	__Specialization__ Target Date __Mon. week 4__					
Month __Feb.__	Task					
	__Initiate food service learning option__					

WEEK	DAY						
	Sun.	Mon.	Tue.	Wed.	Thur.	Fri.	Sat.
1		Group Mtg.	Small Grp.		Student Involvement		
2	News Items	Community group involvement			Inservice Seminar		
3	Radio & TV spots	Pre-enrollment advisement			Enrollment		
4		START LEARNING OPTION					

Fig. 3-14

1. What major components contribute to the successful conduct of an articulated career education program?

Primary aspects of the articulated career education program consist of (a) the educational process which is central to all activity, and (b) supportive elements composed of preassessment and postassessment procedures, curriculum practices, methodology, resources, and facilities.

2. What are the major steps in the planning process for development of articulated career education experiences?

The overall planning process is composed of five interdependent procedures: assessment of societal needs, formulation of educational direction, organization of knowledge, development of instructional strategies, and management of resources.

3. How does a program planner develop a long-range, master plan?

A long-range master plan is developed according to a five-year cycle of events. Goal, program, and management decisions are committed to yearly and monthly implementation deadlines.

4. How does a planner provide for implementation of programs?

Implementation is facilitated through provisions for continuous orientation of both educational and lay personnel. It is an integral part of the long-range plan and provides for continual use of commonly accepted public relations techniques.

ACTIVITIES

1. Utilizing representative census bureau publications, collect population data on your specific geographic region, according to total numbers, age, sex, education, and mobility. Report your findings in writing.
2. Prepare a written summation of your current local, state, and regional employment picture, hiring practices, and occupational outlook. Use manpower data obtained from Department of Labor publications.
3. Using the format in "Formulating Educational Direction" (see Fig. 3-5), write educational directions for a totally articulated K-life career program. Be sure to formulate direction for each phase of the program and carefully answer each question.
4. Modify the world of work classification scheme which categorizes all activity according to major job categories, related divisions, work groups, and specific occupations. Examine the *Dictionary of Occupational Titles* for assistance. Report your revised categorization scheme in writing.
5. Test the classification scheme which you have just developed according to the following: (a) complete coverage of the components of the world of work, (b) insofar as possible, mutually exclusive subcategories, and (c) appropriateness for application to K-life career program activity. Report your findings in writing.
6. Review various sources which deal with analysis techniques and write a list of terms and definitions different from those presented in this chapter.
7. Contrast and compare the list of analysis terms you have developed with those in this chapter. Modify, combine, and/or delete terms into a workable analysis procedure. Justify this scheme in writing.
8. Review resources on automated information processing systems and report in writing possible applications for management of resources.
9. Visit an educational institution which utilizes automated data processing equipment for purposes of program management. Report your observations in writing.
10. Determine and report in writing the predicted five-year population characteristics of a selected community.

    a. Formulate a set of long-range goals for a K-life career program which will serve population needs and characteristics.

    b. Using the planning sheets discussed in this chapter, prepare written statements re program development at each step (year) of the planning cycle.

    c. Prepare a written five-year plan for implementation of this program.

DISCUSSION QUESTIONS

1. Discuss the consequences of interaction between various career program components and summarize their implications for total program development.
2. Compare and contrast the five-step career planning process with alternative methods of program development.
3. Describe what you feel to be the greatest barriers to effective assessment of societal needs. Be prepared to justify your stand.
4. Comment on the statement that "an educational program is and should be built on the real and perceived needs of the men, women, and children who comprise the community for which the school system was created." Do individuals really know what is best for them?
5. Describe what you think are the greatest barriers to the effective development of articulated career program goals.
6. How can career planners best achieve an organization of knowledge which will truly describe the entire realm of the world of work and still achieve categorization of components which can be applied to the learning environment?
7. Determine analysis procedures which are suitable for application to each of the four career development levels.
8. How can planners best provide for coordination of all manner of educational effort at each level of career development?
9. Describe what you feel to be primary deterrents to effective long-range planning activity.
10. Discuss how various career program components might best be combined for maximum effectiveness.

BIBLIOGRAPHY

Bloom, Benjamin S., ed. *Taxonomy of Educational Objectives, the Classification of Educational Goals, Handbook I Cognitive Domain.* New York: McKay, 1956.

Bruner, Jerome S. *The Process of Education.* Cambridge: Harvard U. Press, 1963.

Elam, Stanley, ed. *Education and the Structure of Knowledge.* Chicago: Rand-McNally, 1964.

Ewing, David W. *The Practice of Planning.* New York: Harper, 1968.

Flippo, Edwin B. *Management: A Behavioral Approach.* Boston: Allyn and Bacon, 1970.

Fryklund, Verne C. *Occupational Analysis.* Milwaukee: Bruce, 1971.

Gianchino, J. W., and Gallington, Ralph O. *Course Construction in Industrial Arts, Vocational and Technical Education.* Chicago: American Technical Society, 1967.

Gronlund, Norman E. *Stating Behavioral Objectives for Classroom Instruction.* Toronto: MacMillan, Collier-MacMillan Canada, Ltd., 1970.

Holm, Bart E. *How to Manage Your Information.* New York: Reinhold, 1968.

Mager, Robert F. *Preparing Instructional Objectives.* Palo Alto: Fearon, 1962.

Megginson, Leon C. *Personnel: A Behavioral Approach to Administration.* Homewood, Ill.: Irwin, 1967.

McConkey, Dale D. *How to Manage by Results.* New York: American Management Association, 1967.

Morell, R. W. *Management: Ends and Means.* San Francisco: Chandler Publishing Co., 1969.

Odiorne, George S. *Management by Objectives.* New York: Pitman, 1965.

Richey, Robert W. *Planning for Teaching: An Introduction to Education.* New York: McGraw-Hill, 1968.

Salton, Gerald. *Automatic Information Organization and Retrieval.* New York: McGraw-Hill, 1968.

Silvius, G. Harold, and Bohn, Ralph. *Organizing Course Material for Industrial Education.* Bloomington, Ill.: McKnight, 1961.

Stadt, Ronald W. *Intelligence, Categorical Systems, and Content Organization.* Educational Theory 15:123; 125-126, April, 1965.

Section Two

Structuring Experiences

A number of methods are used to provide order to the many dimensions of the world of work. This section helps the planner to answer questions such as:

1. How do I structure program components to create desired levels of career awareness and technical competence?
2. What should be included in career programs?
3. How do I determine the adequacy and appropriateness of organizations for various career levels and specific career learning experiences?

The alternate organizational schemes discussed in this section are:

Chapter 4. Occupational Cluster Curricula

Chapter 5. Technological Categories

Chapter 6. Business System Analyses

Chapter 7. The Integrated Curriculum

Chapter Four

Occupational Cluster Curricula*

* Credit is extended to the Career Development for Children Project, Southern Illinois University, Carbondale, without whose vast amount of research data this chapter could not have been compiled.

INTRODUCTION

One of the organizational schemes for career education is the occupational cluster approach. This chapter answers the following questions.

- What is an occupational cluster?
- Are occupational clusters and families the same?
- How can occupational clusters be used to structure a curriculum?

Concern to articulate career education at several levels has brought about many new approaches to structuring curricula. Foremost among curricular innovations is the cluster or occupational family approach. This method of content organization requires analysis of elements of various occupations. Once elements of occupations are identified, they are grouped according to given criteria.

Occupational clusters may be based on worker traits, materials utilized, procedures involved, or levels of complexity. Theorists and practitioners who advocate these approaches believe that systematic grouping of occupations makes study more understandable and meaningful.

FEDERAL AND STATE PRIORITIES

The Vocational Education Act of 1963, The 1968 Vocational Education Amendments, and The Education Amendments of 1972 encourage new approaches to categorizing occupations for educational programming. A variety of new and, hopefully, logical groupings of vocational offerings was encouraged. The State of Illinois, for example, at one time, required that all vocational programs consist of offerings in five occupational areas: industrial oriented; health; applied biological and agriculture; personal and public service; and business, marketing, and management.[1] The State of Oregon has also suggested "some four-

---

[1] State of Illinois, Division of Vocational and Technical Education, Springfield, Illinois.

teen to eighteen clusters for purposes of secondary-school instruction and goal setting."[2] These specific clusters will be discussed later.

The career-development movement in American education has also stressed the need for logical clustering of occupations. Projects in the career-development field, funded by the United States Office of Education, have been based on a system of fifteen clusters. Several millions of dollars are committed for the development of instructional materials within each of these clusters.

CLUSTERS AND FAMILIES

The terms "occupational clusters" and "occupational families" will be used synonymously in this book. Perhaps the term "family" is more easily understood, since it implies relationship among sub-elements. However, the majorty of recent research and commentary on this approach to content organization utilizes the term "cluster."

Occupational Families

Sinick has defined two basic types of occupational families.[3] The *formal family* or cluster is based on some formalized system. The clusters utilized by the *Dictionary of Occupational Titles (DOT)*, the U.S. Census Bureau, and federal and state agencies are examples of this technique (Fig. 4-1). Likewise, a cluster system that might be developed by a classroom teacher for use with *all* his students would also fall into the formal category.

Informal families are those cluster techniques designed to specifically fit the needs of an individual learner. Sinick states:

> The idiosyncratic nature of an individual client may limit the applicability of formal families of occupations to his specific needs or characteristics. Unlimited exploration of occupational families is possible if the search proceeds from any of his characteristics as points of departure.[4]

This technique of curriculum organization is particularly useful for tailoring instruction to fit the needs of various disadvantaged and handicapped youngsters enrolled in occupational programs. Both formal and informal families will be treated in depth later in this chapter.

---

    [2] Leonard E. Kunzman, Director of Career Education, *Career Education in Oregon* (Salem, Oregon: Oregon Board of Education, August 1, 1970), p. 6.
    [3] Daniel Sinick, *Occupational Information and Guidance* (Boston: Houghton Mifflin Company, 1970), p. 16-24.
    [4] *Ibid.*, p. 21.

PROJECTED STATE EMPLOYMENT BY MAJOR OCCUPATIONAL FAMILY		
Cluster	State Employment 19_____	State Replacement & growth needs 19_____
Agri-business & Natural Resources		
Business & Office		
Health		
Public Service		
Environment		
Communication & Media		
Hospitality & Recreation		
Manufacturing		
Marketing & Distribution		
Marine Science		
Personal Services		
Construction		
Transportation		
Consumer & Homemaking Education		
Fine Arts & Humanities		

Fig. 4-1

Occupational Clusters for K-8

The cluster procedure is only an organizational technique. Simply clustering old unit prevocational or vocational programs does not meet the intent of federal and state planners nor does it fit the models developed by curriculum designers. Because of what we know of learners and learning, occupational families must be designed to fulfill specific objectives at various stages in the kindergarten-14 articulated continuum. Generally speaking, the cluster characteristics should be very general at the kindergarten level and should increase along the educational ladder. At the early elementary level, occupationally oriented curricular elements should entail simple study of work and its role in society. By the later elementary grades, students should study worker characteristics in broad occupational categories.

At the grade 9-10 level, clusters should be narrowed toward specific occupational families. Finally, grades 11 and 12 should center on jobs. Increasing levels of specificity are necessary if graduating high school seniors are to be employable or ready to move into intensified, specific technical or professional training.

Discussion of the total career development process is not within the scope of this chapter. However, works by Roe and Super listed in the bibliography of this chapter provide information related to career development.

FORMAL FAMILIES

The formal family or cluster system frequently is used as an organizational framework for occupational curricula. However, it is not necessarily a new concept. Hoppock, Super, Roe, and other researchers and theorists in vocational guidance have long endeavored to group occupations into categories in order to enable students to analyze occupational choices more effectively. This goal has changed very little since the early efforts of Super and Roe.

The formal clustering techniques which were developed by the early theorists may be divided into three groups. *One-way classification systems* might be based on any number of occupational elements, but they require the student to analyze only one aspect of the classification. *Two-way classification systems* are based on a matrix analysis procedure where student interests or strengths are specifically related to occupational areas. *Multiple-classification systems* relate several occupational characteristics to student strengths and weaknesses. The complex nature of such systems renders them impractical for curriculum design.

One-way Classification Systems

One-way classification systems can also be classified on the basis of types of elements isolated. For example, job levels, industrial related, prestige ranking, worker traits, and interest-ranking classifications may be utilized.

JOB-LEVEL SYSTEMS

Job-level categorical systems generally are based on the educational- or experience-level requirements of various occupations. Rather than limit the cluster by defining specific materials or processes, such as fermenting, levels along the responsibility ladder are clustered. These clusters cut across industries such as steel, agriculture, and salvage. This system of clustering rests on the assumption that responsibilities at given levels and within certain functions are similar throughout the world of work. For example, frontline supervisors perform essentially the same tasks in nearly all enterprises.

Anne Roe

While noted for her multifactor, two-way classification system, Roe uses job-level ranks as a categorical system.

This classification is based upon degrees of responsibility, capacity, and skill. It should be noted that these are not exactly correlated. Whenever there are marked differences, level of responsibility is considered primary. By level of responsibility is meant not only the number and difficulty of the decisions to be made, but also how many different kinds of problems must be decided. This aspect that has not been much considered, yet in terms of the meaning and value of the occupation to the individual, it is of the utmost importance.[5]

Roe's original list of eight job-level ranks are listed below:[6]

1. Application, Professional
2. Application, Semiprofessional
3. Innovative and Independent Responsibility
4. Support and Maintenance, Skilled
5. Support, Semiskilled
6. Support, Unskilled
7. Transmission, Professional
8. Transmission, Semiprofessional

Moser, Dubin, and Shelsky

Helen P. Moser, William Dubin, and Irving M. Shelsky in a paper based on study related to the Career Pattern Study, and published in the *Journal of Counseling Psychology,* revised Roe's classification by level.[7] They proposed reducing Roe's eight levels to six:

1. Professional and Managerial (Higher)
2. Professional and Managerial (Lower)
3. Semiprofessional and Managerial
4. Skilled
5. Semiskilled
6. Unskilled

In curricula structured according to job-level clustering systems, learning experiences can, of course, foster understanding of an array of

---

[5] Anne Roe, *The Psychology of Occupations* (New York: Wiley, 1966), p. 149.
[6] *Ibid.,* p. 151.
[7] Helen P. Moser, William Dubin, and Irving M. Shelsky, "A Proposed Modification of the Roe Occupational Classification," *Journal of Counseling Psychology,* Vol. 3, No. 1 (1956), p. 27-31.

enterprises. In a course of some duration, activities can be reflective of a good sample of enterprises, e.g., agriculture, mining, manufacturing, construction, and transportation.

The major weakness of this cluster technique is the difficulty of defining lines between the several job levels.

> Much difficulty has been encountered in locating a classification of occupations which uses a single criterion to differentiate all occupations according to level. The major difficulty seems to lie in the establishment of a criterion which would meaningfully differentiate occupations along the entire range of levels extending from professional to unskilled. The classifications generally break down in the middle of the range.[8]

Indeed, more time might be spent in defining the classification system than in using it for analyzing one's world. Nevertheless, this system results in meanings which no other classification system can foster as directly.

INDUSTRIAL CLASSIFICATION SYSTEMS

This clustering system involves divisions of industry. Elements are isolated according to the processes and raw materials utilized, types of products produced, and the nature of services rendered.

Dictionary of Occupational Titles

The Dictionary of Occupational Titles provides a classification system based on industry.[9] There are at least 229 industries or enterprises defined in the DOT. In most cases, jobs are designated by the industry in which they are found. Jobs which occur in several industries are grouped according to occupational requirements and designated as separate industries.

The industry classification of the DOT was arrived at via the following criteria:

1. Character of the services rendered
2. Processes utilized
3. Products manufactured
4. Raw materials employed

---

[8] *Ibid.*, p. 28.
[9] U.S. Department of Labor, *Dictionary of Occupational Titles, Vol. I and II* (Washington, D.C.: U.S. Government Printing Office, 1965).

Occupational Outlook Handbook

The *Handbook* utilizes an industry classification system together with job families.[10] The following major industries are used in this classification system.

1. Agriculture
2. Construction
3. Finance, Insurance, and Real Estate
4. Government
5. Manufacturing
6. Mining
7. Service and Miscellaneous
8. Transportation, Communication, and Public Utilities
9. Wholesale and retail trade

Donald Super

The three-way classification system devised by Super lists the following "enterprise" classifications:[11]

1. Agri-forest
2. Construction
3. Finance
4. Government
5. Manufacturing
6. Mining
7. Services
8. Trade
9. Transport

The industry cluster technique is somewhat complex for use in organizing educational experiences. However, the enterprise classifications by Super are functional and may be of interest to some instructors.

PRESTIGE-RANKING CLUSTER SYSTEMS

Much of the early research which attempted to establish job or occupational categories dealt with the prestige-ranking approach. Students and workers were asked to rate various occupations according to prestige levels. Most ranks were based on attitudes developed via observation of one or two individuals involved in each occupational role. "The major finding which has emerged from studies with most of these prestige scales is that the occupational hierarchy they measure is remarkably

[10] U.S. Department of Labor, *Occupational Outlook Handbook* (Washington, D.C.: U.S. Government Printing Office, 1970-71), p. 859.
[11] Donald Super, *The Psychology of Careers* (New York: Harper, 1957), p. 48.

stable over time and highly generalizable across age, sex, racial, and cultural groupings."[12]

Although laymen utilize this classification system for various and sundry purposes, the writers oppose its use for establishing curriculum components. Its use is especially dangerous with the vast numbers of the young who have had little orientation to the occupational milieu.

WORKER TRAIT CLUSTERS

This classification procedure categorizes workers rather than jobs. It is based on the premise that worker traits can be identified and meaningfully categorized. The worker trait cluster would utilize those traits exhibited by workers in various occupational areas as a system of norms. For example, people in the personal and public service area are usually rather people-oriented. Thus, youngsters interested in careers in this field should possess those same traits. The introverted, analytically oriented youngster will probably be out of place in such an occupation.

The static nature of this technique must not be overlooked. For example, a worker in one job may exhibit traits different from those of another worker in the same job at a different geographic location, working for different pay, and coming from a different socioeconomic or racial group.

Dictionary of Occupational Titles

Whereas, the DOT makes use of the Job Families classification system (see Job Families), it also provides a worker-trait arrangement that is extremely valuable to the vocational guidance counselor and teacher. Sinick has said:

> The Worker Traits Arrangement is the richest vein of the *D.O.T.* mother lode. Each of 22 broad areas of work, from art to writing, is broken down into numerous worker trait groups. Each of these groups is then presented with an amazing amount of succinct information highly pertinent to occupational exploration.[13]

Interest-Ranking Clusters

There has been much work done in the area of interest-ranking techniques and vocational choice. Most of these procedures are designed

---

[12] John O. Crites, *Vocational Psychology* (New York: McGraw-Hill, 1969), p. 58.
[13] Sinick, *op. cit.*, p. 19.

to (1) survey and record the various types of interests youngsters possess, and (2) relate these interests to occupational choices. Interest-inventory instruments such as the Kuder Preference Record, Strong Vocational Interest Blank, and Ohio Vocational Interest Survey can provide necessary information regarding individual interests and related occupational careers.

The interest-inventory classification procedure can be very effective when used in combination with other techniques. The primary disadvantage of this system is the frequency with which most youngsters' interests change. But, interest variation can be used to advantage. That is, the varying interest patterns can be utilized as springboards for studies of various occupations and respective entry requirements.

Holland

Holland proposed a workable system utilizing factors identified on the Vocational Preference Inventory.[14]

Scale	Preference
Realistic	Technical and skilled areas
Intellectual	Scientific
Social	Teaching
Conventional	Clerical
Enterprising	Supervising and sales
Artistic	Art, music, literature

Two-way Classification System

These cluster systems generally make use of two of the aforementioned one-way classification schemes. Probably the best known two-way system is that developed by Anne Roe (Table 4-1). Roe's two-way classification is composed of two subsystems. She defines eight job families and six job levels. Theoretically, all occupations as well as social and hobby activities can be classified in the 48 cells.

One of the major criticisms of Roe's system is that of industry or enterprise effects. That is, one particular occupation may represent a specific level in one enterprise and be totally different in another. In other words, the work-a-day activities of a civil engineer working for a state department of highways may be totally different from those of a civil engineer working for a large mining corporation.

[14] John L. Holland, "A Psychological Classification Scheme for Vocations and Major Fields," *Journal of Counseling Psychology*, Vol. 13, No. 3 (1966), p. 278-288.

Table 4-1. Roe's Two-Way Classification System*

Level	I. Service	II. Business Contact	III. Organization	IV. Technology	V. Outdoor	VI. Science	VII. General Cultural	VIII. Arts and Entertainment
1	Personal therapists Social work supervisors Counselors	Promoters	United States President and Cabinet officers Industrial tycoons International bankers	Inventive geniuses Consulting or chief engineers Ships' commanders	Consulting specialists	Research scientists University, college faculties Medical specialists Museum curators	Supreme Court Justices University, college faculties Prophets Scholars	Creative artists Performers, great Teachers, university equivalent Museum curators
2	Social workers Occupational therapists Probation, truant officers (with training)	Promoters Public relations counselors	Certified public accountants Business and government executives Union officials Brokers, average	Applied scientists Factory managers Ships' officers Engineers	Applied scientists Landowners and operators, large Landscape architects	Scientists, semi-independent Nurses Pharmacists Veterinarians	Editors Teachers, high school and elementary	Athletes Art critics Designers Music arrangers
3	YMCA officials Detectives, police sergants Welfare workers City inspectors	Salesmen: auto, bond, insurance, etc. Dealers, retail and wholesale Confidence men	Accountants, average Employment managers Owners, catering, etc., dry-cleaning, etc.	Aviators Contractors Foremen (DOT I) Radio operators	County agents Farm owners Forest rangers Fish, game wardens	Technicians, medical, X-ray, museum Weather observers Chiropractors	Justices of the Peace Radio announcers Reporters Librarians	Ad writers Designers Interior decorators Showmen
4	Barbers Chefs Practical nurses Policemen	Auctioneers Buyers (DOT I) House canvassers Interviewers, poll	Cashiers Clerks, credit, express, etc. Foreman, warehouse Salesclerks	Blacksmiths Electricians Foremen (DOT II) Mechanics, average	Laboratory testers, dairy products, etc. Miners Oil well drillers	Technical assistants	Law clerks	Advertising artists Decorators, window, etc. Photographers Racing car drivers
5	Taxi drivers General house-workers Waiters City firemen	Peddlers	Clerks, file, stock, etc. Notaries Runners Typists	Bulldozer operators Deliverymen Smelter workers Truck drivers	Gardeners Farm tenants Teamsters, cowpunchers Miner's helpers	Veterinary hospital attendants		Illustrators, greeting cards Showcard writers Stagehands
6	Chambermaids Hospital attendants Elevator operators Watchmen		Messenger boys	Helpers Laborers Wrappers Yardmen	Dairy hands Farm laborers Lumberjacks	Nontechnical helpers in scientific organization		

*From *The Psychology of Occupations* by Anne Roe. Copyright © 1956 by John Wiley & Sons, Inc. Reprinted by permission.

Roe's two-way classification system accounts not only for job functions, but also for levels within functions. This procedure is extremely valuable for identifying the various interactive effects of different occupational levels within the same job family.[15]

MULTIPLE CLASSIFICATION SYSTEM

The three-way or multiple classification system propounded by Super utilizes Roe's job families and levels, but adds a third dimension called enterprise (Fig. 4-2).[16]

Super's three-way classification has the advantage of flexibility and the disadvantage of complexity. Because of the time involved, it would be wrong to expect current junior high school or even senior high school students to establish proficiency with this procedure. For each occupational group, three factors must be analyzed. These factors are *field, level,* and *enterprise.* However, if, in the future, grade school students are provided experiences which develop facility with more basic classification systems and familiarity with the career development process, secondary-school students will one day be able to utilize multiple-factor classification systems.

OCCUPATIONAL CLUSTERS BASED ON JOB FAMILIES

Formal clusters based on logical categories of job families are the most commonly used systems. Occupational educators find these the most meaningful for structuring the content of instruction. Hundreds of job clustering categorical systems have been developed by federal, state, and private agencies. A complete review of such techniques would fill several volumes. Two examples satisfy present purposes.

ILLINOIS CLUSTER SYSTEM

The occupational clusters (areas) defined by the Illinois Division of Vocational and Technical Education encompass five major occupational areas.[17] These basic clusters are diagrammed in Figs. 4-3 through 4-7. The Illinois system of grouping occupations is quite interesting and perhaps ambitious. Only five clusters are used to categorize all jobs which require less than baccalaureate-level preparation. Those who are familiar with vocational education as it existed before the Vocational Education Act of 1963 can see the influence of traditional vocational funding pro-

---

[15] Roe, *op. cit.,* p. 144.
[16] Super, *op. cit.*
[17] State of Illinois, *op. cit.*

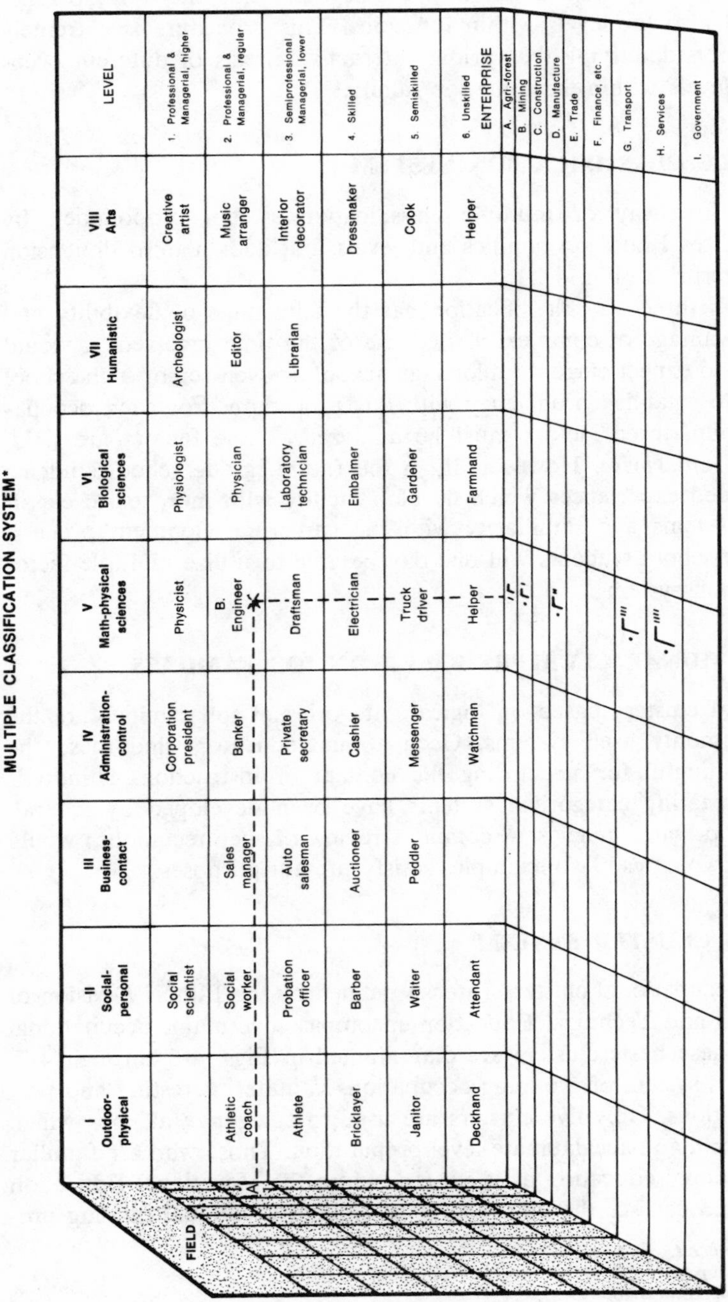

MULTIPLE CLASSIFICATION SYSTEM*

FIELD →	I Outdoor-physical	II Social-personal	III Business-contact	IV Administration-control	V Math-physical sciences	VI Biological sciences	VII Humanistic	VIII Arts	LEVEL
	Athletic coach	Social scientist		Corporation president	Physicist	Physiologist	Archeologist	Creative artist	1. Professional & Managerial, higher
		Social worker	Sales manager	Banker	B. Engineer	Physician	Editor	Music arranger	2. Professional & Managerial, regular
	Athlete	Probation officer	Auto salesman	Private secretary	Draftsman	Laboratory technician	Librarian	Interior decorator	3. Semiprofessional Managerial, lower
	Bricklayer	Barber	Auctioneer	Cashier	Electrician	Embalmer		Dressmaker	4. Skilled
	Janitor	Waiter	Peddler	Messenger	Truck driver	Gardener		Cook	5. Semiskilled
	Deckhand	Attendant		Watchman	Helper	Farmhand		Helper	6. Unskilled

ENTERPRISE

A. Agri.-forest
B. Mining
C. Construction
D. Manufacture
E. Trade
F. Finance, etc.
G. Transport
H. Services
I. Government

Credit: Figure 1, page 48 in *The Psychology of Careers* by Donald E. Super. Copyright © 1957 by Donald E. Super. By permission of Harper & Row, Publishers, Inc.

Fig. 4-2

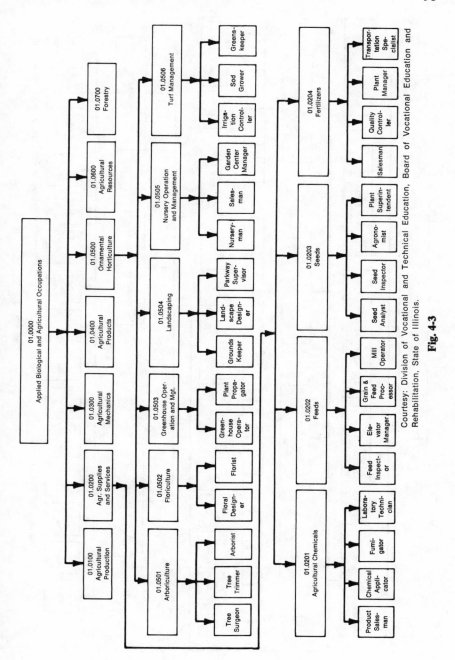

Courtesy: Division of Vocational and Technical Education, Board of Vocational Education and Rehabilitation, State of Illinois.

Fig. 4-3

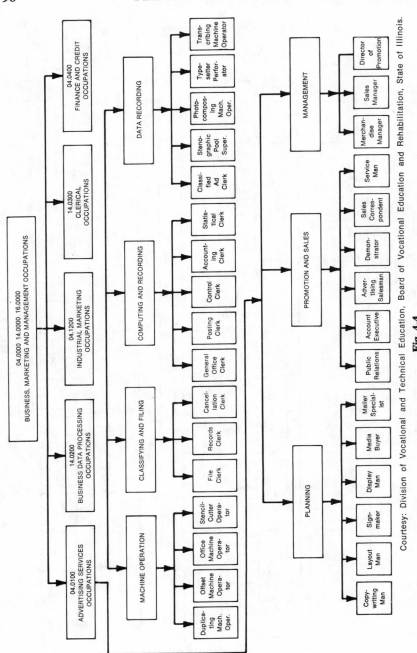

Fig. 4-4

Courtesy: Division of Vocational and Technical Education, Board of Vocational Education and Rehabilitation, State of Illinois.

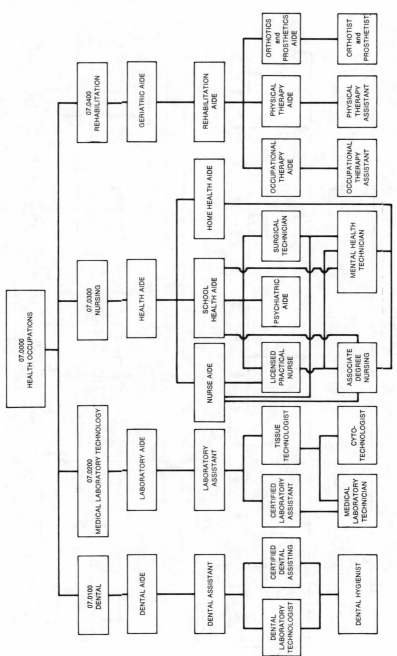

Fig. 4-5

Courtesy: Division of Vocational and Technical Education, Board of Vocational Education and Rehabilitation, State of Illinois.

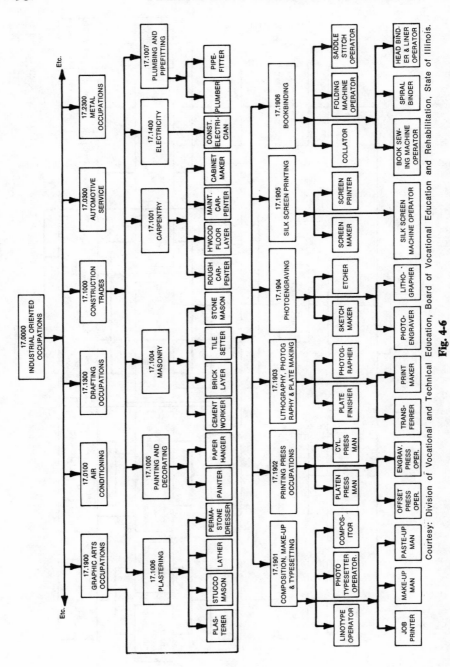

Fig. 4-6

Courtesy: Division of Vocational and Technical Education, Board of Vocational Education and Rehabilitation, State of Illinois.

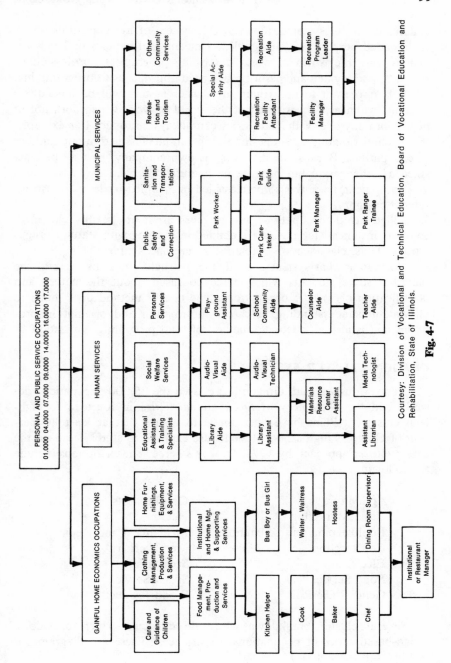

Fig. 4-7

Courtesy: Division of Vocational and Technical Education, Board of Vocational Education and Rehabilitation, State of Illinois.

cedures upon this system. However, this system of five categories serves its intended purpose, i.e., it establishes meaningful handles or labels for dealing with the world of work, describing programs to professionals, students, and laymen and assuring balanced approaches to programming.

It is important to note than any cluster system will be inadequate in some instances. Some aspect of the world of work which does not fit neatly into any one of the categories can always be found. For example, the machinist that opens a one-man shop can be classified in any number of occupations. Because he manages his own company, he may be classified as managerial; but because he manufactures and assembles tools and equipment, he may also be classified in a skilled trade or industrial-related category.

Allied health occupations and workers are more readily classified. In many instances, job duties are defined in keeping with statutory regulations. Thus, classification is relatively pure and simple.

No matter what system is used, the instructor must be alert to the fact that some students will become confused about the nature and classification of specific occupations. The cluster method does much to alleviate misunderstanding in career information and orientation programs and is also an adequate method of total program organization.

OREGON CLUSTER SYSTEM

As previously stated, Oregon has classed the 25,000 occupations described in the *Dictionary of Occupational Titles* in fourteen to eighteen clusters.[18] Plans have been made to assure that at least 80 percent of Oregon's high school students are exposed to study based on the career cluster approach by 1975. Oregon's career cluster options include the following:

Agriculture	Graphic Arts
Basic Marketing	Health
Bookkeeping and Accounting	Mechanical and Repair
Construction	Metalworkers
Electrical	Secretarial
Food Service	Social Service
General Clerical	Wood Products

Several cluster breakdowns illustrate curricula which provide a broad-based series of occupational experiences. These are diagrammed in Figs. 4-8 through 4-14.

---

[18] Kunzman, *op. cit.*

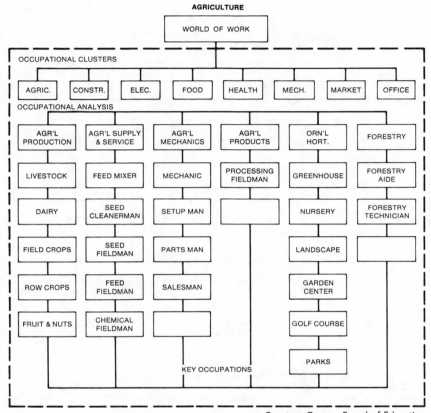

Courtesy Oregon Board of Education

Fig. 4-8

UNITED STATES OFFICE OF EDUCATION CLUSTERS

The United States Office of Education has done much to foster adoption of the cluster approach to curriculum building. The fifteen world-of-work categories developed into clusters by the United States Office of Education (U.S.O.E.) include:

Agri-Business and
    Natural Resources
Business and Office
    Occupations
Communication and Media
Construction

Health Occupations
Hospitality and
    Recreation
Manufacturing
Marine Science
    Occupations

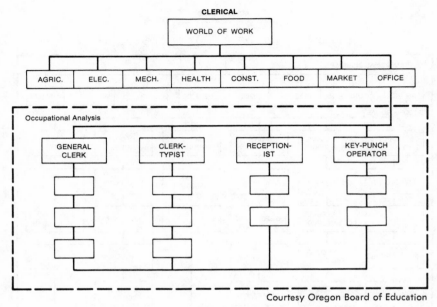

Courtesy Oregon Board of Education

Fig. 4-9

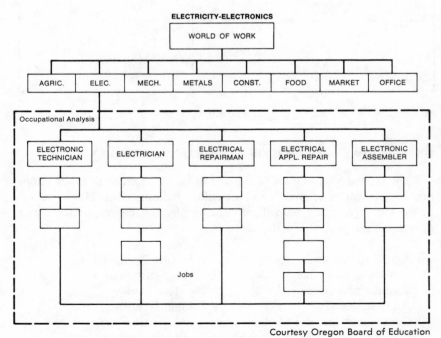

Courtesy Oregon Board of Education

Fig. 4-10

Consumer and Homemaking—
Related Occupations
(Home Economics)
Environment
Fine Arts and
Humanities

Marketing and
Distribution Occupations
Personal Services
Occupations
Public Service
Transportation

Sample clusters for Agri-Business and Natural Resources (Fig. 4-15), Business and Office Occupations (Fig. 4-16), and Communication and Media (Fig. 4-17) are shown here.

FORMAL CLUSTERS AND THE CLASSROOM TEACHER

The majority of the occupational cluster systems previously discussed have resulted from research studies or from the efforts of state

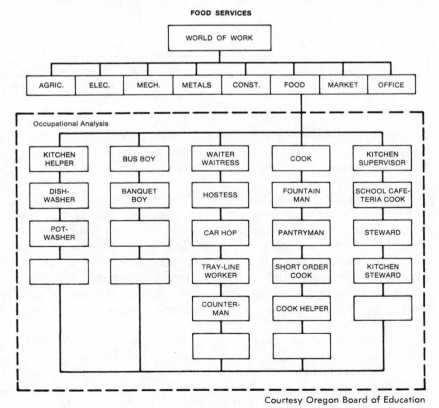

Courtesy Oregon Board of Education

Fig. 4-11

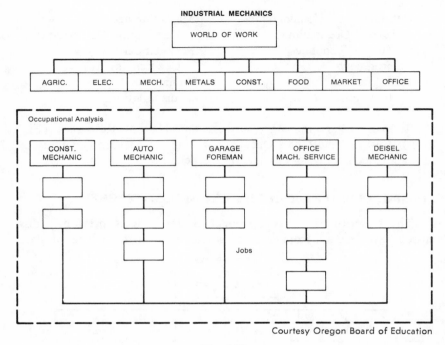

Courtesy Oregon Board of Education

Fig. 4-12

agencies striving to meet the demands of legislation concerning occupational education. The real value of occupational clusters is in the organization of day-to-day learning activities to fit the needs of occupational education.

As occupational orientation becomes central in the curriculum, instructors and curriculum supervisors must assure that the structure and content of instruction provide relevant experiences for youth who are seeking to unravel the mysteries of the world of work. The primary value of studying the occupational environment via clusters lies at the elementary middle school and junior high levels. Cluster-based curricula encourage students in the classroom and in individual school systems to systematically relate their own interests and abilities to various generalized occupational groups.

Individual school systems and class situations will dictate the format which a study of occupations via the clustering technique should take. The classroom teacher must relate community, school, and student needs and goals with a broad knowledge of clustering techniques to determine which of many options is most useful for his particular teaching situation.

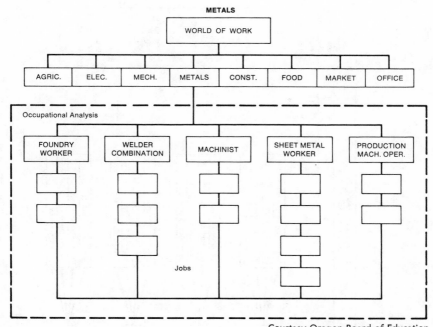

Courtesy Oregon Board of Education

Fig. 4-13

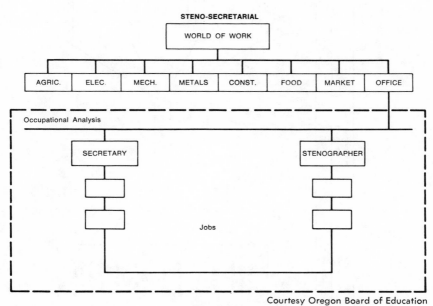

Courtesy Oregon Board of Education

Fig. 4-14

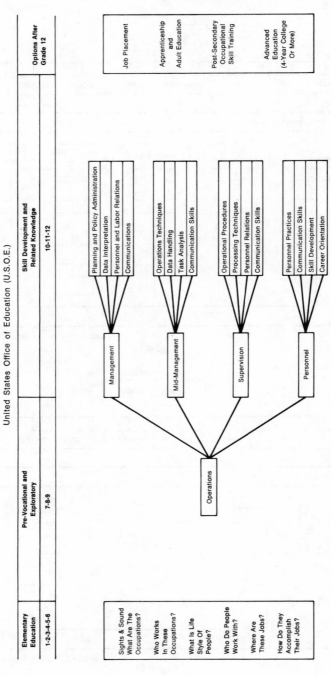

**Cluster for
AGRI-BUSINESS AND NATURAL RESOURCES**
United States Office of Education (U.S.O.E.)

Elementary Education	Pre-Vocational and Exploratory	Skill Development and Related Knowledge	Options After Grade 12
1-2-3-4-5-6	7-8-9	10-11-12	

Sights & Sound What Are The Occupations?

Who Works In These Occupations?

What Is Life Style Of People?

Who Do People Work With?

Where Are These Jobs?

How Do They Accomplish Their Jobs?

Operations

Management
Planning and Policy Administration
Data Interpretation
Personnel and Labor Relations
Communications

Mid-Management
Operations Techniques
Data Handling
Task Analysis
Communication Skills

Supervision
Operational Procedures
Processing Techniques
Personnel Relations
Communication Skills

Personnel
Personnel Practices
Communication Skills
Skill Development
Career Orientation

Options After Grade 12:
Job Placement

Apprenticeship and Adult Education

Post-Secondary Occupational Skill Training

Advanced Education (4-Year College Or More)

Fig. 4-15

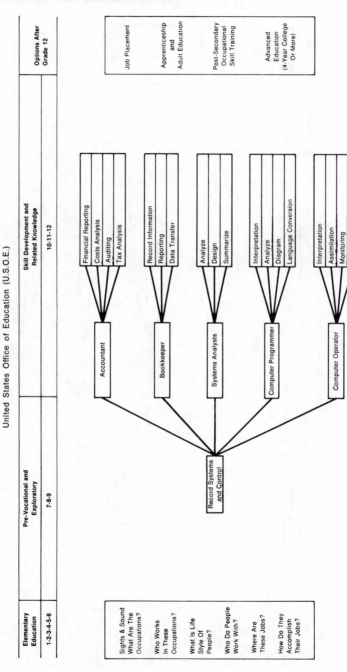

Cluster for BUSINESS AND OFFICE OCCUPATIONS
United States Office of Education (U.S.O.E.)

Fig. 4-16

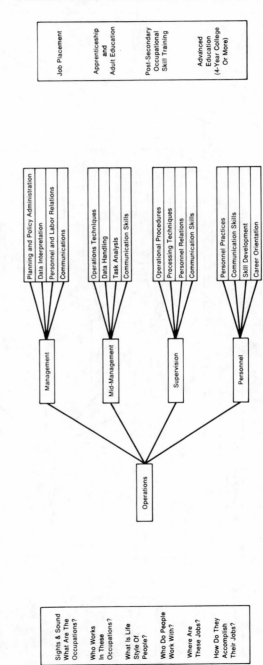

Cluster for
COMMUNICATION AND MEDIA
United States Office of Education (U.S.O.E.)

Elementary Education	Pre-Vocational and Exploratory	Skill Development and Related Knowledge	Options After Grade 12
1-2-3-4-5-6	7-8-9	10-11-12	

Sights & Sound What Are The Occupations?

Who Works In These Occupations?

What Is Life Style Of People?

Who Do People Work With?

Where Are These Jobs?

How Do They Accomplish Their Jobs?

Operations

Management
- Planning and Policy Administration
- Data Interpretation
- Personnel and Labor Relations
- Communications

Mid-Management
- Operations Techniques
- Data Handling
- Task Analysis
- Communication Skills

Supervision
- Operational Procedures
- Processing Techniques
- Personnel Relations
- Communication Skills

Personnel
- Personnel Practices
- Communication Skills
- Skill Development
- Career Orientation

Job Placement

Apprenticeship and Adult Education

Post-Secondary Occupational Skill Training

Advanced Education (4-Year College Or More)

Fig. 4-17

INFORMAL CLUSTERS

As previously defined, informal families or clusters may be designed to fit the needs of an individual learner. As such, the informal family approach seems to be of more value to guidance counselors than to the classroom teachers. However, oftentimes, the "difficult" student will require the extra attention and time required of the instructor to launch into studies in occupational areas in which the majority of the students show little interest.

For example, some students are "turned on" by different types of activities. Past experience may generate interests which peers may not possess. Such was the case of a very typical sixteen-year-old male in a small Midwestern secondary school. Constant discipline problems coupled with a very marked disinterest in schoolwork identified the young man as a potential dropout. When questioned by counselors and teachers regarding these problems, it was obvious that school subjects just were not relevant to him.

After long discussions with this youngster, the occupational education counselor found that he was extremely interested in scuba diving and oceanography. In cooperation with several school personnel, the vocational guidance coordinator developed a program of study based on an oceanography cluster. The need for such subjects as English, basic mathematics, and industrial-related courses was made evident to the youth as he began to study entry-level requirements of jobs in the oceanography cluster.

In this case, curriculum and student interest based on an informal, or impromptu, cluster system saved one youngster from dropping out of school and perhaps never having the basic requirements for work in his area of interest. Of course, the problem may never have become acute if the youth had been provided a broad career education base beginning in kindergarten.

SUMMARY

The occupational cluster approach is frequently used in career education. This chapter answers these questions.

1. What is an occupational cluster?

An occupational cluster is based on systematic grouping of occupations. Grouping may be according to worker traits, materials utilized, procedures involved, or levels of complexity. Occupational clusters or families make the study of occupations much more meaningful.

2. Are occupational clusters and families the same?

Occupational clusters and families are essentially the same. Both refer to a categorical system for analyzing occupations or worker behaviors and traits. Of course, the nature of an occupational cluster or family can be quite different because categories may be based on any number of criteria.

3. How can occupational clusters be used to structure a curriculum?

There are two major occupational procedures that may be utilized to structure a curriculum around the cluster approach. The *formal* family or cluster is based on criteria derived from the occupation itself. The *informal* cluster or family is based on the individual student's interests and abilities.

The occupational cluster approach to curriculum organization and structure is especially useful in career education. It is effective for organizing total kindergarten-14 programs. It is especially useful to the classroom teacher whose instructional objectives revolve around student-centered occupational orientation.

ACTIVITIES

1. Develop an occupational cluster system which could be utilized in structuring an occupational orientation program for both boys and girls at the seventh- and eighth-grade levels.

    a. Develop a series of performance objectives which would serve as basis for such a program.
    b. Describe role-playing activities which may be utilized within each cluster or family.
    c. Develop an educational game which would fit the specific objectives for one of the occupational families or clusters.
    d. Prepare a paper and pencil test which could serve as a unit examination in each of the clusters.

2. Design a two-way classification system which might be utilized by instructors and guidance personnel in assisting youngsters to match their interests with general occupational clusters.

3. Prepare a written paper describing the role that parents, local community leaders, local business people, and instructors from outside your subject matter area might play in a junior high or middle-school occupational cluster program.

4. Write to various sources, such as those described in this chapter, and request material which might be kept on file to aid development of an occupational cluster curriculum which might be needed at some future date.

DISCUSSION QUESTIONS

1. What is an occupational cluster or family?
2. Differentiate between a formal occupational family and an informal occupational family.
3. What is a job level cluster? An interest cluster? An occupational cluster?
4. In your opinion, what is the major drawback of prestige-ranking systems?
5. What is the major problem in utilizing multiple classification systems for junior high youngsters?
6. At what level within the kindergarten-14 continuum is the cluster or family system of exploring occupations most effective?
7. How can a curriculum organized around formal families help bridge the gap between traditional school classes and occupational programs?
8. What role should guidance personnel play in the organization of curricular families or clusters in relation to students served? Resources utilized? Evaluation?

BIBLIOGRAPHY

Crites, J. O. *Vocational Psychology*. New York: McGraw-Hill, 1969.

Gibson, Robert L. *Career Development in the Elementary School*. Columbus, Ohio: Charles E. Merrill, 1972.

Gribbons, W. D., and Lohnes, P. R. *Emerging Careers*. New York: Columbia University, 1968.

Hamachek, Don E. (Ed.). *The Self in Growth and Learning*. Englewood Cliffs, N.J.: Prentice-Hall, 1965.

Hodge, R. W., Siegel, P. M., and Rossi, P. H. "Occupational Prestige in the United States, 1925-63, "*American Journal of Sociology,* Vol. 70, No. 3, November, 1964.

Holland, J. L. "A Psychological Classification Scheme for Vocations and Major Fields," *Journal of Counseling Psychology,* Vol. 13, No. 3, 1966.

Isaacson, L. E. *Career Information in Counseling and Teaching*. Boston: Allyn and Bacon, 1966.

Law, Gordon F. (Ed.). *Contemporary Concepts in Vocational Education*. Washington, D.C.: American Vocational Association, 1971.

Mills, C. W. "The Middle Classes in Middle-sized Cities," *American Sociological Review,* Vol. II, October, 1946.

Moser, H. P., Dubin, W., and Shelsky, I. M. "A Proposed Modification of the Roe Occupational Classification," *Journal of Counseling Psychology,* Vol. 3, No. 1, 1956.

National Opinion Research Center, "Jobs and Occupations: A Popular Evaluation," *Opinion News,* Vol. 9, No. 4, 1947.

Peters, Herman J., and Hansen, James C. *Vocational Guidance and Career Development*. New York: Macmillan, 1966.

Roe, A. *The Psychology of Occupations.* New York: Wiley, 1966.

Sinick, D. *Occupational Information and Guidance.* Boston: Houghton Mifflin, 1970.

Super, D. E. *The Psychology of Careers.* New York: Harper, 1957.

Super, Donald E., *et al. Vocational Development: A Framework for Research.* New York: Columbia University, 1965.

Chapter Five

Technological Categories

INTRODUCTION

Many occupational education programs have been organized according to analyses of technology. This chapter answers the following questions:

- What are the characteristics of occupational programs which are organized according to technological categories?
- How may a program planner analyze technology to establish major units for occupational programs?
- How may the adequacy of a given technological structure be tested for appropriateness in specific educational situations?

Some educators feel that youth and adults can maximize career opportunities through educational experiences which are derived from analysis of the technological aspects of productive society. Many suggest that emphasis be placed upon skill development related to (a) selected crafts and trades, (b) processes, (c) materials, and (d) products. Programs based upon analyses of technology result in psychomotor, affective, and cognitive behaviors. Classroom, laboratory, and cooperative work experiences can develop manipulative skills, desirable work attitudes, understanding of the general duties of selected occupations, and mental job skills. Learner utilization of such competencies for self-fulfillment and occupational fulfillment is the major concern, or the thrust, of occupational programs which are organized by technological categories.

RATIONALE

It is assumed that technologically based occupational programs and the constituent experiences integrate work activities with the life styles and patterns of learners. Hence students are better able to select future goals and subsequently assume occupational roles which fit their interests and abilities. Through real and simulated experiences with the tools, processes, materials, and products of crafts, trades, and professions, learners develop individual abilities which enable them to engage in worthwhile and profitable work roles. That this is a widely held belief is evidenced by a sampling of the vast number of programs which have been derived from analyses of inherent technological characteristics of occupations.

Representative craft, trade, and semiprofessional occupational programs are titled air traffic management, automotive body and fender, building maintenance, clerk-typist, floristry, food processing, fish husbandry, mortuary science, ornamental horticulture, physical therapy, practical nursing, and real estate. As do the others, building maintenance and food processing programs entail educational experiences organized according to the technological functions of individuals employed in the respective job categories.

The structure and content of building maintenance programs are derived from analyses of the techni-functions which are performed by practicing building maintenance personnel. Results of such analyses suggest that the following experiences and time allotments best meet learner and occupational needs.

UNIT	HOURS
orientation	6
blueprint reading	60
math	60
general safety	6
carpentry	102
painting	60
electrical	150
plumbing	60
machine shop practice	102
sheet metal work	60
cementing & plastering	30
welding	72
TOTAL	768

Source: H. E. W. Bulletin OE-87043.

Food processing programs are based on analyses of techni-functions performed within many and varied segments of the food production industry. Techni-functions of laboratory technicians, quality control technicians, production supervisors, and technical salesmen are identified and codified for purposes of content organization. Food processing experiences for the learner include:

A. commercial canning of fruits, berries, seafoods, vegetables, etc.
B. freezing of fruits, berries, meats, vegetables, prepared foods, etc.
C. manufacturing ice cream, cheese, cultured milk products, butter, etc.
D. fermentation of sauerkraut, pickles, etc.
E. dehydration of food products.
F. manufacture of jams and jellies.
G. seafoods—salmon, tuna, shrimp, crab, oyster, fish varieties.
H. milling products—flour, cake mixes, dried foods, starch, gelatin.
I. meat and poultry products.
J. bakery products—bread, crackers, cookies, cereals.
K. beverage products.
L. delicatessen—food kitchen products.

Supplementary experiences aid and abet facility with food processing technology:

mathematics
communication skills
business economics
statistical quality control
quality assurance
plant and environmental
  sanitation

industrial safety
food packaging
food processing machinery
employer-employee relations
supervision

Source: Mt. Hood CC Food Processing Technology Bulletin, Gresham, Oregon, The College, 1970, mimeograph p. 2.

A third technologically based occupational program also illustrates structure and content which are derived from a core of commonly used materials and processes. Supporters of this approach contend that the many dimensions of a technological society are best described through a sequence of educational experiences organized about recurrent industrial practices and commonly worked materials. A technologically based occupational program entitled "Materials & Processes" is outlined below.

Materials and Processes

I. Introduction

    A. Overview of technological functions
    B. Major technological functions
    C. Humanistic functions

II. Material Removal

    A. Turning
    B. Shaping
    C. Planing
    D. Drilling
    E. Boring
    F. Etching
    G. Shearing
    H. Milling
    I. Mechanical cutting
    J. Heat cutting
    K. Separating
    L. Occupations

III. Combinations and Assembly of Materials

    A. Coating
    B. Fastening
    C. Positioning
    D. Mixing
    E. Classifying
    F. Laminating
    G. Occupations

IV. Materials

    A. Forming
    B. Heat-treatment
    C. Measurement
    D. Identification
    E. Occupations

Source: Oregon State University, I. Ed. Dept. Bulletin

Another example of technologically based programs illustrates organization according to a clearly defined material limitation. Content is derived from a study of the characteristics, properties, applications, and occupations appertaining to woods, metals, ceramics, plastics, textiles, soils, chemicals, etc. Supporters of this organizational scheme maintain that self-awareness, occupational awareness, and technical competence are best facilitated through experiences and simulations which assure interaction with a body of knowledge concerning a single or small group of specific materials. A representative material-based occupational outline ranging from an overview of the wood industries to laminating and bending follows.

Woodworking

Unit I. Overview of wood and wood-related industries
    II. Career opportunities
    III. Planing
    IV. Joinery
    V. Assembling
    VI. Finishing
    VII. Hardware Application
    VIII. Tool and Equipment Maintenance
    IX. Cabinetmaking
    X. Furniture Making
    XI. Boat Building
    XII. Building Construction
    XIII. Laminating and Bending

Source: Industrial Arts in Oregon Schools, Oregon Board of Education

A final example of a technology based program is the Industrial Arts Curriculum Project. Basic concepts and foundations of contemporary industrial technology are organized according to two one-year experiences: the "World of Construction" and the "World of Manufacturing." The "World of Construction" is a one-year exploratory experience derived from study of primary knowledges and techniques common to the construction industry. Representative units of study and learning options follow:

Buying real estate	Bridge building
Soil testing	Road building
Estimating	Writing specifications
Clearing the site	Building walls
Building forms	Landscaping homesites
Mixing concrete	Housing people
Installing utilities	Managing community developments
Laying floors	Collective bargaining

The "World of Manufacturing" fosters awareness and understanding of the fundamental processes of management, personnel, and production techniques which create finished goods in a plant or factory. Content is derived from study of the characteristics, methods, and occupations of organized manufacturing systems. Learners investigate, design, engineer, and manufacture products of varying materials utilizing unique and specific processes. Units of study and learning activities include:

The evolution of manufacturing
Manufacturing technology
Organization, ownership, and
   profit
Researching and developing
Making working drawings
Automating processes
Estimating cost
Supplying equipment and
   materials

Hiring and training
Extracting raw materials
Casting or molding
Making assemblies or
   finished products
Combining components
Preparing for distribution
Forming a corporation
Manufacturing in the future

PROCESS

Educational experiences which maximize opportunities for individual career goal development and subsequent entry into an appropriate occupation need to be formulated with the greatest of pedagogical competence. Achieving self-fulfillment in the world of work is facilitated through a series of experiences derived from critical analyses of men at work, occupations, jobs or tasks, and instructional principles. The process by which structure and content is conceptualized for purposes of occupational program development is illustrated in Fig. 5-1. Consisting of five interdependent phases, the total system aids and abets development of actual and simulated activities which enhance occupational career development for learners at all stages of occupational maturity.

Phase I assures that curriculum development will be carried on in view of the individual student's quest for identity and career fulfillment. This is important to planning activities at all levels of the occupational education continuum from preschool to adult retraining experiences. The planner must isolate and analyze those aspects of man and his work which tend to maximize individual potential and self-actualization. Resultant goals should define expected program outcomes, pertinent constraints under which such results will be expected to occur, and measures by which success or failure will be determined.

Phase II involves occupational analyses. These analyses emphasize identification and definition of selected occupations. Major and minor duties, requirements, and environments are analyzed. Based upon available employment data, this phase provides realistic guidelines for developing programs which benefit the majority of the citizenry. This phase provides a means by which a myriad of occupations can be categorized for pedagogical purposes. Information on man at work is classified according to one or a combination of the four following codification systems: (a) trade, craft, profession; (b) process; (c) material; and (d) product. The categorization system by which content is to be structured

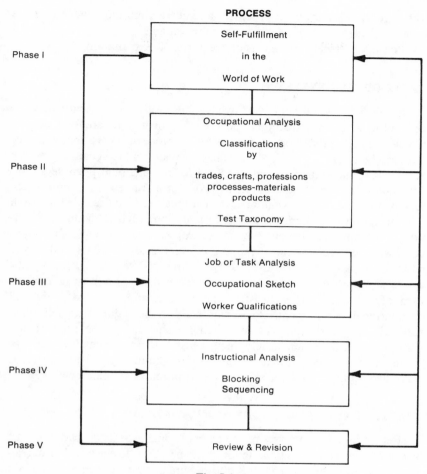

Fig. 5-1

and organized is likewise tested for universality, exclusiveness, and appropriateness to instructional environments.

Phase III concerns job or task analysis. These are treated at length in Section III. Selected job duties are outlined, tasks are identified for each duty, and standards of performance are specified. Corresponding "knowing" and "doing" activities are identified as a result of these endeavors.

In Phase IV, Instructional Analysis, instructional concepts or principles are identified as pedagogical blocks or units. Concepts are fitted to a hierarchical structure, revised, and arranged into a logical, simple-to-complex order. Finally, a system of checks and balances is employed to assure that development processes and curriculum implementation are monitored for purposes of program improvement.

Phase V, Review and Revision, requires no explanation.

CATEGORICAL SYSTEMS

Man's participation in worthwhile and productive activity may be conceptualized for educational purposes according to analysis of (1) selected trades, crafts, or professions; (2) processes; (3) materials; or (4) products (Fig. 5-2). All schemes provide viable means by which knowledges and skills may be organized for instructional purposes. Cognizance of such codification systems provides a framework within which to develop actual and simulated educational experiences. While each scheme requires a slightly different orientation, each demands recognition of a common element, i.e., man. All curriculum work should be done with full recognition of the many and varied life styles and career patterns of the population to be served. Analysis, selection, and organization of a body of knowledge for instructional purposes must be done in light of individual characteristics and their relationships to functional occupational requirements. Programs need to be tailored to individual aptitudes, interests, temperaments, competencies, and subsequent job parameters. Curriculum development must foster a successful marriage of human and occupational characteristics. Similarly, programs should maximize opportunities for individuals to progress at their own rates.

CRAFT, TRADE, AND PROFESSION ANALYSIS

Before in-depth analyses of the technological aspects of trades, crafts, or professions can be begun, action must be taken to ensure that curriculum development incorporates those humanizing elements which aid and abet learners in their quest for self-actualization and fulfillment of career goals. Essentially, the planner must seek to answer this question:

> Within the total planning effort, how can the entire program relate to the career patterns of individual students in a manner which will enable them to maximize their ability to select goals leading toward a full and rewarding life?

Obviously, there is no single answer. There are candidate answers. Several alternate routes exist for humanizing the process of occupational orientation and subsequent acquisition of job skills and knowledges. Each attempts to incorporate human and technological elements through provision for:

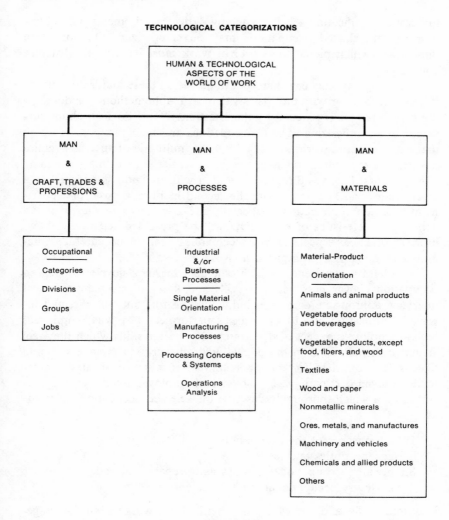

TECHNOLOGICAL CATEGORIZATIONS

HUMAN & TECHNOLOGICAL ASPECTS OF THE WORLD OF WORK

MAN & CRAFT, TRADES & PROFESSIONS

MAN & PROCESSES

MAN & MATERIALS

Occupational
—
Categories

Divisions

Groups

Jobs

Industrial &/or Business Processes
—
Single Material Orientation

Manufacturing Processes

Processing Concepts & Systems

Operations Analysis

Material-Product Orientation
—
Animals and animal products

Vegetable food products and beverages

Vegetable products, except food, fibers, and wood

Textiles

Wood and paper

Nonmetallic minerals

Ores, metals, and manufactures

Machinery and vehicles

Chemicals and allied products

Others

Fig. 5-2

1. Individual competencies,
2. Interesting and stimulating activities,
3. Relevant and need-satisfying experiences, and
4. Pursuit of individual interests.

After assuring commitment to these human considerations, the curriculum planner may proceed to Phase II of the developmental process. In Phase II, effort is directed toward determination of a suitable structure which describes dimensions of the world of work. The planner must identify a classification scheme whereby duties, requirements, and environments of selected occupations may be categorized. One or more dimensions which pierce the world of work must be used to structure content.

The program planner is hard put to decide on these major dimensions if he is not familiar with the vast array of available methods for developing programs. He is plagued by the question: "How do I go about surveying and synthesizing various occupations and their many tasks which make up the entire world or work?" Of the multitude of specific avenues open to the curriculum planner, two routes emerge as primary planning aids. The first involves direct consultation with individuals engaged in a given trade, craft, or profession; the second involves perusal of Department of Labor publications, especially the *Dictionary of Occupational Titles*. Characteristics of each route will be presented separately; however, in practice, aspects of both techniques need to be carefully integrated to maximize program successes.

To identify experiences which will help learners develop increased occupational awareness and job skills and knowledges, planners must interview appropriate employed individuals. Effort must be directed toward identification of (1) exact tasks performed, (2) what employees believe employers expect of them, and (3) specific skills which they feel should be emphasized in the educational enterprise. Employers should likewise be consulted for their perceptions of what constitutes competence in given occupations. Employer and employee interviews may result in data which thoroughly describe the selected occupations in terms of:

1. the purpose of the occupation,
2. general duties and tasks,
3. preentry occupational abilities and preparation, and
4. postentry occupational conditions.

Required skills and knowledges, described by workers and management and codified by curriculum developers, may be organized into task descriptions. However, program organization and structure should not be dependent on information derived from these sources alone. Programming decisions should also be based upon data secured from publications of the U.S. Department of Labor.

For example, invaluable planning assistance is to be had from Volume 1 of the *Dictionary of Occupational Titles,* wherein occupational terminology is reviewed, synthesized, and standardized. The D.O.T. is derived from well over 75,000 individual job studies and reflects relationships among occupations in terms of work performed and required competencies. The third edition, Volume I, *D.O.T.*, contains a composite alphabetical listing of over 35,550 occupational definitions. The planner can obtain a wealth of descriptive information because each listing includes "what" gets done, "how" it gets done, and "why" it gets done.[1]

Example:

Paper Boy (glass mfg.) 920.887

What	*Pulls lites, stacked on end, slightly forward while*
How	*simultaneously inserting paper between them to*
Why	*protect glass from surface damage. Pastes labels*
What	*on lites, preparatory to packing.*

Additional developmental assistance can be gained from definitions which describe worker functions, prominent aptitudes, interests, temperaments, physical demands, and working conditions.[2]

Example:

Worker Functions   Physicist, Theoretical (profess. & kin.) 023.088 *Interprets results of experiments in physics, formulates theories consistent with data obtained, and predicts results. Synthesizing of experiments designed to detect . . .*

Review and synthesis of information about occupations is also aided by D.O.T. lists of major required aptitudes, interests, and temperaments.[3]

Example:

Aptitudes, Interests, & Temperaments

(aptitude)		*(interests)*
verbal ability	Editorial Writer (print. & publ.) 132.088. *Writes comments on topics of current interest to stimulate or mold public opinion in accordance with viewpoints & policies of publication . . .*	people & the communication of ideas

(temperaments)   Influencing people's opinions, attitudes, or judgments on ideas. Interpreting feelings, ideas, and facts in terms of personal viewpoint.

---

[1] U.S. Department of Labor, *Dictionary of Occupational Titles*, 3rd ed. (Washington, D.C.: U.S. Government Printing Office, 1965), Vol. I, p. 515.

[2] *Ibid.*, p. 15.

[3] *Ibid.*, p. 16.

Required worker abilities and activities are subsumed under the heading of aptitudes and were derived from the "General Aptitude Test Battery" of the U.S. Employment Service. Characteristics which represent interests disclose definite preferences for given productive activities. Job temperaments are indicative of special characteristics which are as essential as specific skills.

Physical requirements and working conditions are likewise defined in each job description.[4]

Example:

	High climber (logging) 949.-781. climber; high rigger; rigger; squirrel man; topper. Installs blocks (pulleys), cables, and other rigging tackle on tree to be used for yarding	(physical
(working cond.)	logs from forest. *Climbs tree,*	demands)
outside	*using climbing spurs and safety*	climbing
hazards	*rope . . .*	balancing

Additional assistance for curriculum planning and organization may be obtained from *D.O.T.* job definitions which are identified by industrial classification in 229 industries, categorized according to (a) character of services rendered, (b) products, (c) primary processes, and (d) raw materials consumed. Definitions are coded according to the industry in which the job is found, the type of activity, or both.

A six-digit codification scheme aids classification of the 35,550 titles. The system combines occupational groups and worker trait categorizations. The first method provides a means of discerning various relationships among occupations with common traits. Jobs are classified according to a composite of service area, purpose, material, product, subject matter, service, generic term, and/or industry as evidenced in the first three digits of the code. Nine general categories emerge as being representative of all defined occupations. The nine categories are coded 0 to 9 and are evidenced in the first digit of the "dot" code as:[5]

0
1 } Professional, technical, and managerial occupations
2 Clerical and sales occupations
3 Service occupations

[4] *Ibid.*
[5] *Ibid.,* p. 17.

4	Farming, fishery, forestry, and related occupations
5	Processing occupations
6	Machine trades occupations
7	Benchwork occupations
8	Structural work occupations
9	Miscellaneous occupations

The nine generalized categories are delineated into 84 two-digit divisions and these are further subdivided into 603 three-digit groups. Hence the original nine general divisions are defined as categories, divisions, and groups.[6]

Example of category definitions—2 Clerical and sales occup.
Example of division definitions—20 Stenography, typing, filing, and related occup.
Example of three-digit group definitions—201 Secretaries

Based upon findings of the U.S. Employment Service, the remaining three digits of the *D.O.T.* code infer:

a. Every job requires the worker to, in varying degrees, relate to data, people, and things.
b. These relationships can be arranged in a complex hierarchy, simple to complex, with each successive function including simpler ones and excluding complex functions.
c. Identification of highest function in each hierarchy will illustrate the job's relationships to data, people, and things.
d. Taken together, the last three digits express total functional complexity of job in question.[7]

Example:

DATA	*PEOPLE*	*THINGS*
0 synthesizing	0 mentoring	0 setting-up
1 coordinating	1 negotiating	1 precision working
2 analyzing	2 instructing	2 operating-controlling
3 compiling	3 supervising	3 driving-operating
4 computing	4 diverting	4 manipulating
5 copying	5 persuading	5 tending
6 comparing	6 speaking-signaling	6 feeding-offbearing
7 no significant relationship	7 serving	7 handling
	8 no significant relationship	8 no significant relationship

[6] *Ibid.*
[7] *Ibid.*, Vol. II, p. 649.

When grouped according to worker traits, jobs are classified by a consolidation of requisite educational competencies, aptitudes, interests, temperaments, and physical demands. The 114 worker trait groups provide the program planner with descriptions of necessary worker traits and abilities, and occupations which share these requirements. The following are described by these groups:[8]

Art

Business

Clerical work

Counseling, guidance, & social work

Crafts

Education & training

Elemental work

Engineering

Entertainment

Farming, fishery, & forestry

Law & law enforcement

Machine work

Managerial & supervisory

Math & science

Medicine & health

Merchandising

Music

Photography & communication

Transportation

Writing

In addition to employer-employee interview data and Volume I of the *D.O.T.*, the curriculum developer should study Volume II of the *Dictionary of Occupational Titles*. This volume facilitates further clarification of the thousands of jobs which are defined in the first volume. The program planner will find the second volume useful for determining unique and specific relationships within and between various occupations. The volume describes groupings of jobs which possess like occupational, industrial, and/or worker characteristics. These help the planner to develop programs which serve large groups of student and employer clientele. Program developers will find Volume II most beneficial for categorizing content according to specific occupational categories, divisions, and groups; according to areas of work and worker trait groups; and according to industry groups.

Curriculum planners must also be aware of wide ranges of employment opportunities in a vast number of work environments. Information of this nature is readily available through the many publications of the Bureau of Labor Statistics. Representative titles include: *Occupational Outlook Handbook, Occupational Outlook Quarterly, Occupational Outlook Report Series,* and *Monthly Labor Review.* The *Occupational Outlook Handbook* provides valuable descriptions of the character of work, preemployment requisites, occupational outlook, employment locations, earnings, and working conditions for approximately 700 jobs. It synthe-

[8] *Ibid.,* Vol. I, p. 18.

sizes significant aspects of the entire occupational-employment spectrum for those who would organize, and implement instructional programs.

In sum, program designers must utilize information from a number of sources such as employer representatives, labor organizations, trade associations, professional societies, governmental agencies, and standard reference works. Information from these and other sources is used to develop curriculum outlines for appropriate levels and divisions in the total kindergarten-to-adult occupational education program. Development of specific craft, trade, or semiprofessional programs is best carried out within the context of their relationships to the entire spectrum of the world of work. In Fig. 5-3, this type of relationship is traced for the specific job *stenographer* (clerical). Another prerequisite to curriculum development is consideration of the total work environment and its human and occupational elements. Attention must be given to the relationship of man and his work. The curriculum planner must be cognizant of worker motivations and the changing nature of work. The program developer should familiarize himself with standard works on these subjects: Among them are: *The World of Work, Why Men Work, Work and the Nature of Man,* and *The Motivation to Work.*

To understand his work, the planner must employ a scheme for categorizing jobs. One of the best available methods is the aforementioned six-digit *Dictionary of Occupational Titles* code. It provides a means of discerning the many and varied relationships among occupations in terms of common traits. The nine resulting *D.O.T.* job categories which result from a combination of service area, purpose, material, product, subject matter, service, generic term, and/or industry are illustrated in Step 2 of Fig. 5-3.

Since we are attempting to delimit the job of stenographer, the next logical step is to examine in detail the specific one-digit occupational category which includes this job. The clerical and sales occupational category D.O.T. code (2) is defined to include:

> occupations concerned with preparing, transcribing, transferring, systematizing, and preparing written communications and records; collecting accounts; distributing information; and influencing customers in favor of a commodity or service. Includes occupations closely identified with sales transactions even though they do not involve actual participation.[9]

The clerical and sales occupations category which consists of eight two-digit related occupational divisions is diagrammed in Fig. 5-3.

---

[9] *Ibid.,* p. 17.

OCCUPATIONAL PROFILE

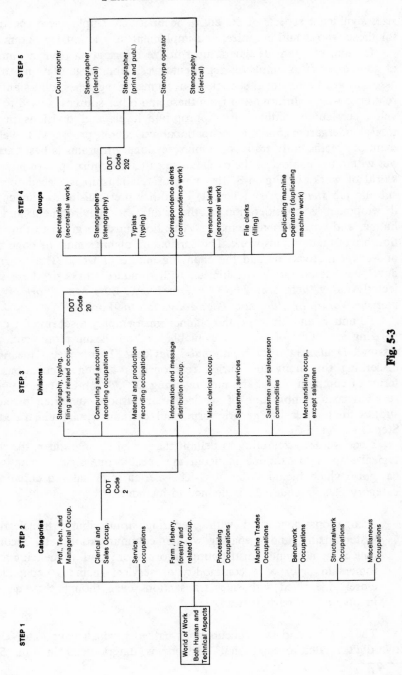

Fig. 5-3

Divisions are representative of jobs which range from stenography, typing, filing, and related occupations; miscellaneous clerical occupations; to salesmen and salespersons dealing in commodities. The two-digit D.O.T. code (20), stenography, typing, filing, and related occupations division, is defined to include:

> Occupations concerned with making, classifying, and filing records, including written communications.[10]

As is indicated in Step 4, Volume II of the D.O.T. further delineates this division into seven distinct occupational groups including secretaries, stenographers, typists, correspondence clerks, personnel clerks, file clerks, and duplicating-machine operators. Step 5 depicts an even finer distinction within the stenographers (stenography) group D.O.T. code (202) which results in the listing court reporter, stenographer (clerical), stenographer in print shop (print & publ), and stenotype operator.

This five-step process makes use of the analyses which underlie the D.O.T. for purposes of describing a specific occupation. The basic steps involved analysis of (1) occupational and human interaction and (2) selection of a one-digit occupational category, (3) selection of a two-digit occupational division, (4) selection of a three-digit occupational group, and (5) identification of a specific occupation. This procedure not only benefits development of specific trade-oriented programs, but also assists development of occupational family or clusters programs. (Refer to Chapter 4 for additional information on application.)

We have now arrived at the point in Phase II when the selected taxonomy, i.e., the classification of program elements according to specific occupational categories, divisions and groups, must be tested for universality, exclusiveness, and appropriateness to both specific and generalized occupational aims. First, the reasoning by which the planner has delineated the occupation of stenographer (clerical) must be examined for inclusiveness of like characteristics as applied to the categories of clerical and sales occupations. Failure to meet all criteria of this category suggests review and revision. Secondly, groupings must be tested for inclusion of elements which apply exclusively to that occupation. Finally, the revised structure needs to be considered for impact on achievement of specific program objectives within the context of overall, articulated program goals.

Analysis and subsequent acceptance of the occupational taxonomy will enable the planner to further delimit the selected occupation for pedagogical purposes. At this stage much valuable assistance can again be obtained through consultation with competent workers and leaders

---

[10] *Ibid.*, p. 18.

from all affected segments of society. Taken in combination with information from Department of Labor publications, resultant data provide a composite picture of the specific occupation, its general duties, environmental influences, and worker requisites.

Development of a program for a specific occupation also requires preparation of a detailed written summation of the human and technological requirements of the occupation. This process is best facilitated by preparation of an occupational sketch and qualifications profile. This profile (see Occupational Sketch and Qualifications Profile in Fig. 5-4) identifies and clarifies the following aspects of the selected occupation.

General description of job	Interests
Work performed	Temperaments
Worker requirements	Physical demands
Special vocational preparation	Working conditions
General educational requirements	Tasks
Aptitudes	

To illustrate preparation of an occupational sketch and qualifications profile, we shall continue to describe the job titled stenographer (clerical). Detail will follow the profile format and is a composite of information derived from interviews with competent workers and managers and from the *Dictionary of Occupational Titles,* volumes I and II.[11]

Occupational Sketch
&
Qualifications Profile

Example:

Description General.

Stenographer (clerical) DOT code 202.388
Takes dictation in shorthand of correspondence, reports, and other matter, and transcribes dictated material, using typewriter. Performs variety of clerical duties (Clerk, General Office), except when working in stenographic pool. May transcribe material from sound recordings. (Transcribing-Machine Operator). May perform stenographic duties in professional offices and be designated as Legal Steno . . .; Medical Steno . . .; Technical Steno. . . . May take dictation in foreign language and be known as Foreign Language Stenographer. May be designated according to department in which employed as Police Stenographer (gov. ser.). May work for public stenographic service and be designated Public Stenographer.

---

[11] *Ibid.,* p. 692.

OCCUPATIONAL SKETCH & QUALIFICATIONS PROFILE

Directions: Through consultation with qualified individuals and study of various publications write out descriptions of the following items.

Name of occupation _____

Job description:

Work performed:

Worker requirements:

Special vocational preparation:

General educational requirements:

Specific required aptitudes:

Specific required interests:

Specific required temperaments:

Physical demands:

Working conditions:

Specific occupational tasks:

Fig. 5-4

This job's relationship to data, people, and things follows:
(.388)

    3—data—(compiling) gathering, collating, or classifying information about data, people, or things. Reporting and/or carrying out a prescribed action in relation to the information is frequently involved.
    8—people—(no significant relationship)
    8—things—(no significant relationship)

Example:
Work Performed.

Work activities in this group primarily involve taking shorthand or machine and transcribing it with a typewriter.

Example:
Worker Requirements.

An occupationally significant combination of: The ability to understand the meaning and relationships of words and sentences; finger dexterity and eye-hand coordination for taking dictation or typing; form perception to recognize shorthand symbols; adaptability to routine, repetitive and uninvolved tasks; attention to detail in dictation or typed materials to avoid error; willingness to work according to instructions; ability to work with specialized terminology, such as that in the medical, legal, or engineering fields.

Example:
Special Vocational Preparation.

Completion of typing, shorthand, and other business courses in high school or business school. Successful performance on clerical aptitude and achievement tests.

Example:
General Educational Requirements.

Reasoning Development; Apply principles of logical or scientific thinking to define problems.
Mathematical Development; Perform ordinary arithmetic, algebraic and geometric procedure in standard, practical applications.
Language; Transcribe dictation, make appointments for executive and handle his personal mail, interview and screen people wishing to speak to him, and write routine correspondence on own initiative.

Example:
  Aptitudes.

  General Intelligence; above-average or high degree of general intelligence required by this job.
  Verbal; above-average, high, and extremely high degree of verbal ability.
  Numerical; medium to below-average degree of numerical ability.
  Spatial; below-average to low degree of spatial aptitude.
  Form Perception; above-average or high degree of form perception.
  Clerical Perception; ability to perceive detail in verbal or tabular material.
  Motor Coordination; above-average or high degree of motor coordination.
  Finger Dexterity; medium degree of finger dexterity.
  Manual Dexterity; medium degree of manual dexterity.
  Eye-Hand-Foot Coordination; negligible degree.
  Color Discrimination; negligible degree.

Example:
  Interests.

  Situations involving a preference for activities of a routine, concrete, organized nature versus situations involving a preference for activities of an abstract and creative nature.
  Situations involving a preference for activities concerned with people and the communication of ideas versus situations involving a preference for activities dealing with things and objects.

Example:
  Temperaments.

  Situations involving doing things only under specific instruction, allowing little or no room for independent action or judgment in working out job problems.
  Situations involving the precise attainment of set limits, tolerances, or standards.
  Situations involving repetitive or short-cycle operations carried out according to set procedures or sequences.

Example:
  Physical Demands.

  Light work—lifting 20 pounds maximum with frequent lifting and/or carrying objects up to 10 pounds.

Reaching, handling, fingering, and/or feeling.

Talking and/or hearing

Seeing

Example:

Working Conditions.

Inside: protection from weather conditions, but not necessarily from temperature changes.[12]

Example:

On-the-Job Tasks.

Take dictation in shorthand

Transcribe dictation on typewriter

Transcribe from sound recordings

Compose and type routine correspondence

Compile and type statistical reports

Answer phone

Route calls to appropriate official

Place outgoing calls

Greet visitors and send to appropriate official

Give information to callers

Schedule appointments

Read and route incoming mail

Locate and attach appropriate file to correspondence to be answered by employer

File correspondence and other records

Analyses of the human and technological aspects of crafts, trades, and professions provide viable means by which the complex nature of man at work may be structured and organized for application in educational enterprises at several levels of occupational maturity. Opportunities for learner self-realization are provided by educational experiences which are derived by occupational, job or task, and instructional analysis. The many dimensions of the world of work are described according to nine generalized occupational categories, 84 divisional titles, 603 specific groupings, and approximately 36,000 detailed job descriptions. Composed of an occupational group scheme and worker traits codifications, this taxonomy facilitates program development along lines of clearly defined crafts, trades, and professions.

Development of programs by employing occupational groupings and worker traits is guided by information elicited by questions such as:

---

[12] *Ibid.*, p. 651-656.

A. What is the general nature of the occupation?
B. What kinds of specific work activities are performed by persons employed in this occupation?
C. What are the unique and specific worker requirements deemed necessary for successful participation in this occupation?
D. What are the prerequisites to job entry?
E. What specific worker aptitudes, interests, and temperaments are required in this occupation?
F. What physical activities are required of an individual employed in this occupation?
G. What is the composition of the physical environment in which the worker must exist in order to successfully carry out job requirements?
H. What specific tasks must an individual perform in order to hold down this job?

Answers to these questions are obtained from interviews and discussions with qualified members of the world of work and through investigation and analysis of published guides, manuals, reports, and books. Curriculum development should be carried on in light of overall occupational program goals (kindergarten-to-adult). Specific program outcomes should be in keeping with a planned and articulated program which enables learners to enter, progress, and exit at appropriate developmental stages whenever and wherever exhibited competencies demand. Structure should be tested for universality, exclusiveness, and appropriateness to educational activities. Adequacy of aforementioned factors to overall program goals facilitates movement toward the final stage of developmental effort. The specific aspects of instructional analysis dealing with blocking, sequencing, and timing will be dealt with in Chapter 9, while techniques for review and revision of program are discussed in Chapters 10 and 11.

PROCESS ANALYSIS

A second technological categorical system is process analysis. Instead of analyzing crafts, trades, and professions, occupational program developers may analyze industrial and/or business processes. Process analysis results in educational experiences patterned after productive activities which utilize such representative processes as forming, material removal, finishing and coating, joining, and physical property modification. Such programs are best described in terms of a process-based continuum, which is shown in Table 5-1.

Table 5-1. Process-Material Continuum

PROCESSES APPLIED TO SPECIFIC MATERIALS[a]	MANUFACTURING PROCESSES[b]	COMMON PROCESSING CONCEPTS[c]	OPERATIONS ANALYSIS[d]
Single material orientation	Application to many materials	Manufacturing Processing concepts and systems	All industrial and/or business processes
Shaping plastic	Shaping	Assembly	Record system unit operations
Machining plastic	Machining	Casting, molding, etc.	
Finishing plastic	Finishing	Metallurgical	Unit operations in process industries
Joining plastic	Assembly	Finishing	Material handling operations
Physical property change	Physical property change	Inspection and quality control	Forming operations
		Manufacturing management	Material removing operations
		Manufacturing systems	Miscellaneous
		Material forming	Fastening operations
		Material removal	

[a] Traditional unit material-process experiences, i.e. wood, metal, ceramic, textile, etc.
[b] Department of Industrial Education, Oregon State University, Corvallis.
[c] American Society of Tool and Manufacturing Engineers.
[d] Arthur D. Little.

Organized according to processes used to alter or modify a specific material, traditional industrial-oriented programs deal almost exclusively with manufacturing processes. Representative programs are structured according to specific processes performed on metal, wood, plastic, ceramic, rubber, and similar materials. Each program is unitized and carried out independently of process application to any other material. An example of a unit material process organization follows:

Example:
Unit Material Process; Metalworking

A. Shaping metal
    1. Extraction from ore

    2. Casting
    3. Hot and cold working
    4. Powder metallurgy forming
  B. Machining metal
    1. Traditional chip removal
    2. Nontraditional machining
  C. Surface finishing metal
    1. Removal
    2. Polishing
    3. Coatings
  D. Joining metal parts and materials
  E. Changing physical properties of metals

Since this structure limits study in a given program to fundamental processes applied to a single material, many educators feel it does not adequately describe the many dimensions of human and technological interaction in the world of work. Many have sought to provide a broader understanding of manufacturing processes and occupations through program organizations which reflect applications of processing concepts to many and varied materials. Classification of common manufacturing processes results in the following structure.

Example:
Representative applications of manufacturing processes to all manner of materials.

A. SHAPING
  forging
  swaging
  spinning
  vacuum-forming
  explosive-forming
B. MACHINING
  turning
  boring
  electromechanical
  electron beam
  other

C. SURFACING
  parkerizing
  anodizing
  honing
  lapping
  other
D. JOINING
  welding
  adhesives
  riveting
  screw fastening
  other

  E. PHYSICAL PROPERTY CHANGE
    heat-treating
    hot and cold working
    shot peening
    other

Within this structure, shape change, machining, finishing, joining, and physical property alteration might well include processing concepts and materials of the following nature:

Processing Concept	*Materials*
Extracting	minerals, wood products, or agricultural products
Casting	iron, plastic, or plaster
Spinning	aluminum or wool
Rolling	steel or paper
Shaping	clay, wood, or rubber
Cutting	metal, stone, or cloth

Processes are organized and structured without regard to traditional material and/or industrial limitations. Hence, learners may engage in common processing activities which touch upon manufacture of textile, ceramic, plastic, wood and metal products. It is assumed that exposure to common processes employed by many and varied manufacturing industries will result in a more versatile and qualified graduate.

A third classification system also disregards traditional material and/or industrial limitations. Like the previous system, it categorizes processes regardless of materials. This system was developed by the American Society of Tool and Manufacturing Engineers to better describe the complex nature of the manufacturing industry. Three categories were added to the obvious process divisions: Inspection and quality control; Manufacturing management; and Manufacturing systems. Added to assembly, casting, molding, and metallurgical processing, finishing, forming, and material removal, these categories foster experiences which create awareness and develop understanding of:[13]

A. Activities and occupations required to maintain high product standards in compliance with all manner of regulations.
B. Occupations and functions related to the organization of scientific principles, men, money, and resources, for purposes of manufacture and distribution.
C. Occupational tasks and related jobs which seek to regulate and control manufacturing operations.

Although this system provides for broader coverage of manufacturing occupations and processes, some educators maintain that this codification is still too restrictive. They suggest that the complex nature of

[13] American Society of Tool & Manufacturing Engineers, *ASTME Technical Divisions* (Dearborn, Michigan, The Society, 1965).

productive activity is better understood by application of operations analysis. Processes (operations) are analyzed to include all manufacturing and information processing industries. The resulting classification incorporates 94 unit operations, relevant to the processing of all manner of information and materials. These are categorized into seven groupings as follows:[14]

1. Record system unit operations—conversion, arranging, selection, merging, transmission, storing, editing, processing, controlling, transferring, and interpretation.

2. Unit operations in processing industries—crystallization, screening, classification, flotation, sedimentation, filtration, centrifugation, solid-liquid extraction, liquid-liquid extraction, vapor-liquid transfer, fractionation, adsorption, evaporation, drying, peeling, combining, mixing, working, agitation, gas-liquid transfer of heat and mass, size reduction of solids, curing, heat transfer fluids and solids, heat transfer-vapors and liquids, and heat transfer-radiation.

3. Materials handling operations—pumping and compression, lifting and carrying, fluidized transport of solids, transport of fluids by flow.

4. Forming operations—vacuum deposition, casting, pressing and sintering, forging, rolling, stamping, bending, drawing, and extrusion.

5. Material-removing operations—turning, shaping and planning, drilling, boring, milling, broaching, sawing, grinding.

6. Miscellaneous operations—etching, molding, vacuum form and blow, laminating, cutting, shearing, combing, spinning, winding, felting, warping, knitting, braiding, weaving, buffing, polishing, deburring, painting, printing, dyeing, calender coating, electroplating, oxide coating, porcelain enameling, location, orienting, filing, evacuating.

7. Fastening operations—welding, brazing and soldering, pinning, sewing, seaming and curling, shrinking, pressing, gluing, and sealing.

There is evidence that the results of operations analysis have application to program organization in the areas of:

Agriculture   Public utilities
Forestry   Wholesale trade

[14] Arthur D. Little, Inc., *Analysis of Automation Potential by Means of Unit Operations Analysis* (Washington, D.C.: U.S. Department of Labor, 1965), C-66411.

Mining   Retail trade
Construction   Finance
Manufacturing   Insurance
Transportation   Real estate
Communication   Services

Organization of programs according to common processing concepts found within each of these areas has great potential for fostering improved learning. Attention is directed toward identification of many and varied processes, many of which, with minor modification, are applicable to all manner of materials regardless of the nature and structure of the industry. Common processing concepts organized to cross traditional material subject-matter lines include:

Peeling wood products and splitting animal hides.
Mixing construction aggregates and foodstuffs.
Rolling metal, paper, and felting.
Casting metal, plastic, or plaster.
Extruding plastics, metals, or candies.
Drilling in soil, stone, or wood.
Molding foodstuffs and plastics.
Laminating cookies, plywood, and fibers.
Cutting paper, textiles, and glass.
Polishing furniture, windows, or automobiles.
Painting houses, pictures, and vehicles.
Printing newspapers, billboards, and posters.
Filling gasoline tanks, cigarette machines, and pastries.
Pinning cloth, aluminum, or wood.
Sealing jars, packages, or pumps.

This organizational scheme makes possible categorization of many and varied occupations engaged in the processing of:

metal and metal products
ore refining and foundry products
food, tobacco, and related products
paper and related products
petroleum, coal, natural and manufactured gas
chemicals, plastics, synthetics, rubber, paint, and related products
wood, wood products, and related products
stone, clay, glass, and related products
leather, textiles, and related products

Programs so organized attempt to relate specific processes to many and varied occupations representing all manner of productive endeavor. The learner will perform selected operations, e.g., mixing of materials, such as sand, gravel, grain, liquids, and powders, as in construction, food processing, petroleum, and pharmaceutical industries. Hence, the learner not only gains competence with a given process but also becomes aware of the broader application of, and demand for, his newly acquired expertise.

Occupational programs may be organized according to one of the four systems of categorizing processes described in Table 5-1. They may also be organized according to an eclectic framework. That is, the best of several schemes may be employed. Prevailing philosophy and/or goal orientation will (and should) determine the extent to which one or a combination of classifications is utilized in curriculum development. Regardless of the system employed, the planner must identify both the human and the technological characteristics which affect man in the occupational arena. Emphasis upon only manipulative skill development will result in ill-equipped graduates. Here, as with other organizational patterns, provisions must be made for development of varying levels of competence. Appreciation of desirable work attitudes, job purposes and duties, worker and job requirements, and employment outlook and conditions are as important as skills with specific processes.

With process analysis, as with any other approach to organizing content, development should be carried out within the established kindergarten-to-adult, articulated occupational program philosophy, goal, and structure. The ideals of easy entry, easy exit, progression at one's own rate, and others must be maximized by the program model and individual experiences. The curriculum organization must also be tested for applicability to articulated program goals, exclusiveness of classification elements, and match with the human and technological needs of society. If the selected process taxonomy meets the above criteria, effort may be directed toward identification of specific work tasks associated with identified categories of human and material behavior. Task identification and sequencing are treated in Chapters 9 and 10.

MATERIAL-PRODUCT ANALYSIS

A third method of categorizing elements of technology for organizing occupational programs is dependent on simultaneous classification of materials and products. Some of the more common, traditional material-product oriented programs are entitled woodworking, metalworking, and plastics technology. Such classifications are usually the product of trade associations, technical societies, production enterprises, and governmental agencies. Such schemes group items belonging to the same

Table 5-2. Alternate Material-Product Categorizations

Scheme A	Scheme B	Scheme C	Scheme D
Animals and animal products	Foods	Textiles	Vegetable products
Vegetable food-products and beverages	Textile fibers	Leather	Animal products
Vegetable products, except food, fibers, and wood	Crude forest products	Wood	Mineral products
Textiles	Metals and sulfurs	Paper	Synthetic products
Wood and paper	Fuels and power	Rubber	
Nonmetallic minerals		Glass	
Ores, metals, and manufactures		China	
Machinery and vehicles		Metals	
Chemicals and allied products		Gold, silver, platinum	
Miscellaneous		Gems	
		Petroleum	
		Paints and varnishes	
		Cosmetics	
		Foods	

area within distinct categories such as textiles, machinery and vehicles, and food products.

In recent years, leaders in all sectors of the economy have become cognizant of the need to expand career education experiences beyond the ordinary limitations of traditional materials and products. Such thinking is especially appropriate in a world of endless varieties of synthetics and diminishing natural resources. The demand for and short supply of many materials, and introduction of new substitute materials, has created a decided need for better understanding and utilization of materials and products. Development of new and improved materials has been given impetus by space exploration, new communications devices, and the demand for a higher standard of living. Ceramics, plastics, and exotic materials are being utilized in increasing quantity for products which heretofore employed copper, steel, animal products, vegetable derivatives, or wood products.

Expansion and development of programs according to contemporary material-product categories may be based on one or more of the classification systems in Table 5-2. Examination of alternate material-product codifications provides valuable insight into the development of program rationale and structure. One such taxonomy, Scheme A in Table 5-2, categorizes need-satisfying materials and products into ten divisions representing:

Animal & animal products
Vegetable food-products &
  beverages
Vegetable products, except food,
  fibers, & wood
Textiles
Wood & paper
Nonmetallic minerals
Ores, metals, & manufactures
Machinery & vehicles
Chemicals & allied products
Commodities not
  classified elsewhere

Planning of a program for a selected material-product area, such as vegetable food-products and beverages (see Commodity Classification in Fig. 5-5) can be facilitated by examining the subcategories of:

Grains and preparations
Fodders and feeds
Vegetables
Fruits and nuts
Oil seeds and vegetable oils and fats
Cocoa, coffee, tea, spices, and leavening agents
Sugar, molasses, syrup, honey, confectionery
Beverages

Analysis of such subdivisions is important to decision-making re program structure and content.

Investigation of the fourth classification method, or Scheme D in Table 5-2, is described in Material-Product Categorization (Fig. 5-6). All manner of materials and products are classed into four major categories called vegetable, animal, mineral, and synthetic products. The subcategories also are listed.

Whereas these four schemes describe materials and products in varied ways, they all provide a frame of reference by which educators may develop rationale and structure for occupational programs. Each scheme possesses distinct characteristics which may or may not satisfy

COMMODITY CLASSIFICATION*

Animals and animal products (except wool and hair)
  Meats
  Dairy products
  Fish
  Animal and fish oils, fats, and greases
  Leather and leather manufactures
  Miscellaneous animal products
Vegetable food products and beverages
  Grains and preparations
  Fodders and feeds
  Vegetables
  Fruits and nuts
  Oil seeds and vegetable oils and fats
  Cocoa, coffee, tea, spices, and leavening agents
  Sugar, molasses, sirup, honey, confectionery
  Beverages
Vegetable products, except food, fibers, and wood
  Rubber and similar gums and manufactures
  Gums, resins, and balsams
  Tobacco
  Starch and vegetable glue
  Miscellaneous vegetable products
Textiles
  Cotton, cotton fabrics, and knit goods
  Manufactures of cotton fabric
  Jute and jute manufactures
  Flax, hemp, and ramie
  Miscellaneous vegetable fibers, straw or grass
  Wool and hair and manufactures
  Silk and manufactures thereof
  Miscellaneous textile products
Wood and paper
  Lumber (logs, timber, and other unmanufactured or partly manufactured wood)
  Lumber for building and factory use

Manufactures of wood (except furniture)
Furniture of wood
Paper (except printed matter)
Books and other printed matter
Miscellaneous paper products
Nonmetallic Minerals
  Coal, petroleum, asphalt, and mineral wax
  Stone, sand, and cementitious material
  Glass and glass products
  Clay and clay products
  Abrasive materials, asbestos, and chalk
  Mica, rare minerals
  Precious stones and imitation stones
  Sulfur, magnesia, salt, and graphite
  Miscellaneous nonmetallic minerals
Ores, metals, and manufacturers (except machinery, vehicles, and electrical supplies)
  Iron and steel
  Iron and steel manufactures
  Ferro-alloying ores and metals, and alloy steel manufacturers
  Aluminum, antimony, bismuth, cadmium, and cobalt
  Copper, brass, and bronze
  Precious metals, metal jewelry, and plated ware
  Clocks, watches, and dials
  Tin and zinc
  Miscellaneous ores, metals, alloys, and metal maufactures
Machinery and Vehicles
  Power generating equipment, except electrical
  Electrical machinery and supplies
  Vehicles, except agricultural vehicles and steam locomotives
  Agricultural machinery and implements
  Construction, conveying, and hoisting machinery

Mining, oil well, and pumping machinery

Metalworking machinery

Textile, sewing, and shoe machinery

Industrial plant machinery

Miscellaneous machinery

Chemicals and allied products

Coal-tar products

Medicinal and pharmaceutical preparations

Acid (except coal-tar) and anhydrides, alcohol, etc.

Chemical compounds (except medicinals, acids, alcohols, and coal-tar products)

Paints, varnishes, lacquers, and related products

Explosives, fireworks, and ammunition

Soaps, cosmetics, and toilet preparations

Disinfectants and water treatments

Miscellaneous chemical products

Commodities not elsewhere classified

Scientific and professional apparatus and supplies

Office, printing, lithographic and educational supplies

Toys, athletic and sporting goods, and insignia

Containers

Fire extinguishing apparatus and supplies

Brushes and brooms

Miscellaneous articles

*National Bureau of Standards, Supplement to National Directory of Commodity Specifications; Washington, D.C.: United States Department of Commerce; 1947; page 3.

Fig. 5-5

criteria set forth by individual planners. Selection of an appropriate material-product organizational pattern is dependent upon prevailing philosophy, articulated program goals, and short-range instructional objectives.

After the major material-product classification system is selected, general and specific areas may be organized for purposes of instruction. There are several alternate methods for accomplishing this task. These are analyses according to (a) nature and structure of materials, (b) production consequences, and (c) product utility and consumption (Fig. 5-7). Whereas each of these schemes will be discussed separately in actual practice, they are applied in concert when and where they are deemed most appropriate in material-product organizational patterns or systems.

The first technique holds that raw materials for any processed part, machine or foodstuff have many and varied properties. Content is structured according to numerous characteristics which determine the suitability of material to all manner of industrial processing. Structure and content are derived from analyses of the nature of both metallic and nonmetallic materials and of both organic and inorganic materials. Metallic substances such as ferrous and nonferrous materials are organized according to metal solidification, heat-treating, and lattice dislocation. Each division includes:

MATERIAL-PRODUCT CATEGORIZATION

Vegetable Products
  fibers
  rubber & allied products
  oils, fats, & waxes
  food products
  beverages
  gums & resins
  spices & condiments
  vegetable dyes & pigments
  tanning materials
  woods
  miscellaneous plant products

Animal Products
  fibers
  hides & skins
  furs, hairs, bristles, feathers, &
    plumage
  horns, bones, ivory, & allied pro-
    ducts
  pearls, shells, & other marine pro-
    ducts
  animal oils, fats, waxes, perfumes
    & pigments
  miscellaneous animal products

Mineral Products
  coal
  petroleum
  building & ornamental stones
  abrasives
  miscellaneous rocks & minerals
  lime, sand, and gravel
  clays
  asbestos
  asphalt & allied substances
  phosphatic deposits
  gems or precious stones
  mineral pigments
  ores of metals
  nonmetallic elements

Synthetic Products
  utilization of waste & by-products
  coal tar derivatives
  synthetic dyestuffs
  synthetic drugs and chemicals
  celluloid
  casein
  synthetic resins & plastics
  artificial fibers

*Henry J. Vanstone. The Raw Materials of Commerce. London (NY), Pitman, 1929. 428 pp.

Fig. 5-6

Metal Solidification
  crystallization
  atomic lattice
  crystal structure
Heat-Treating
  solid solutions
  precipitation
  age hardening
  quenching and tempering
  annealing and normalizing

Lattice Defects & Dislocation
  plastic deformation
  dislocation
  hardening
  recrystallization
  recovery
  creep, sharp, point, and
    strain hardening

Nonmetallic substances are further categorized as either inorganic or organic. The resultant two-part taxonomy includes the following:

MATERIAL-PRODUCT ORGANIZATIONAL PATTERNS

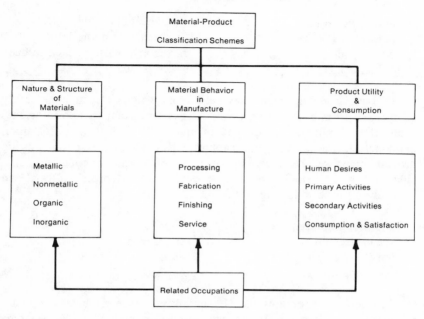

Fig. 5-7

Inorganic Substances
  cement
  ceramics
  glass
  graphite
  minerals

Organic Substances
  leather
  paper
  petroleum products
  plastics
  rubber
  wood

Each is, in turn, investigated and codified according to representative divisions labeled:

Rubbers
  elastomers
  natural rubber
  synthetic rubber

Refractory Materials
  ceramics
  fire clay
  magnesite, chromite, graphite,
    and dolomite
  silica

The bonds of each are then identified and organized according to ionic or heteropolar, covalent or homopolar, and secondary valence or cohesive bond.

Study of the physical state of materials should entail:

allotropic	body-centered cubic lattice
amorphous	face-centered cubic lattice
crystalline	hexagonal, close-packed lattice
polymorphic	space lattice

Of equal concern are the several factors which determine suitability of material to manufacturing process. It is important to know the mechanical and physical properties of materials and their effect upon manufacturing processes. Physical properties within the manufacturing process might well be categorized in terms of thermal conductivity, specific heat, and thermal expansion. Specific material property tests lend themselves to the following codification:

compression strength	ductility
shear strength	endurance
tensile strength	hardness
torsional strength	impact

Instructional programs may be organized to describe how a material behaves in given manufacturing processes and may, at the same time, create varying levels of occupational awareness and technical competence. The consequences of production processes for the functioning of materials and for man may be made known to learners. Understandings and skills may be fostered by educational experiences which involve:

deformation processes
fabrication
finishing
heat-treating
material formation from liquid states
material formation from particle states
material removal

Note the sample material-product based occupational program outline in Fig. 5-8. First, the primary classifications of thermoplastics and thermosetting plastics were established. Second, plastic materials were further categorized for application and use as production materials. They were classified according to thermal, flow, elastic, solid-liquid flow characteristics. Finally, a distinct category was formulated for durable and nondurable goods production. Applications of end-product manufacture

PROGRAM OUTLINE
Plastics and Their Manufacture

Primary classifications
  thermoplastics
  thermosetting

Acrylic resins
Amino resins
Cellulose derivatives
Epoxy resins
Phenolic resins
Polymides
Polyesters
Polyethylene
Silicones
Styrenes derivatives
Silicones
Vinyl compounds

Plastics as Production Materials

Thermal energy transfer
Flow characteristics

Elastic-visco-elastic behavior
Reversal of solid-liquid change

End-Product Manufacture

Plastics molding
Plastic extrusion
Calendering
Vacuum forming
Blow molding
Hand lay-up
Spray lay-up
Matched metal molding
Electroplating
Spray-coating
Dip coating

Occupations in the Plastics Industry

Direct employment opportunities
Related employment opportunities

Fig. 5-8

to plastic materials were classified as molding, extrusion, calendering, and similar processes.

Whereas this structure was derived from a material-product basis, no attempt was made to de-emphasize the role of man. Man and his interaction with technology is the central theme, the purpose and thrust, of program development. Analysis of a specific material; its nature, structure, and properties; its behavior in production processes; and its relationship to final product, provide the planner with a framework for fostering varying degrees of occupational awareness and expertise in program development.

Categorization of utility forms and consumption patterns are an alternate method of organizing material-product oriented programs. All forms of productive activity result in utility in the form of goods or services. Utility means usefulness or want-satisfying potential. Because man strives to satisfy his desires through production and subsequent consumption of goods and services, it is logical to assume that occupational programs might well be benefited by being organized according to the economics of utility and consumption.

This point can best be illustrated by the following utility-consumption model.

Basic human physiological, social, and emotional needs are satisfied through individual or collective productive effort. Man is first of all concerned with gratification of basic needs involving food, clothing, and shelter. Upon satisfaction of these desires, effort is directed toward gratification of social and emotional needs such as acceptance, integration, health, intellectual growth, social reform, peace, solitude, and repose. Vast quantities of human energy are spent in search of the best means by which to gratify these needs. Since goods and services are produced in order to sustain life and to fulfill higher level social and self-fulfilling needs, men produce for one reason alone—for the express purpose of satisfying personal desires through consumption.

This being the case, productive effort is categorized (Fig. 5-9) according to form, time, and place utility. Effort to create utility thus can be categorized into primary and secondary productive activity. Such effort involves materials, products, and occupations related to agricultural, forestry, mining, and manufacturing activities. Representative primary utility categories and subdivisions include:

Primary Utility Institutions	Materials & Products	Occupations
Plant farming	Vegetable, grain, fruit, and nuts	farmer, cash grain farmhand driver, agricultural seed cutter orchardist fig caprifier
Forestry	forests, forest tracts, and woodlands	jumpmaster fire lookout forester aid tree pruner box cutter greens picker
(Manufacturing) Food processing	food, tobacco, and related products	honey grader cheese blender dough mixer noodle mixer noodle pressman batter mixer

PRODUCT UTILITY AND CONSUMPTION CATEGORIZATION

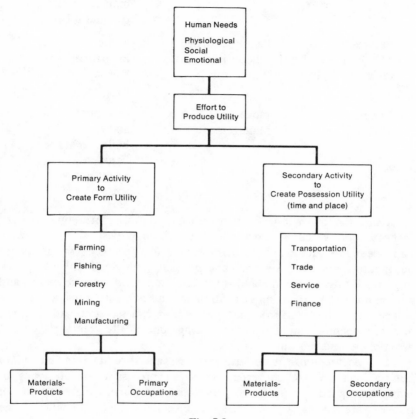

Fig. 5-9

Effort to make goods and services available at the right time and appropriate place is carried out by secondary institutions normally classified as commercial business units. Commercial agencies seek to satisfy human wants by facilitating possession of goods and services through transportation, trade, service, and financial endeavors. Sample secondary utility agencies and their major material-product and occupational categories are:

Secondary Utility Institutions	Materials, Products & Services	Occupations
Transportation	public vehicle transport for	baggageman bus driver

	passengers and freight	depot master manager, traffic manifest clerk gas and oil man
Service (Barbering and cosmetology)	beauty and/or related individual treatments	barber manicurist hair stylist wig dresser
Finance	monetary management	accountant auditor budget manager bank cashier credit analyst trust officer

Thus, the product utility and consumption organizational pattern seeks to codify man's efforts to gratify human desires into primary and secondary activities. Primary productive activity centers about occupations, materials, services, and products concerned with (a) growing, harvesting, catching, and gathering land and aquatic plant and animal life[15] (b) extraction of coal, metal and nonmetal ores, and rocks, stone, gravel, and sand from underground and surface excavations . . .[16] and (c) refining, mixing, compounding, chemically treating, heating, assembling, and finishing.

The occupations, materials, services, and products of secondary business activity are concerned with (a) provision for all types of public transportation for passengers and freight, including operation of public warehousing and storage establishments,[17] (b) facilitating the most efficient exchange of desired goods and services, and (c) obtaining suitable financing for the conduct of business as it relates to consumption.

Should this classification scheme be selected as appropriate for purposes of organizing programs, it must be subjected to the same tests and analyses prescribed for previous categorization techniques.

DEVELOPMENTAL GUIDELINES

Attempts to organize content which deals with both the human and technological aspects of the world of work should satisfy several impor-

[15] *D.O.T., op. cit.,* Vol. II, p. 78.
[16] *Ibid.,* p. 595.
[17] *Ibid.,* p. 597.

tant developmental criteria. These appear in the Developmental Checklist for technology-based occupational programs (Fig. 5-10). They provide a series of checks and balances for the planning effort.

The curriculum development process involves three interdependent phases (see Fig. 5-10). The first involves clarification of educational thought, specification of program objectives, and analysis of the compatibility of specific versus articulated program goals. The second entails the organization of knowledge. Available categorizations are investigated and analyzed for application to the task at hand. An organizational scheme is selected and delimited for its respective parts. The third and final stage evaluates the other two and facilitates revision.

DEVELOPMENTAL CHECKLIST

DIRECTIONS: Complete, in order, each of the following aspects when attempting to develop a rationale and structure for technology-based occupational programs.

I. Determine Educational Direction:

 A. State prevailing philosophy.

 B. State specific technology-based program objectives.

 C. State the extent to which specific objectives contribute to fulfillment of overall kindergarten-to-adult articulated program objectives.

II. Select and Organize Body of Knowledge.

 A. Search available resources and list potential classification schemes.

 B. Identify and list what you consider to be the best scheme.

 C. List the major units of the selected scheme.

III. Test and Revise Scheme

 A. Does the selected classification scheme represent the entire spectrum or field of a given occupation, processing activity, material, or product? YES_____, NO_____. If no, state why, and then how it might be altered to include all of the affected area.

 B. Does the scheme possess mutually exclusive subcategories? YES_____, NO_____. If no, state why, and how you propose to remedy the situation.

 C. Is the scheme practical for purposes of occupational simulation? YES_____, NO_____. If no state why, and how it must be altered to be appropriate for occupational education activities.

Fig. 5-10

An example will illustrate the use of the checklist. Assume that a planner has been directed to identify and structure a body of knowledge and skills required of dental laboratory technicians. The ultimate purpose of the program is to develop salable job competencies. The planner must first consider the role of the program within the total articulated occupational program. He must consider occupational needs, learner characteristics, community composition, educational resources, and appropriate pedagogical structures. Analyses of these factors enable the planner to formulate a philosophy which will guide development efforts. Analyses of alternate classification schemes, e.g., technology, occupational families, business system, and integrated, define direction and thrust. A statement of prevailing philosophy for item I-A on the Developmental Checklist might read:

Checklist, Item I-A

An articulated kindergarten-to-adult occupational program designed to develop salable entry level skills for employment as a dental laboratory technician may best be structured through consideration of alternate technology-based categorizations including (a) craft, trade and profession, (b) process, and (c) material-product analysis.

Specific technology-based program objectives thus can be formulated in keeping with the statement of philosophy. Such objectives might read:

Checklist, Item I-B

1. The learner will demonstrate knowledge and understanding of the construction and repair of dental appliances through completion of oral, written, laboratory, and on-the-job experiences.
2. The learner will demonstrate knowledge and understanding of dental laboratory technician worker requirements, special vocational preparation, general education requirements, aptitudes, interests, temperaments, physical demands, and working conditions through completion of oral, written, laboratory, and cooperative work experiences.

Effort then would be directed toward development of a statement regarding how specific program objectives will, in fact, enhance overall articulated program effort. A statement of this nature might well read:

Checklist, Item I-C

This is a specialized occupational experience designed to provide learners with salable job skills facilitating employment as dental laboratory technicians. Intended primarily for postsecondary level, it deals with those individuals who, having successfully completed exploratory experiences in health-related activities, have indicated a desire and exhibited potential for employment in this field. Upon completion of this experience, learners may pursue a number of alternatives: (a) enter the labor market as a dental laboratory technician, (b) seek related health care work, (c) enter a related health education program, (d) seek a totally different field of work, or (e) continue advanced education in dental or allied health fields.

Structure and organization of the body of knowledge representing the occupation of dental laboratory technician is facilitated through study of appropriate categorization schemes. A listing of major pedagogical units can be derived from analysis, delimitation, and selection of a workable classification scheme. An investigation of appropriate schemes which give order to the many dimensions of the occupation of dental laboratory technician could result in a listing of these alternatives.

Checklist, Item II-A

Craft, trade, and profession   process, materials, and products.

When considering each categorization technique, the planner must seek answers to questions such as:

"Can all of the factors which act upon the successful work of a dental laboratory technician be fully described through organization of content based upon _____ analysis?"

This question must, in turn, be asked of each classification scheme. For example, if the craft, trade, and profession scheme were selected as the means by which to structure the occupation of dental laboratory techician, item II-B would read as follows:

Checklist, Item II-B

Craft, trade, or profession classification scheme.

Major pedagogical units derived from this structure could include the following:

Checklist, Item II-C

Full and partial denture fabrication
Crown, inlay, and wire-frame construction
Porcelain tooth construction
Appliance polishing

The third phase is concerned with test and revision of the selected organizational scheme (see Fig. 5-10). The planner must determine whether the taxonomy allows for and incorporates all the many and varied aspects of the dental laboratory technician occupation. If any phase or segment is not accounted for, appropriate action must be taken to remedy the deficiency. The scheme must likewise be examined for clearly defined organizational categories. If unrelated items appear in the pattern, they must be rejected. Simply stated, exclusive pedagogical groupings should not be contaminated with apples and oranges if the purpose is to study pears. The scheme should also be examined for ease and effectiveness of application to real-life learning situations. If the scheme cannot be implemented readily, it is of no practical value. Finally, the planner must determine whether the scheme will actually achieve the purpose for which it was intended. Should the response to any one of the above be "No," action must be taken to rectify the situation.

The identification and sequencing of unique and specific instructional concepts will be discussed at length in subsequent chapters.

SUMMARY

This chapter has described the alternate technology-based organizational schemes which facilitate analysis along several dimensions of the world of work. Narratives and examples were used to provide answers to the following questions:

1. What are the characteristics of occupational programs which are organized according to technological categories?

A program which derives structure from technological foundations seeks to develop skills through participation in real and simulated experiences with the tools, processes, materials, and products of crafts, trades, and professions. Supporters of technology-based programs contend that such experiences best integrate work roles with life styles and patterns of learners.

2. How may a program planner analyze technology to establish major units for occupational programs?

Those who attempt to organize knowledge so that learning experiences incorporate all manner of technological activity may employ several alternate schemes. Primary schemes which provide guidance and direction in the developmental process include analyses of (a) crafts, trades, or professions, (b) processes, or (c) materials and products. These technological categorizations were illustrated in Fig. 5-2.

3. How may the adequacy of a given technological structure be tested for appropriateness in specific educational situations?

The adequacy of an organizational structure may be tested with the aid of three basic criteria. The first determines whether the selected taxonomy includes all characteristics of the technical area in question. A second test ascertains the exclusive nature of each of the classification scheme's subcategories. A third test is designed to determine the extent to which the structure will actually achieve the purpose for which it was intended.

ACTIVITIES

1. Secure detailed information on one of the following programs and write a summarization of its pedagogical structure and content.

Auto mechanic	Nurses aide
Carpenter	Plumber
Computer programmer	Policeman
Dietician	Private pilot
Electronic technician	Salesclerk
Florister	Sheet metalworker
Fry cook	Typist

2. Select one of the technology-based analysis techniques discussed in this chapter and write your own rationale for its use as a basis for selection and organization of content for purposes of occupational program development.
3. Develop a rationale and structure for an occupational program based upon analysis of a technique discussed in this chapter. Use the developmental checklist as your guide in preparation of program. Include a written:

   a. Classification scheme
   b. Evaluation structure and content
   c. Statement of program objectives
   d. Statement of your philosophy

4. Prepare a written justification and structure for an occupational program organized according to the *Dictionary of Occupational Titles*.
5. Prepare a written plan by which you would account for varied life styles and career patterns in the development of an occupational program.
6. Utilizing the *Occupational Outlook Handbook,* prepare a written profile of a given occupation. Describe the character of the work,

preemployment requisites, occupational outlook, employment locations, earnings, and working conditions.

7. Select an occupation which is of interest to you and arrange for a personal interview with a competent representative of industry, labor, or a professional society. Ask questions which will elicit information re:

Aptitudes	Special vocational preparation
General educational	Temperaments
requirements	Work performed
General nature of the job	Worker requirements
Interests	Working conditions
Physical demands	

8. Utilize the *Dictionary of Occupational Titles* to prepare a written worker qualifications profile for an occupation of your choice.
9. Develop a rationale and structure for an occupational program dealing exclusively with manufacturing processes in the metalworking industry.

DISCUSSION QUESTIONS

1. Which characteristics best describe an occupational program organized according to an analysis of the technological foundations of the world of work?
2. Through which organizational scheme might occupational program objectives best be accomplished? Be prepared to defend your choice.
3. Contrast and compare process versus material-product based occupational course organization.
4. What relationship should exist between specific technology based programs and the total K-to-adult occupational continuum?
5. Differentiate between craft-, trade-, and profession-oriented programs and material-product-based programs.
6. How can the program planner tie the entire program to the career patterns of individual learners in a manner enabling them to maximize their ability to select goals leading toward a full life?
7. What are the drawbacks of utilizing the "Data, People, Things" categorization for purposes of program organization?
8. Discuss the most important aspects of man's motivation to work.
9. Discuss the changing nature of work and its effects upon program planning effort.
10. Discuss the pros and cons of the product utility and consumption categorization for purposes of program development.

11. What problems do you anticipate in attempting to design a program based on identification and analysis of technology levels?
12. Describe what you think are the greatest barriers to effectively categorizing the many dimensions of the world of work.

BIBLIOGRAPHY

Begeman, Myron L., and Amstead, B. H. *Manufacturing Processes*. New York: Wiley, 1969.

Campbell, James S. *Principles of Manufacturing Materials & Processes*. New York: McGraw-Hill, 1961.

Datsko, Joseph. *Material Properties & Manufacturing Processes*. New York: Wiley, 1966.

DeGarno, Paul E. *Materials & Processes in Manufacturing*. New York: Macmillan, 1962.

Dubin, Robert. *The World of Work*. Englewood Cliffs, N.J.: Prentice-Hall, 1958.

Edgar, Carroll. *Fundamentals of Manufacturing Processes and Materials*. Reading, Mass.: Addison Wesley, 1965.

Heron, Alexander. *Why Men Work*. Stanford, California: Stanford U. Press, 1948.

Herzberg, Frederick. *The Motivation to Work*. New York: Wiley, 1959.

Herzberg, Frederick. *Work and the Nature of Man*. Cleveland, Ohio: World Publ., 1966.

Killough, Hugh B., and Killough, Lucy W. *Raw Materials of Industrialism*. New York: Crowell, 1929.

Lux, Donald G., et al. *A Rationale & Structure For Industrial Arts Subject Matter*. Columbus, Ohio, 1966, Series C-002.

Marin, Joseph. *Engineering Materials*. Englewood Cliffs, N.J.: Prentice-Hall, 1952.

Paustian, John H. *Engineering Materials & Manufacturing Processes*. Dubuque, Iowa: W. C. Brown, 1952.

Reich, Edward, and Siegler, Carlton. *Consumer Goods and How to Use Them*. New York: American Book, 1937.

Scheller, Gilbert S. *Engineering Manufacturing Methods*. New York: McGraw-Hill, 1953.

Scoby, Mary Margaret. *Teaching Children About Technology*. Bloomington, Ill.: McKnight, 1970.

Thomas, Geoffrey G. *Production Technology*. London (N.Y.): Oxford Press, 1970.

United States Department of Labor. *Dictionary of Occupational Titles*. 3rd ed., Washington, D.C.: U.S. Government Printing Office, 1965. Vol. I and II.

United States Department of Labor. *Occupational Outlook Handbook*. No. 1650. Washington, D.C.: U.S. Government Printing Office, 1970-71.

Vanstone, Henry J. *The Raw Materials of Commerce*. London, N.Y.: Pitman, 1929, Vol. I and II.

Venn, Grant. *Man, Education, and Work*. Washington, D.C.: American Council on Education, 1964.

Chapter Six

Business Systems Analyses

INTRODUCTION

Program planners charged with the responsibility of developing simulated occupational experiences from the entire spectrum of business activity are beset with numerous problems and questions. This chapter answers the following:

- What are the characteristics of occupational programs organized and structured on the basis of business system analysis?
- How does a program planner conceptualize a structure of business system operational units as a basis for selection of activities and experiences for occupational education endeavors?
- How does a program planner test the adequacy of a given taxonomy for application to unique and specific educational environs?

Some curriculum builders identify content and organize instruction according to interpretations and analyses of elements of the American business system. Supporters of this approach de-emphasize skill development and craft activities. They emphasize familiarization of young and old alike with contemporary productive society and performance models in the world of work. They advocate content which entails both the technical and the human aspects of all manner of productive effort. Coursework and related experiences create awareness of and lend understanding to the problems of organizing, directing, controlling, and evaluating the efforts of men, money, machines, and materials in efficient combination. The manner in which these resources are utilized in various and sundry enterprises is the primary concept which interpretation and analysis of the business system make clear.

RATIONALE

Those who support this concept contend that experiences in occupational education should foster intelligibility of man's effort to produce and distribute goods and services within the framework of the American business system. Pioneers in curriculum development recognized the need to study large fields of human interaction when developing new or revised educational programs. As early as 1928 the respected curriculum expert, Henry Harap, suggested, "There is almost unanimous agreement among leaders in curriculum-making that revision should be made by studying the large fields of human activity."[1]

That this belief is widely shared is evidenced by the work of Face and Flug, Stern, and Kirby and Brown. Wesley Face, Eugene R. Flug, and others identified knowledges necessary to understand American industry. Their conceptual model is explained in Fig. 6-1. The structure

[1] Henry Harap, *The Technique of Curriculum Making* (New York: Macmillan, 1928), p. 268.

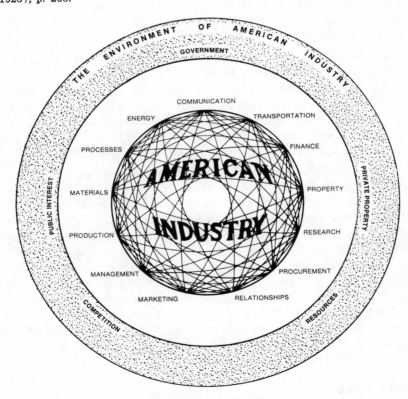

A CONCEPTUAL STRUCTURE OF THE KNOWLEDGES NECESSARY
TO UNDERSTAND AMERICAN INDUSTRY

(Courtesy: American Industry, Stout State University, Menomonie, Wisconsin)

Fig. 6-1

implies that exploration of industry can best be accomplished through study of communication, transportation, finance, property, research, procurement, relationships, marketing, management, production, materials, processes, and energy. After an extensive analysis of the business system, the thirteen concepts were proposed as a structure which should establish greater consistency across occupational education endeavors. Level 1 is outlined in Fig. 6-2.

The belief that educational activities should be "for" and "about" industry prompted Jacob Stern to identify common functions of industry. The resultant "Functions of Industry" program was developed to provide a structure for instruction pertaining to industry. Industrial activity was divided into two distinct categories: product-producing endeavor and product-servicing activity. Divided according to function, product production consisted of research, development, planning, and production. Service of products was divided into diagnosis, correction, and testing.

Kirby and Brown were likewise cognizant of the fact that American industry was not being interpreted via traditional curricula. After studying American industry, they proposed that *Industriology* constitute a study of American enterprise through analysis of the principle functions of basic industries, classified as (1) primary, (2) manufacturing, (3) distribution, and (4) service. Major activities, representative of many industries include: development and design, internal finance and office services, manufacturing or processing, marketing, industrial relations, and purchasing. The conceptual model of Industriology is diagrammed in Fig. 6-3.

Justification for this content organization is based in the belief that current educational experiences emphasize technology at the expense of creating awareness of contemporary productive society and its impact on modern man. Cochran put it: "The rationale for such programs is derived from the fact that this aspect of our society is not properly presented in any other curricular area."[2]

Thus, occupational educators should be charged with the responsibility of identifying content and organizing instruction so that the educational experience entails systematic effort, employing both human and technological resources and is directed toward discernable ends. Instruction should respond quickly to changes in technology and to respective occupational roles. It should become relevant to American enterprise and the contemporary needs of real people with real learning characteristics and real career pattern potentialities. The nature of contemporary

---

[2] Leslie Cochran, *Innovative Programs in Industrial Education* (Bloomington, Ill.: McKnight, 1970), p. 38.

LEVEL I—AMERICAN INDUSTRY COURSE OUTLINE

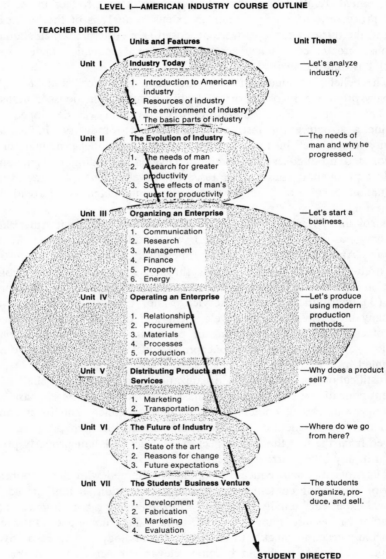

TEACHER DIRECTED

Units and Features

Unit Theme

Unit I — **Industry Today**
—Let's analyze industry.
1. Introduction to American industry
2. Resources of industry
3. The environment of industry
4. The basic parts of industry

Unit II — **The Evolution of Industry**
—The needs of man and why he progressed.
1. The needs of man
2. A search for greater productivity
3. Some effects of man's quest for productivity

Unit III — **Organizing an Enterprise**
—Let's start a business.
1. Communication
2. Research
3. Management
4. Finance
5. Property
6. Energy

Unit IV — **Operating an Enterprise**
—Let's produce using modern production methods.
1. Relationships
2. Procurement
3. Materials
4. Processes
5. Production

Unit V — **Distributing Products and Services**
—Why does a product sell?
1. Marketing
2. Transportation

Unit VI — **The Future of Industry**
—Where do we go from here?
1. State of the art
2. Reasons for change
3. Future expectations

Unit VII — **The Students' Business Venture**
—The students organize, produce, and sell.
1. Development
2. Fabrication
3. Marketing
4. Evaluation

STUDENT DIRECTED

(Courtesy: American Industry, Stout State University, Menomonie, Wisconsin)

Fig. 6-2

INDUSTRIOLOGY

the science of industry

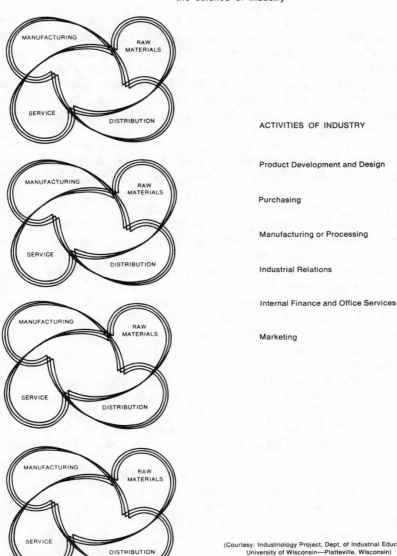

ACTIVITIES OF INDUSTRY

Product Development and Design

Purchasing

Manufacturing or Processing

Industrial Relations

Internal Finance and Office Services

Marketing

(Courtesy: Industriology Project, Dept. of Industrial Education, University of Wisconsin—Platteville. Wisconsin)

Fig. 6-3

enterprise and its impact on modern man must be understood by those who would find their rightful place in the world of work.

Identification of developmental stages and subsequent selection of simulated occupational experiences must follow a plan involving clearly defined behavioral objectives, suitable taxonomy, adequate hardware and software resources, and provisions for program management. The planner must isolate and analyze those aspects of the economy which can result in instructional elements which will assure desired behavioral outcomes. In order to successfully achieve this end, he must describe accurately the experience which is to be simulated for students. Program development must focus on expected program outcomes, the conditions under which learning will be expected to occur, and the measure(s) by which successes or failures will be determined.

The second phase of the program development process is the establishment of a taxonomy which is compatible with stated measurable objectives. During this stage, the planner must become familiar with various and sundry classification schemes and other tools for analyzing the world of work. Awareness and understanding of categorical systems such as functional, activity, product, ownership, size and level of mechanization facilitate conceptualization of structures for simulated occupational experience which will be representative of the world of work.

Selection of an appropriate taxonomy facilitates organization of resources for instruction. Only if a matrix is established, can on-the-job experiences, and simulated situations be selected for inclusion in an instructional program. Similarly, identification and selection of instructional resources can only be intelligent if the major components of the curriculum, the major real and simulated experiences, are selected and ordered beforehand.

The final stage of curriculum development entails making provisions for organization and management of such programs. Provisions for implementation, evaluation, and revision of program elements are of primary and central concern. Program management includes the functions of total program planning, organization, coordination, control, review, and revision.

In summary, the curriculum development process entails four interdependent phases: (1) determination of educational direction, (2) selection of an appropriate taxonomy, (3) preparation of instructional strategies, and (4) initiation of management functions.

DEFINITION OF TERMS

What this chapter says regarding each of these phases can be better understood if a common terminology is established. In order to clearly define program thrust and direction, it is essential that the planner understand what is meant by business system, business, industry, and enterprise.

Business System: The business system is the combination of all resources, organizations, and institutions which are directly or indirectly related to the production and distribution of goods and services for the satisfaction of human need.[3]

The business system includes both public and private enterprises. Some economic theorists suggest that two distinct categories of enterprises exist: those which have profit as a motive and those which do not. The institution which assembles television sets, the discount department store, and the local loan company are truly business since they are subject to profit or loss. The operation of a school district, religious institution, county highway maintenance section or national forest is not considered by some to be a business because profit is not a goal. This study will show striking similarities between the functional characteristics of profit- and nonprofit-oriented institutions. Be alert to these commonalities.

Business: Any person or organization which produces useful goods or services is called a business.[4]

Industry: A collection of companies which utilize like processes in the creation of allied products and services, i.e., the paper, automobile, or electronics industry.

Enterprise: An operational unit which is directly engaged in business activity.

CLASSIFICATION SCHEMES

The occupational program planner must have tools for categorizing all manner of productive endeavor. Awareness and understanding of categorical systems provide for understanding various and sundry aspects and activities of the business world. Only if the larger segments of the economy are understood can identification of key work roles and selection of appropriate educational experiences be intelligent.

---

[3] Bayard Wheeler, Business: An Introductory Analysis (New York: Harper, 1952), p. 2.
[4] Bernard Shilt and Harmon Wilson, Business Principles & Management (Cincinnati, South-Western, 1961), p. 2.

There are untold ways to categorize the many millions of enterprises. The establishment of a simplified system of categorizing business units is not, however, an easy task. For many years the Bureau of the Budget, Bureau of the Census, Internal Revenue Service, American Association of Manufacturers, investors services, and individuals in education such as Warner, Olson, Lux, Ray, Stern, and Ziel have wrestled with the problem of deriving a widely acceptable codification system. A universally accepted classification system has not come to the fore. One never will. This is a result of two reasons: (a) the complexity and diversity of the business system, and (b) divergent ideologies of those who would analyze business system units into their constituent parts. Neither reason will ever go away and either is reason enough to prevent resolution of the quest for a universal categorized system which so many have undertaken. These efforts have not, however, been initially wasted. The resultant business system classifications provide fertile ground for the program planner who wishes to develop programs based upon the strong points of many and varied categorical systems. Representative business system classification systems appear in Fig. 6-4. A large number of business system categorizations were analyzed and condensed into this simplified structure. For present purposes, they were grouped into six types: (a) differentiation of function, (b) analysis of activity, (c) product analysis, (d) ownership pattern, (e) organizational size, and (f) level of technology.

The first, functional differentiation, gives order to analyses of business system activity by identification of common activities and functions. Activity analysis is similar to functional differentiation. However, it is used to group enterprises according to industrial operations, ranging from extraction of natural resources to sales and servicing of consumer goods. The third categorization technique attempts to classify operating enterprises according to types and kinds of goods produced. An analysis of different forms of business ownership is the fourth method by which development of a rational structure for occupational simulations may be derived. Selection of educational experiences can also be based upon categorization of enterprises according to size. The final taxonomy seeks to organize content and structure simulations according to the level of technology employed by various business system units.

These six schemes are only representative of many business system characteristics which might be used as bases for developing instruction. Alternate systems for categorizing business system efforts include: degree of competition, location, economic importance, scale of production, marketing methods, degree of concentration in the industry, kinds of competition, cost structure in industry, life cycle of industry, total num-

REPRESENTATIVE CATEGORICAL SYSTEMS

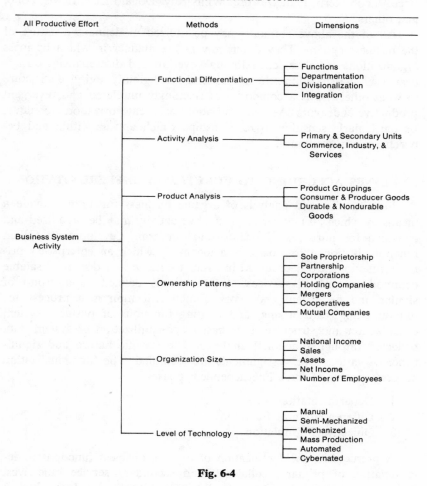

Fig. 6-4

ber of employees, number of firms, and value of products. This list of characteristics could go on and on for pages. The creative and innovative program planner thus needs to familiarize himself with various classification schemes which adequately describe the efforts and activities of the entire business system. Specific data regarding the aforementioned traits is readily accessible in the *Census of Manufactures, Moody's Industrial Manual, Enterprise Statistics, Standard Industrial Classification,* and *Standard Commodity Index Classification,* to name only a few. Likewise, attention should be directed toward the scholarly efforts of program planners such as William Warner, Delmar Olson, Donald Maley, Wesley

Face, Jacob Stern, Paul DeVore, Willis Ray, Donald Lux, Lewis Yoho, and others.

All of the above methods may be utilized to define the nature of the business system. They differ only in the manner in which business organizations are classified. Although overlap and discrepancies do appear, such classification schemes do lend intelligibility and give structure to what otherwise is a composite of seemingly unrelated and divergent productive endeavors. As you read about each categorization technique, be particularly sensitive to relationships which appear within and between various groupings.

ANALYSES ACCORDING TO FUNCTIONAL DIFFERENTIATION

Identification and analysis of organic business functions provide a means by which all manner of productive activity may be organized and classified for purposes of occupational program development. Called functionalization, this process is a means by which an enterprise's primary functions are determined in order to create and distribute salable commodities and/or services. A function is defined as a group of similar and dependent endeavors. Functionalization is a process for differentiating, categorizing, and relating functions of business system organization and structure. It is based upon utilization of system data collected through functional analyses. The specific nature and significance of various work assignments are identified. The functionalization process consists of three interdependent phases:

1. Departmentation
2. Differentiation of Functions
3. Objective Formulation

A prerequisite to identification of organic business functions is determination of primary, collateral, and secondary service objectives. Primary service objectives specifically state the salable values which a productive unit proposes to create and distribute to the general public. A wholesale frozen dinner processor will illustrate. The firm converts raw foodstuffs into ready-to-eat dinners and subsequently distributes them to commercial customers. Primary service objectives define the specific kinds of dinners produced, dinner quality, and cost of dinners. Primary objectives also set the boundaries in which collateral and secondary objectives are developed. The program planner seeking to differentiate unique and specific functions of a given enterprise must therefore carefully ascertain primary service objectives as an initial developmental step.

The next developmental step is to determine the selected enterprise's collateral objectives. They are considered to be humanistic in nature, since they are characterized by attention to man's role in productive activity in terms of both economic and societal influences. Often, business enterprises have been looked upon as economic institutions with little or no empathy for anyone or anything other than the dollar. While the profit motive is still very much alive, it is being tempered by a powerful current of social awareness. Witness increased emphases on pollution control, product quality and safety, employee welfare and safety, and work as a socializing force. Subsequently, management, labor, government, and consumers are moving to maximize opportunities for individual and group self-fulfillment. Action to improve working conditions, recognition of employee performance, products and services, and overall condition of the environment; as well as wages, profits, and dividends serve to benefit all segments of society. The enterprise as a social institution might well have as its collateral objectives the following:

1. To provide customers with quality goods and services at a just price.
2. To provide equitable opportunities for all employees.
3. To provide ethical and constructive action to industry as a whole.
4. To provide opportunities for economic and social advancement for the whole of society.
5. To provide shareholders with successful results.

Primary and collateral service objectives are implemented with the utmost of economy and efficiency through implementation of secondary objectives. These are the facilitating elements which constitute the final stage of the business unit's goal formation stage. A wise curriculum planner would do well to familiarize himself with a productive agency goal structure before attempting to differentiate functions for purposes of occupational simulation.

An awareness of a productive unit's primary service goals will enable the program planner to intelligently begin the differentiation process. Several examples will serve to point out this relationship. If the primary objectives of a selected enterprise have to do with manufacture and sale of shoes, the organic business functions which facilitate movement toward fulfillment of these objectives are production and sales. When primary objectives concern operation of a discount department store, organic functions deal with operations and merchandising. A large chemical company would have multiple functions, such as refining, transportation, and marketing. As the size and complexity of an enterprise increases, it may well form a conglomerate of separate businesses each with its own organic business functions. System units of this nature include Ford, General Motors, American Telephone and Telegraph, and General Foods.

Therefore, as a productive agency grows and prospers, say from a family-owned dry goods store into a chain of department stores, it requires an ever-increasing number of operatives to assist with functions heretofore performed by the owners. This gives rise to functionalization and subsequent departmentation. To reiterate, functional differentiation is a process whereby functions are grouped for purposes of job assignment. The process by which functions are grouped is dependent upon the "Principle of Functional Emergence" wherein:

> The tendency of a given function toward differentiation and independent grouping tends to vary directly with (1) the degree of dissimilarity between the particular functions and the functions with which it is grouped, (2) the degree of correlation between its growth and development and the growth of the organization as a whole, and (3) the tendency of the function to become increasingly complex and technical with growth.[5]

(1) The first corollary suggests that the program planner must carefully examine the myriad of business functions for those which share common or like objectives, similar work characteristics, and common barriers to efficiency and economy.

(2) Upon identification of these characteristics, attention must be given to the second functional emergence corollary. This corollary states that business growth results in the need for additional operatives. As a business grows and expands operations, additional help will be required. Furthermore, the functions which expand the most will, of course, be the ones requiring the greatest number of new operatives.

(3) Finally, the program planner must be cognizant of the third emergence corollary which implies that a function tends to become more complex and technical as the business unit grows. The third corollary has particular application to departmentation, which will be discussed shortly.

Through application of the *Principle of Functional Emergence* and its inherent strategy, i.e., (1) identification of common objectives, like characteristics, and similar barriers, (2) comparison of growth and new employees, and (3) analysis of business growth and specialization; functions of the business system may be determined. A comprehensive

---

[5] Ralph C. Davis, *The Fundamentals of Top Management* (New York: Harper, 1951), p. 375.

listing of like activities derived through functional differentiation includes:[6]

Accounting	Planning
Advertising	Production control
Assembling	Protection
Auditing	Public relations
Building & grounds	Publicity
Collections	Purchasing
Credit	Quality control
Finance	Research
Inventory control	Sales
Legal	Sanitation
Machining	Secretarial
Maintenance	Transportation
Personnel & training	

In a small business, the owner would no doubt perform many of these functions himself. However, as a business expands, he will need to hire additional employees, assign specialized tasks, and organize the whole for efficient operation. This gives rise to departmentation wherein jobs are categorized into like organizational units with clearly defined lines of command. Departmentation is an organizational tool by which businesses account for company growth, increasing numbers of employees, and specialization. In keeping with the second and third functional emergence corollaries, jobs are categorized by means of one or several of the following methods: (a) functional, (b) product or service, (c) customer, (d) regional, or (e) process or equipment analysis.

The basic form of departmentation is the functional organization pattern (Fig. 6-5), wherein all activities are subsumed under four basic headings entitled executive, finance, production, and sales. An extremely simple and logical organizational pattern, it avoids duplication of effort and is widely used by small businesses.

When sales, income, assets, employees, or products become so great that an enterprise can no longer operate efficiently under functional departmentation, reorganization may occur along the lines of product orientation. A product organization pattern for a household appliance manufacturer can be found in Fig. 6-6. Within this pattern a great deal of duplication occurs, since the divisions each carry out their own finance, production, and sales functions. Giants, such as DuPont and General Electric, operate under a product-oriented pattern characterized

---

[6] William Withers, *Business in Society* (New York: Appleton-Century Crofts, 1966), p. 245.

FUNCTIONAL ORGANIZATION

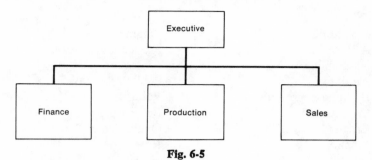

Fig. 6-5

by specialization, duplication, divisionalization, and decentralization of control.

As size and specialization demand, productive agencies organize according to regional or territorial pattern. A chart representing regional organization is diagrammed in Fig. 6-7. Activities which often take on this form of organization include: generation of electric power, telephone communication, cement production, and food processing and preparation.

When striking differences occur in consumer taste and demand for a firm's product, organization may well follow a customer pattern. A

PRODUCT ORGANIZATION

```
                          ┌──────────────┐
                          │  President   │
                          └──────────────┘
         ┌────────────────────┼────────────────────┐
┌──────────────────┐ ┌──────────────────┐ ┌──────────────────┐
│  Vice-President  │ │  Vice-President  │ │  Vice-President  │
│      Major       │ │     Radio &      │ │      Hand        │
│Kitchen Appliances│ │   Television     │ │   Appliances     │
└──────────────────┘ └──────────────────┘ └──────────────────┘
┌──────────────────┐ ┌──────────────────┐ ┌──────────────────┐
│    Finance       │ │    Finance       │ │    Finance       │
│    Production     │ │    Production    │ │    Production    │
│    Sales         │ │    Sales         │ │    Sales         │
└──────────────────┘ └──────────────────┘ └──────────────────┘
```

Fig. 6-6

REGIONAL ORGANIZATION

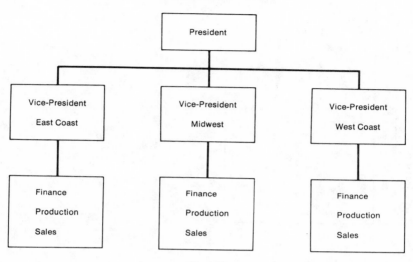

Fig. 6-7

customer organizational plan for a quick-copy machine company which services commercial, financial, government, and industrial markets is provided in Fig. 6-8. Business system operational units utilize all four departmentation techniques in order to deal effectively with growth,

CUSTOMER ORGANIZATION

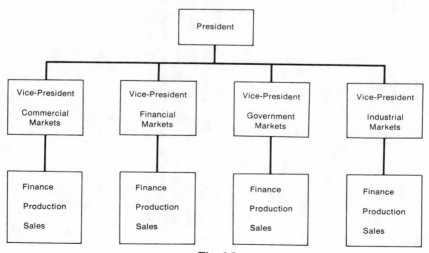

Fig. 6-8

Table 6-1. Comparative Structures of Functional Integration

Fayol[a]	Jucius[b]	Mooney[c]	Northcutt[d]	Smith[e]	Wheeler[f]
Technical operations	Production	Finance	Sales	Finance	Sales
Commercial operations	Sales	Sales	Production	Sales	Finance
Financial operations	Finance	Supply	Personnel	Supply	Personnel
Security operations	Personnel	Service	Finance	Manufacturing	Purchasing
Accounting operations			Standards and Records		Engineering and Research
Administrative operations					

[a] Fayol, Henri. *Industrial & General Administration*, International Management Institute, 1930.
[b] Jucius, Michael J. & Terry, George. *Introduction to Business*, Irwin, 1961.
[c] Mooney, James D. & Reiley, Alan C. *Onward Industry*, Harper, 1931.
[d] Northcutt, C. H., et. al. *Factory Organization*, Pitman, 1928.
[e] Smith, Edgar. *Organization & Operating Principles*, American Management Association, General Management Series No. 112, 1930.
[f] Wheeler, Bayard. *Business: An Introductory Analysis*, Harper, 1962.

employment, and specialization. Health organizations change and alter organizational form periodically to meet changing conditions.

A number of authorities have attempted to reduce the number of specific functional categories. Northcutt, Sheldon, Wardropper, and Urwick have discussed functional integration. They have combined functions in order to define a simplified taxonomy. They hypothesized that every business has a (a) sales function, (b) production or purchasing function, (c) personnel function, (d) finance function, and (e) standards and records function. Several other attempts to integrate functions along departmental or divisional lines are illustrated in Table 6-1.

Functional analysis has likewise been applied to selected industries, i.e., collections of companies which utilize like processes in the creation of allied products and services. Sufficient evidence is available to suggest that the organic functions of the transportation industry incorporate maintenance, traffic, and finance; while plant, traffic, and commercial activities constitute the telephone industry's major activities. Investigation within the insurance industry reveals sales, claims, and finance as the primary organic functions. The functions of distributive industries appear to be procurement, merchandising, and finance. A sample of manufacturing concerns suggests the primary organic functions of production, distribution, and finance. Each of the aforementioned analyses is a logical derivation of functional differentiation theory.

Selection of an appropriate taxonomy may be greatly facilitated through awareness and understanding of the following principles:[7]

A. As an organization grows in size, functions must be differentiated and jobs created. (Functional Emergence or Functionalization).

B. The degree of specialization in an organization varies directly with its size.

C. The creation of jobs in an organization requires their accurate description and definition to avoid confusion and overlapping of functions.

D. Before jobs can be grouped, a basic pattern of grouping must be chosen. The patterns commonly used are functional, product, territorial, and customer patterns.

E. As organizations become large, they find it necessary to employ the product, territorial, and customer patterns.

This section has dealt with the selection of a taxonomy for selection and ordering of simulated occupational experiences. It is important

---

[7] *Ibid.*, p. 258.

to note that this phase of the curriculum development process must be carried out in harmony with Phase I and the predetermined philosophy and objectives set forth therein. If the program planner is, in fact, committed to the idea that all manner of business activity can best be organized for instructional purposes through functional differentiation, he should proceed as follows:

First, he should consider the impact of goal formation; i.e., primary, collateral, and secondary service objectives on the structure and organization of enterprise. He also should consider the significance of the business system as a social as well as an economic institution. Finally, organic business functions, departmentation, and divisionalization of selected enterprises should be defined for incorporation in the structure and content of simulated occupational experiences. The derived business system classification scheme should be tested for adequacy by answering the following:

A. Does it encompass business system activities in the whole of society?
B. Does it contain mutually exclusive subcategories?
C. Is it practical for occupational simulation purposes?

If a taxonomy satisfies these conditions, the third and fourth phases of the curriculum development process should be undertaken. These phases involve (3) organization of materials and information and (4) implementation, evaluation, and revision. General and specific aspects of these phases are presented at the end of this chapter.

ANALYSES ACCORDING TO ACTIVITY

Activity analysis involves identification of broad business and/or industrial purposes, whereas functionalization involves a more detailed analysis of a given enterprise. Activities range from extraction of raw materials to retailing of finished goods and rendering of personal services. Numerous classification schemes will be described.

The first scheme assumes that units of the business system are concerned with creation of utility. In developmental terms, "utility," is defined to mean usable goods or services. This scheme also assumes that enterprises engage in either primary or secondary endeavors. Advocates of this approach submit that the beginning of all economic pursuits involve the extraction of fuel, resources, or food from nature. Since raw materials are not available in a usable form, they must be given utility. The need for form utility has thus given rise to the process of farming, mining, and manufacturing. Called primary or industrial businesses, they change the nature and/or form of raw materials into goods capable of satisfying human needs.

Enterprises engaged in secondary operations or processes are classified as commercial business units. Such agencies are concerned with making manufactured goods available to the general public, i.e., they facilitate possession utility. Typical activities are transportation, trade, service, and finance.

The second scheme divides business system activity into three broad classifications: (a) commerce, (b) industry, and (c) services. Those establishments which deal with related aspects of goods transportation are categorized as commerce. The program planner would therefore include the collection, grading, storage, movement, insurance, and finance of goods in transit within this category. This division likewise includes retail sales outlets and various and sundry service organizations. The industrial category entails three major headings: genetic, extractive, and manufacturing. Forestry, agriculture, and fish propagation are genetic industries. Industries which engage in mining, lumbering, hunting, and fishing are called extractive industries.

Manufacturing industries alter the form of raw materials or partially fabricated goods. Changes wrought by these industries are chemical, physical, or both. Manufacturing establishments may further be divided according to analytical, synthetic, processing, integrated, fabrication, and construction industries. Petroleum, chemical, and coal derivative enterprises are analytical industries. Such enterprises refine materials into need-satisfying materials. For example, the petroleum industry processes raw oil into gasoline, diesel oil, heating oil, grease, asphalt, tar, medicinal products, insecticides, face creams, and other products. Whenever a manufacturer derives a product from the combination of two or more materials or parts, it is described as a synthetic industry. Plastics is one of the major synthetic industries.

Representative processing industries are meat packing, flour milling, and steelmaking. The mode of operation of unique and specific processing establishments determines whether they are classified as analytical or synthetical.

Fabrication industries take manufactured materials through orderly sequences to combine them into composite usable products. Such enterprises are often integrated with firms providing raw and manufactured materials. Nearly all fabrication activity occurs within the confines of a factory. Representative fabrication industries are automobile, airplane, home appliance, farm implement, and shoe manufacturers.

Enterprises which entail activities in two or more of these categorical systems are said to be integrated. Several sectors of the economy illustrate this point. Tire production involves two basic procedures: (a) treatment and/or processing of chemicals, fabric, and rubber, and (b) fabrication of the tire, i.e., combining processed materials, shaping, vulcanizing, molding, and casing. Similarly, iron and steel production are typified by a combination of extraction, processing, and fabrication. These are highly integrated, interdependent technologies or activities. The typical steelmaking firm owns (a) mines and quarries, (b) furnaces, ovens, and rolling mills and (c) fabrication facilities which create higher level utility.

The last manufacturing category, construction industries, is characterized by enterprises which are dependent upon external sources for raw materials. They erect and/or fabricate products on the site. Examples of construction products include residential, commercial, and industrial buildings, canals, roads, docks, dams, bridges, tunnels, and airports.

The third and final broad business system sector consists of those activities dealing with services. Enterprises which fall within this division provide services such as:

Advertising	Lodging
Communication	Medicine
Credit	Motion pictures
Education	Personal services
Government services	Repair service
Legal service	Transportation

Representative enterprises which warrant classification under the communication services division include: Western Union, International Telephone & Telegraph, Columbia Broadcasting, Comsat, and American Broadcasting. Some which provide transportation services are Greyhound, Union Pacific, Yellow Cab, United Airlines, Pacific-Intermountain Express, and Sea-Lanes. Some which provide lodging and related services are Hilton, Holiday, Ramada, and Sheraton Inns. As was indicated earlier, other activity analysis schemes exist. The two which have been described are practicable. For purposes of program development, the following and more may be categorized:

Agriculture	Mining and quarrying
Communication	Public utilities
Construction	Real estate
Finance	Retail trade
Forestry and fisheries	Services
Insurance	Transportation
Manufacturing	Wholesale trade

The program planner should employ this codification system for content selection and organization of simulated experiences, if it is compatible with what is for him and the clients of his agencies the prevailing educational philosophy and program objectives. If the taxonomy is in harmony with the dominant educational thrust, it should be subjected to two questions: Does the taxonomy pertain to all economic activity which affects clientele? Are the subcategories mutually exclusive and workable for purposes of occupational education? If answers to these questions are positive, the program planner should proceed to Phases 3 and 4 of the curriculum development process. These are introduced at the end of this chapter and treated in detail in subsequent sections.

ANALYSES ACCORDING TO PRODUCT

Structures for categorizing and integrating simulated occupational experiences may also be established according to types of goods or products produced. Several such methods are obviously useful. The rationale of the first scheme assumes that productive agencies can be categorized after observing an industry's products. *Moody's Industrial Manual* lists twenty-six industrial product groupings:[8]

Aircraft and airplanes	Machinery and machine tools
Automobiles	Meat packing
Building	Metals (nonferrous)
Cement	Paper
Chemicals	Petroleum
Coal	Railroad equipment
Cotton	Rayon
Electrical equipment	Retail trade
Electronics	Rubber and tires
Food industries	Shipping and shipbuilding
Leather and shoes	Steel and iron
Liquor	Sugar
Lumber and plywood	Tobacco

A second scheme assumes that business system units can best be classified according to specific characteristics of products and their intended customers. Operational units can be categorized into (a) enterprises which produce consumer goods and (b) agencies which supply producer goods. Agencies in the first division provide goods which

[8] Moody's Industrial Service, Inc., *Moody's Industrial Manual* (New York: The Service, 1971), p. a-2 to a-15.

are consumed directly by the purchaser, e.g., dairies, restaurants, and furniture manufacturers. Business system units in the second category provide materials to intermediary processors, e.g., lumber companies, mining and machine tool, and processing equipment manufacturers.

A third business system classification scheme divides products into durable and nondurable goods. Representative durable goods producers are manufacturers of furniture, metal products, automobiles, and aircraft. Nondurable goods producers include enterprises in food, tobacco, leather, petroleum, and many other industries.

A fourth classification system for identifying program elements results from a synthesis of four product-based classification systems: (a) *Indexes to the International Standard Industrial Classification of All Economic Activities,* (b) *U.S. Industrial Outlook,* (c) *Standard Industrial Classification Manual,* and (d) *Classified Index of Occupations and Industry.* Similarities and only a few differences which are not accounted for by the eight categories are indicated in Table 6-2:

Agriculture	Transportation
Manufacturing	Communication
Mining	Utilities
Construction	Services

Singularly or in combination, the four product classification systems provide frameworks for selection and organization of content in occupational education.

ANALYSES ACCORDING TO OWNERSHIP

An analysis of different forms of ownership may be used for systematic development of instruction in occupational education. A relatively small number of legally defined ownership structures can serve as a simplified system for categorizing economic endeavors. Approximately a dozen forms are in current use. They include single proprietorships, general and limited partnerships, limited partnership associations, joint ventures or syndicates, joint stock companies, business trusts, corporations, holding companies, cooperatives, and mutual companies. Description of several representative ownership styles will illustrate possibilities for use by the curriculum planner. The most frequently employed form of ownership is the sole proprietorship. Consisting of enterprises owned and controlled by one individual, they represent 75% of nonfarm enterprises. Enterprises best suited to operation as sole proprietorships are those which (a) can be owned by a single proprietor and operated by persons hired by him and (b) which require little capi-

Table 6-2. Product-Based Industrial Classification Systems*

International Standard[a]	Industrial Outlook[b]	Standard Industrial[c]	Classified Index[d]
Agriculture, Forestry, Fishing & Hunting	Agriculture	Agriculture, Forestry, & Fishing	Agriculture, Forestry, & Fishing
Mining & Quarrying	Mining	Mining	Mining
Manufacturing	Manufacturing	Manufacturing	Manufacturing
Construction	Contract Construction	Contract Construction	Construction
Transport, Storage & Communication	Transportation	Transportation, Communic., Electric, Gas, & Sanitary Servs.	Transportation, Communics., & Public Utilities
	Communications		
Electricity, Gas, Water & San. Services	Public Utilities		
Commerce	Wholesale & Retail Trade	Wholesale & Retail Trade	Wholesale & Retail Trade
Services	Services	Services	Services: Bus. & Repair, Personal, Entertainment & Rec., Prof. & Related
Activities Not Adequately Described	Others	Non-Classified Establishments	
	Finance, Ins. & Real Estate	Finance, Ins. & Real Estate	Finance, Ins. & Real Estate
	Government	Government	Pub. Admin.

[a] *Indexes to the International Standard Industrial Classification of All Economic Activities*, United Nations, New York, 1959.

[b] *U.S. Industrial Outlook*, U.S. Department of Commerce, 1964.

[c] *Standard Industrial Classification Manual*, U.S. Technical Committee on Industrial Classification, U.S. Government Printing Office, 1957.

[d] *Classified Index of Occupations and Industry*, U.S. Department of Commerce, 1964.

* Courtesy of: "A Rationale & Structure for Industrial Arts Subject Matter," (Columbus, Ohio, Industrial Arts Curriculum Project, The Ohio State University, November, 1966), Pg. 138. ED 013-955.

tal. The largest group of enterprises which are suited to this form of ownership is personal service organizations and retail outlets. Personal service establishments include painters, plumbers, carpet layers, veterinary clinics and animal hospitals, maintenance services, barber shops, dental offices, and similar establishments. Sole proprietor retailing establishments include: automobile dealerships, news agencies, filling stations, independent grocery stores, etc.

A business owned by two or more persons is called a partnership. Accounting for 11 percent of nonfarm enterprises, the partnership may assume the sub-forms of a general or limited partnership association. The general partnership is common to the numerous productive enterprises, wherein more than one product or service is provided. The individual partners usually assume the separate business functions for which each has special expertise. General partnerships are common among clothing stores, radio and television sales and service, photographic stores, and hotels and motels.

Limited partnerships are almost exclusively brokerage houses. They are seldom manufacturing, merchandising, or service enterprises.

Corporations are enterprises owned by stockholders. They function as legal agencies under authority and franchise granted by State governments. They account for 14 percent of nonfarm enterprises and 77 percent of total receipts from sales of goods and services. The corporate form of organization is attractive to entrepreneurs because of its long life, limited liability of owners, easily convertible securities, and capital attraction potential. Mining, manufacturing, public utilities, railroads, and airlines are almost exclusively corporate structures.

Corporations take the sub-forms of closed, open, private nonstock or public. Corporations whose securities are traded through brokerage or securities exchanges are regarded as open. Representative open corporations are Consolidated Edison, Xerox, Boeing, General Foods, American Hospital, Brunswick, and Parke Davis. Securities of closed corporations are not readily available to the general public. Such corporations, which have recently gone public, include the Ford Motor Company and the Great Atlantic and Pacific Tea Company. Under state laws, educational, religious, and charitable organizations are allowed to incorporate. Called private, nonstock corporations, these institutions issue no stock, seldom seek profit, and reinvest internally. Public corporations are usually established by municipalities, states, and federal agencies, to better serve societal needs. They are nonprofit and normally nonstock. Agencies illustrative of public corporations include: city-owned sewer systems and waterworks, state universities and medical centers, and some electric utilities.

Holding companies represent still another form of business system ownership. A holding company controls a group of businesses through ownership of controlling blocks of securities in each establishment. The holding company does not directly operate its subsidiaries, but owns enough stock in each to exert control over its management and operation. Such companies are the Standard Oil Company of New Jersey, Borg-Warner Corporation, and American Telephone and Telegraph.

Enterprises owned and operated by their members are known as cooperatives. Their primary purposes are to provide inexpensive goods and services to members and to distribute profits to participants. There are consumer, retail, service, wholesale, producer, and marketing cooperatives. One of the simplest organizations, the consumer cooperative, is formed to make joint purchases of goods and services, such as household appliances, paints, and hardware. Grocery, general merchandise, and petroleum product cooperatives are the major groups in the retail cooperative category. Rapid growth in service cooperatives is attributable to child care, storage and moving, feed supply, water supply, and recreation industries. Wholesale cooperatives are designed to facilitate large-scale purchase of goods for local retail co-ops. Sample wholesale cooperatives which engage in purchasing as well as production activities include: the National Cooperatives, Inc., Farm Bureau Cooperative Association, and National Cooperative Refinery Association. Producers of grain, cotton, vegetables, and fruits often cooperate in the harvest, storage, and marketing of their crops. Examples of fruit growers cooperatives are: *Sun-Maid* raisins, *Welch* grape juice, *Sunkist* oranges, and *Blue Diamond* walnuts.

The final form of ownership to be described here is the mutual company. Mutuals are similar in structure to cooperatives. They issue no stock and distribute profits to the participating members. Numerous savings banks and insurance companies are mutual companies.

As was said at the beginning of this section, enterprises can be categorized according to forms of ownership. Occupational education experiences may be selected from such categories. The three most commonly used forms of ownership, sole proprietorship, partnership, and corporation account for 75 percent, 11 percent, and 14 percent of nonfarm business. Corporations account for 77 percent of receipts from the sale of goods and services. Proprietorships account for 15 percent and partnerships account for 8 percent. Because each ownership form is important, occupational education should entail instruction for:

Sole proprietorships	Holding companies
Partnerships	Cooperatives
Corporations	Mutual companies

For some purposes, this taxonomy will be all-inclusive of business characteristics, have mutually exclusive categories, and be applicable to instructional endeavor.

ANALYSES ACCORDING TO SIZE

Components of the world of work may likewise be analyzed for instructional purposes according to magnitude. The economy can be investigated in terms of organizational size, from the small "mom and pop" grocery store to the large corporate enterprise which employs thousands of workers. At first, it appears that all agencies may be categorized into a small number of classes. Three categories would yield small, medium, and large groupings. Such a classification system could well include small businesses such as specialty shops in metals fabricating, costume jewelry, men's wear, food service, and repair service, and large enterprises such as steel, automobile, aircraft, tires, construction, and chemicals. However, this taxonomy is oversimplified and difficult to defend because so many characteristics influence organizational size.

To categorize agencies according to size, it is necessary to ascertain magnitude in terms of several specific criteria, such as (a) number of employees and geography, (b) sales, (c) assets, (d) national income, (e) net income. These are representative of numerous measures of size. When two or more measures are used, operational units of the business

Table 6-3. National Income by Industry Division*

Industry Group	Billions of Dollars	% of Total
Manufacturing	195.2	29.9
Nondurable	75.5	11.6
Durable	119.7	18.3
Wholesale & Retail Trade	97.5	14.9
Government & Government Enterprise	93.8	14.4
Services	78.5	12.0
Finance, insurance, & real estate	71.9	11.0
Contract construction	33.2	5.1
Transportation	25.2	3.9
Agriculture, forestry, & fisheries	21.6	3.3
Electric, gas, & sanitary services	12.6	1.9
Communication	13.1	2.0
Mining	6.3	1.0
Rest of World	4.5	.7
All division totals	653.3	100.0

* *Census of Manufacturers,* 1971, p. 3.

system can be better described in terms of size, i.e., largest employer of labor with the least assets. Explanations of the five criteria follow.

A perspective of the comparative size and relative impact of industry groups in terms of gross national income is presented in Table 6-3. This synthesis of national income by industrial divisions provides the program planner with one hierarchy of productive giants. The data suggest that the leading income-producing groups are manufacturing, wholesale and retail trade, and government and government enterprises with 195.2-, 97.5-, and 93.8-billion-dollar total annual national income. However, the apparent magnitude of these industrial giants should not be allowed to dominate program planning strategy. The remaining nine industry divisions also contribute significantly to the economic and social well-being of society.

Curriculum development can be facilitated by simultaneous examination of sales, assets, net income, and number of employees. In Table 6-4, the ten largest industrial firms are ranked according to sales. General Motors, Standard Oil (N.J.), and Ford emerge as the leaders in gross sales. But, when institutional size is determined by measures other than total sales, some marked reversals occur. Ranking by total assets causes the industrial giants to change order, with the resulting ranking: Standard Oil (N.J.), General Motors, and Texaco. A still more decided shift in rank order occurs when net income is the measure of institutional size. Note that Standard Oil (N.J.) remains a leader, but International Business Machines and Texaco, ranked fifth and ninth according to gross sales, move up to second and third place respectively. Ranking according to number of employees yields General Motors first, Ford second, and General Electric third. Note that the petroleum group, Standard Oil, Mobil, and Texaco, employs the least number of operatives while accounting for a great share of sales, assets, and net income. Other changes in rank which occur when the criterion measure is altered can be noted in Table 6-4. The program planner must be alert to these and other assessments of size.

Because occupational education planners have properly been concerned with employment data, several comments regarding labor force and business system units are in order. The distribution of business firms by the number of employees can be found in Table 6-5. The program developer should be alert to the fact that approximately half the 305,680 economic establishments reported had less than ten employees. The Bureau of the Census states that such small establishments account for less than three percent of the total value added by manufacture.[9]

---

[9] U.S. Department of Commerce, *Census of Manufacturers,* Vol. I (Washington, D.C.: U.S. Government Printing Office, 1971), p. 3.

Table 6-4. Ten Largest Industrial Corporations Ranked by Sales.*

Rank	Company	Sales $(000)	Assets $(000)	Net Income $(000)	Employees
1	General Motors	18,752,354	14,174,360	609,087	695,796
2	Standard Oil (NJ)	16,554,227	19,241,784	1,309,537	143,000
3	Ford Motor	14,979,900	9,904,100	515,700	431,727
4	General Electric	8,726,738	6,309,945	328,480	396,583
5	International Business Machines	7,503,960	8,539,047	1,017,521	269,291
6	Mobil Oil	7,260,522	7,921,049	482,707	75,600
7	Chrysler	6,999,676	4,815,772	7,603	228,332
8	International Telephone & Telegraph	6,364,494	6,697,011	353,307	392,000
9	Texaco	6,349,759	9,923,786	822,016	73,734
10	Western Electric	5,856,160	3,743,623	253,447	215,380

* "Fortune Directory of the 500 Largest Industrial Corporations," *Fortune*. Vol. LXXXIII, NO. 5, May 1971, p. 172-3.

Table 6-5. Distribution of Business Firms by Number of Employees per Firm*

Number of Establishments	Number of Employees
117,514	1 - 4
39,349	5 - 9
41,678	10 - 19
48,949	20 - 49
24,923	50 - 99
19,762	100 - 249
7,749	250 - 499
3,450	500 - 999
1,639	1000 - 2,499
674	over - 2,500
Total 305,680 all Establishments	

* *Census of Manufacturers,* Vol. 1, 1971, p. 2-4.

Education *about* industry, travel, business, and commerce could well be designed with factors other than where the jobs are. Education *for* employability must be designed with employment statistics foremost in mind.

A structure of the business system can be conceptualized for pedagogical purposes through an analysis of the relative size of industrial groups and/or specific operational units. It is, however, extremely difficult, if not impossible, to categorize all business system units as small, medium, or large. Too many variables affect the measures of size. Competent program planners will utilize national income, sales, assets, net income, number of employees, and other measures of size. When confronted with the task of classifying productive units by size, they will ask, "In terms of what measure?" If a body of knowledge which represents the entire spectrum of business activity is structured according to specific size criteria, simulations of occupational situations can be selected and developed to sample appropriate parts of the economy. When a specific structure for the body of knowledge has been selected, it should be subjected to the test for universality, exclusive categories, and applicability in education.

ANALYSES ACCORDING TO LEVEL OF TECHNOLOGY

A sixth structure for development of occupational programs depends upon analysis of the technology of production employed by business system units. Some feel that the character of American enterprises is best described through analysis and study of technology. Aspects of the economy can be classified as (a) manual, (b) semi-mechanized, (c) mechanized, (d) mass-production, (e) automated, and (f) cybernated (Table 6-6). Admittedly, it is difficult to make fine distinctions between levels, but these classifications provide a degree of structure for development of occupational experiences.

Table 6-6. Levels of Technology

Technology Level	Characteristics	Business System Sector
Cybernation	Communication & control involving mathematics, servosystems, communication, computers, & finite automata	Medicine Finance Management
Automation	Integrated units utilizing self-regulated control & decision making	Electricity Petroleum Chemicals
Mass Production	High-volume production Standardization of components Assembly line	Automobiles Appliances
Mechanized	Performance of several operations at once Low-medium volume production Application of power & energy sources Separation of labor & management	Building materials Fabrication Food services
Semi-Mechanized	Hand & simple machines/elementary tools Semi-custom products & goods	Carpentry shops Custom retail outlets Repair establishments
Manual	Absence of technology Single operation at one time	Maintenance work Agricultural tasks Unskilled services

A relatively small segment of the economic arena operates on the first level. At this level, tasks are performed directly by hand with the assistance of only simple hand tools such as shovel, hoe, pick, wedge, broom, pencil, brush, or hammer. The decided absence of refined technology prohibits individuals from performing more than one operation at a time.

The semi-mechanized level of technology accounts for those productive endeavors in which tasks are performed directly by hand but with assistance from simple machines as well as elementary tools. Demand for semi-customized commodities has spurred the growth and well-being of many semi-mechanized businesses, which produce and distribute such goods. Enterprises employing this level of technology include antique and furniture rebuilding shops, cabinet shops, custom auto-parts wholesalers, welding shops, special apparel shops, and specialty hobby suppliers.

Productive units which employ full-scale mechanized technology are capable of performing several operations at one time. This is possible, primarily because of various forms and applications of power. At this level, one will find the beginnings of factory-type organization, involving a separation of labor and management. Agencies within this category of technology include material service yards, food service and processing institutions, and various types of low-volume consumer product fabricators.

When high volume and standardization of component parts or work units combine, higher-level technology, or mass production is possible. Mass production is characterized by an application of the principles of specialization and integration. Specialized work tasks are integrated, often along a production line, but also in other forms, depending upon the agency's function.

Automation is a refinement of the mass-production level of technology. In automated systems, divergent tasks are organized into a single, integrated unit for increased output and efficiency, made possible by application of self-regulated control and decision-making apparatus. Generation of electricity, production of chemicals, office work, food and drug processing, printing and binding, appliance manufacture, warehousing, and many other aspects of the economy lend themselves to automation.

Cybernetics is the sixth and perhaps final stage of technological achievement. Though few, if any, fully cybernated systems exist, the theory of communication and control in man and machine foretells productive systems heretofore unheard of. A composite of mathematics, communication theory, servosystems, computers, and finite automate, cybernetics has been employed in medicine, voice-controlled computers, finance, postal service, traffic control, and business system management.

The multitude of divergent enterprises which comprise the economy may be analyzed for educational purposes according to level of prevailing technology. Though, as with other taxonomies, it is difficult to define boundaries between categories, this classification system enables the program planner to conceptualize a structure for the study of the totality of the world of work. A minimal listing of levels of technology include: manual, semi-mechanized, mechanized, mass production, automated, and cybernated.

DEVELOPMENTAL GUIDELINES

Identification and organization of content for occupational programs may be facilitated through utilization of developmental guidelines depicted in the Developmental Checklist (Fig. 6-9). A simulated program

---

DEVELOPMENTAL CHECKLIST

DIRECTIONS: Write out the answers to the following questions or statements to develop a rationale and structure for busi-system based occupational programs.

I. Determine Educational Direction:

    A. State prevailing philosophy.

    B. State overall business system program objectives.

    C. How compatible are objectives to total occupational education program objectives, K-adult?

II. Select and Organize Body of Knowledge.

    A. Search available resources and list potential classification schemes.

    B. Identify best scheme.

    C. List the major units of the selected scheme.

III. Test and Revise Scheme.

    A. Does the selected classification scheme represent the whole of productive activity? YES_____, NO_____. If no, state why, and then how it might be altered to include all of business system effort.

    B. Does the scheme possess mutually exclusive subcategories? YES_____, NO_____. If no, state why, and how you propose to remedy the situation.

    C. Is the scheme practical for purposes of occupational simulation? YES_____, NO_____. If no, state why, and how it must be altered to be appropriate for occupational education.

Fig. 6-9

development assignment will illustrate this procedure. Suppose, for example, that a program planner has been charged to identify and structure content for an occupational program which will aid and abet the learner's awareness and understanding of the multitude of work situations within the spectrum of business and industrial activity.

A rationale and structure of content is derived from a (a) clarification of educational direction, (b) selection and organization of content, and (c) provisions for control and revision. Certification of direction requires (1) statement of philosophy, (2) formulation of program objectives, and (3) an indication of how the program is to be articulated with other levels, kindergarten-to-adult, in the occupational program. At a given moment, philosophy results from a combination of factors which impinge upon the whole of occupational education. The many variables include learners, parents, community, business, industry, labor, teachers, etc. All should have opportunity for input to program planners. The planner must recognize divergent and vested interests and pattern the total program so that it will do the most good for a majority of the populace. A statement of prevailing philosophy for Item I-A on the checklist might read:

Checklist, Item I-A

> An occupational program designed to create awareness and understanding of the entire spectrum of opportunities for employment can best be accomplished through investigation, study, and participation in activities representative of the entire spectrum of business activity.

Overall program objectives can then be derived from the statement of philosophy. Representative program objectives might well be:

Checklist, Item I-B

1. The learner will understand the nature of contemporary productive society and its relative impact upon modern man. He will demonstrate competence through completion of oral, written, laboratory, and cooperative work experiences.
2. The learner will demonstrate knowledge and understanding of respective occupational roles through completion of oral, written, laboratory, and cooperative work experiences.

A definition of educational direction is not complete without a statement of objective compatibility. Herein the planner must state the ways in which his specific program compliments and enhances the total kindergarten-to-adult educational effort. Such effort should include statements on prerequisites, grade levels, time, competencies, etc. A statement of this nature would include:

Checklist, Item I-C

> A ten-week exploration of the entire business system and its subsequent work environment, this experience is intended for 7th grade boys and girls as part of the total career education

program. Upon completion of this experience, learners will possess increased understanding of many and varied job opportunities.

Selection and organization of a relevant body of knowledge is facilitated through (a) a study of business system classification schemes, (b) analysis, delimitation, and design of a workable scheme, and (c) listing of major instructional units. A study scheme which describes the whole of business system activity could result in a listing of these techniques:

Checklist, Item II-A

Activity Analysis	Ownership Analysis
Functional Differentiation	Product Analysis
Level of Technology	Size Analysis

To consider each technique, the planner must seek answers to questions such as: "Can all business system effort and occupations be fully described through content organized according to a 'product' analysis?" This question must, in turn, be asked for each categorization technique. This process is repeated until all unacceptable techniques have been rejected. Assume, for example, the product analysis has been selected as the best means by which to order and classify the whole of productive effort. Futhermore, assume that, of the several alternate methods of product analysis, the 26 industrial-product groupings of *Moody's Industrial Manual* have been selected to delineate business system endeavors. Consequently, the developmental checklist for item II-B would read:

Checklist, Item II-B

Moody's Industrial Manual Classification

Checklist, Item II-C

Aircraft and airlines	Machinery and machine tools
Automobiles	Meat packing
Building	Metals (nonferrous)
Cement	Paper
Chemicals	Petroleum
Coal	Railroad equipment
Cotton	Rayon
Electrical equipment	Retail trade
Electronics	Rubber and tires
Food industries	Shipping and shipbuilding

Leather and shoes   Steel and iron
Liquor   Sugar
Lumber and plywood   Tobacco

Then, major instructional units need to be defined according to the 26 industrial-product headings.

Finally, the selected taxonomy is subjected to a test of universality, exclusiveness, and appropriateness to program. The planner must first determine whether the taxonomy can be used to categorize all varieties of productive effort in the business system. If answers to questions such as "Has any sector or segment been unintentionally deleted?" are positive, the taxonomy should be revised. If the scheme is truly universal in scope, it should be tested for mutually exclusive categories. This test measures the extent to which groupings of similar business system activities overlap one another. Rules for classifying content suggest that such groups should not overlap. If categories are found to overlap, they must be deleted, revised, integrated, and/or divided to provide exclusive groupings. Once the taxonomy has been cleared for categorical exclusiveness, basic concepts and principles within each content area may be determined. Finally, the taxonomy must be subjected to the test of appropriateness. The instructional scheme must be tested in educational settings to ascertain whether stated purposes are attained. Variables such as professional talent, learner characteristics, finances, time, community, and instructional resources may or may not be controllable, but are sure to affect achievement of predetermined objectives.

As material is tested in real educational situations, units of content may be well defined. For example, concepts may be analyzed, placed in hierarchical order, and arranged in a logical, simple-to-complex order.

PROGRAM CHARACTERISTICS

Occupational programs for which structure and content are derived from analysis of business system activity exhibit several common characteristics. Classroom, laboratory, self-study, and on-the-job experiences illuminate and clarify concepts which facilitate efficient combination of men, money, machines, and materials. A sample introductory level course outline appears in the Sample Business System Based Course Outline (Fig. 6-10).

Classroom experiences foster intelligibility of human, financial, and technological aspects of all manner of productive effort. Study facilitates understanding of work roles. For example, understanding of the public relations, recruiting, hiring, training, wages and incentives, job evalu-

SAMPLE BUSINESS SYSTEM BASED COURSE OUTLINE
Introductory Level

Unit I. Nature & Structure of Business System
   organization & composition of system
   business as a societal institution
   business as an economic institution
   unique and specific goal structures
   technological considerations
   occupational & career implications

Unit II. Personnel
   employment
   education & training
   safety & medical
   research
   employee services
   employee relations
   occupational simulation

Unit III. Manufacturing
   research & development
   plant engineering
   product engineering
   maintenance
   servicing
   production
   testing
   inspection
   simulation & role playing

Unit IV. Finance
   forms of ownership
   methods of financing
   financial Institutions
   securities
   risk
   insurance
   accounting
   occupational role playing

Unit V. Marketing & Distribution
   buying
   selling
   information
   advertising
   transportation
   warehousing
   standardization
   packaging
   dividing
   pricing
   financing
   risk assumption
   occupational simulation & role playing

Unit VI. Enterprise Simulation
   define activity
   personnel selection
   structure organization
   raise capital
   market analysis
   cost considerations
   secure materials
   production
   distribution
   sales
   accounting & evaluation
   occupational simulation & role playing

Fig. 6-10

ation, safety, and labor negotiations, functions of occupations in industrial and personnel relations would be developed by a unit outlined in the Sample Instructional Unit Outline: Industrial and Personnel Relations (Fig. 6-11).

Classroom experiences may also develop intelligibility of specific aspects of business system finance. Learners would study sources of capital, credit, collections, purchasing, and accounting procedures. Tech-

SAMPLE INSTRUCTIONAL UNIT
Outline: Industrial and Personnel Relations

EMPLOYMENT

Recruiting
Interviewing
Testing
Induction
Placement
Change of status
Merit rating
Counseling
Separation Interviews
Employment records

EDUCATION & TRAINING

Standards
Libraries
Readings
Company schools
Operative training
Supervisory training
Executive training
Visual aids
Records & statistics

SAFETY

Safety standards
Safety inspections
Safety publicity
Mechanical safeguards
Safety engineering
Safety contests
Safety education
Accident investigation
Safety rules
Records & statistics

RESEARCH & STANDARDS

Job analysis
Job descriptions
Job evaluation
Job grading
Wage analysis
Labor market surveys
Organizational planning
Record & report design
Manuals & forms

EMPLOYEE SERVICES

Recreation
Group insurance
Pensions
Profit sharing
Credit unions
Employees associations
Cafeteria
Miscellaneous services
Legal assistance
Records & statistics

EMPLOYEES RELATIONS

Collective bargaining
Wage & Salary administration
Grievance systems
Suggestion systems
Morale studies
Union relations
Public & government relations
Hours & working conditions
Group interests
Records & statistics

MEDICAL

Health standards
Sanitation control
Physical examinations
Personal hygiene
Professional services
First aid
Health education
Case histories
Records & statistics

Fig. 6-11

nological characteristics of the business system would be investigated from the standpoints of planning, production, and distribution. The planning efforts of enterprise are normally examined for work roles involved in management, office services, systems design, design and development, operations research, and similar roles. The many and varied aspects of production require study of production planning and control, plant layout and location, quality control, time and motion study, packaging, and manufacture. Representative distributive activities include storage and warehousing, stores control, traffic, transportation, sales, marketing, insurance, and service. A sample marketing instructional unit is outlined in the Sample Instructional Unit, Marketing (Fig. 6-12).

SAMPLE INSTRUCTIONAL UNIT, MARKETING

BUYING

Determination of needs
Location of sources
Price negotiation
Terms agreement

MARKET INFORMATION

Information gathering
Information dissemination
Quantities of goods
Trends on prices & demands
New outlets

STORAGE
Holding of commodities
Time of production
Rate of production
Coordination

PACKING

Protection of goods in storage
Protection of goods in transit
Containerization
Coatings

SELLING

Determination of buyers
Creating a demand
Advertising
Price & terms agreement

TRANSPORTING

Physical movements
Managerial considerations
Legal considerations

STANDARDIZING
Designation of quality
Commodity classification
Characteristics of standards
Consumer needs & desires

DIVIDING

Separation of products
Techniques
Mass production to one item sale

PRICING

Offers & bids
Competitive pricing
Market analysis
Discount bargaining

FINANCING

Cash
Credit
Banks & finance companies

RISK ASSUMING

Price fluctuations
Changing consumer tastes
Goods deterioration
Future markets

Fig. 6-12

Laboratory experiences develop awareness and understanding of the business system and work roles through simulated production activities. Learners engage in the formation of a business unit. For example, they form a company, raise capital, recruit and train a work force; secure essential materials; prepare appropriate tools, dies, or fixtures; produce goods or services; distribute commodities; and account for assets and liabilities. Students are required to engage in a variety of jobs in order to understand many and varied work situations. Day-care centers, bicycle repair shops, small engine and appliance repair shops, building and grounds maintenance, concession stands, stenographic services, and light manufacturing can be readily simulated in the school.

The level of sophistication of activities will vary a great deal, the primary restraints being learner and institutional characteristics. The combined forces of student maturity, interest, and experience, together with institutional objectives, professional talent, and resources, limit the types of simulation which can be selected. The exact nature of a given occupational simulation is best determined through analysis of concepts which facilitate increased self-awareness and fulfillment of articulated program objectives. The wise program planner never loses sight of the need to recognize opportunities for promotion of activities which assist students in realizing their full potential.

At what stage of development, then, does a program of this nature find application? There is, of course, no simple answer to this question. When designed with the learner in mind, this program can find application at all levels of the educational continuum. Whenever and wherever program objectives call for an educational experience depicting the whole of business system activity, simulations of varying complexity may be employed.

An actual business system simulation, described in some detail, will illustrate. The sample endeavor involved formation, planning, and operation of a mass production experience in the laboratory. The students employed the program and evaluation review technique (PERT) as a network system for planning and scheduling the simulation. Learners identified key activities, a sequence of activities, and time limitations. Student analysis identified 36 critical activities which include product selection, market survey, wage determination, procurement of raw materials, and manufacture. The complete list of activities is provided in PERT Events (Fig. 6-13).

An integral part of the student's planning efforts was preparation of the PERT network diagrammed in Fig. 6-14. The entire enterprise effort was broken down into tasks. The tasks were organized as events (circles) which were then connected by activities (arrows). Students assumed work roles to forecast volume of production and complete a breakeven analysis by determining the relationship of fixed and variable costs (Fig. 6-15).

PERT EVENTS

1 Enterprise defined
2 PERT program developed
3 Officers selected and their duties defined
4 Product chosen
5 Method of providing capital selected
6 Approximate product cost determined
7 Necessary business forms developed
8 Enterprise named
9 Approximate selling price determined
10 Financial records set up
11 Market survey taken
12 Sales commission decided
13 Sales goals set
14 Capital provided
15 Selling price more exactly determined
16 Number of units determined
17 Potential of total revenue determined

18 Salaries of officers set
19 Wages decided
20 Break-even analysis completed
21 Production method decided
22 Fixed costs determined
23 Material costs noted
24 Production facilities determined
25 Raw materials purchased
26 Equipment for manufacture obtained
27 Raw materials obtained
28 Equipment setup
29 Workers hired
30 Product manufactured
31 Product sold
32 Wages, salaries, fixed and variable costs paid
33 Records concluded
34 Market data correctness evaluated
35 Efficiency calculated
36 Financial gains reported and distributed

Courtesy—Enterprise: Man & Technology

Fig. 6-13

Learners also engaged in role-playing activities to understand physical and psychological aspects of the manufacturing process. Students became familiar with the fundamentals of flow-process charting in hopes of eliminating unnecessary operations, combining activities, sequencing events, simplifying procedures, and minimizing unnecessary delays or storage. A graphic representation of operations, transportation, storage, inspections, and delays of the student-conducted enterprise appears in Fig. 6-16. While engaged in the multitude of activities involved in the conduct of a business venture, learners are exposed to many and varied aspects of the world of work. At every turn, emphasis is placed upon awareness and understanding of occupations and self. Learners are motivated to identify the purpose and other characteristics of the work roles they have assumed. They also determine preentry job requirements and postentry employment conditions.

Some programs have provisions which enable learners to obtain actual experience through placement in a real-life operational business system unit. Depending on maturity level, the student is engaged in activities which range from simple observation to operation of equipment

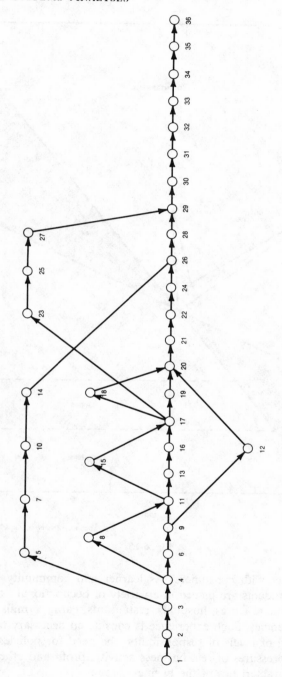

PERT PROGRAM FOR I-D ENTERPRISE

Courtesy: Enterprise: Man & Technology

Fig. 6-14

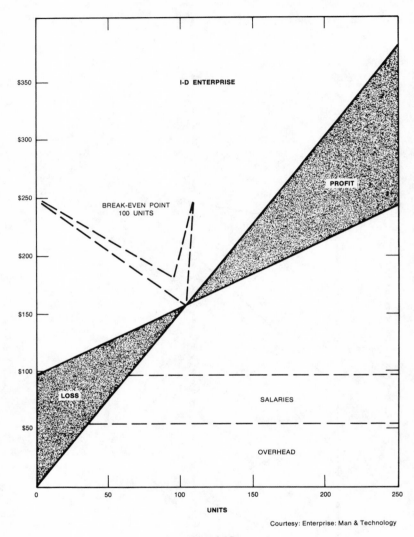

Courtesy: Enterprise: Man & Technology

Fig. 6-15

and/or contact with consumers. As learner and community characteristics allow, students are placed in a variety of occupational situations in
banks, department stores, hospitals, restaurants, garages, mills, and governmental agencies. Such experience is considered necessary to facilitate
understanding of levels of responsibility, the need for policies and procedures, the pressures of real business activity, profit and other motives,
and other characteristics of the business arena.

PRODUCT FLOW-PROCESS CHART FOR I-D ENTERPRISE

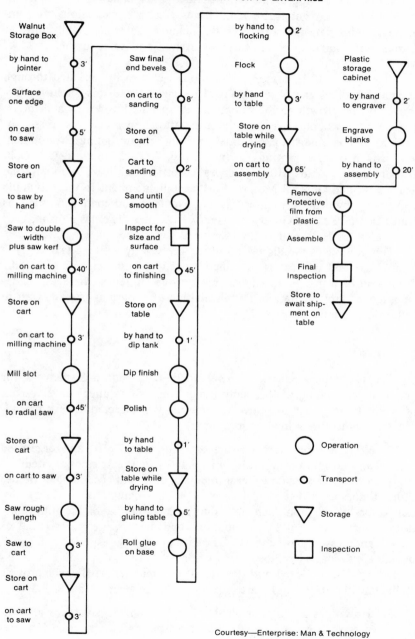

Courtesy—Enterprise: Man & Technology

Fig. 6-16

Visitations to representative business units enhance the effort of student-conducted enterprise simulations. Planned excursions to commercial, industrial, and service establishments contribute significantly to learner understanding of the business system and roles in the world of work.

Classroom and laboratory simulations can also be enriched through assigned readings and observations of business system biographies. Narratives of the growth and development of specific businesses and industries serve as valuable assets to the occupational awareness process. Numerous sources report the oft-times exciting and intriguing development and growth of organizations such as Ford, Xerox, Standard Oil, Colt, DuPont, MacDonalds, Hilton, General Electric, American Telephone and Telegraph, and General Motors. Further enlightenment re the economic sector is provided by biographies of inventors and managers such as Gail Borden, Charles Goodyear, Henry Bessemer, Thomas Edison, Carl Benz, Charles Hall, and Willis Carrier.

This completes the discussion of the process by which a taxonomy is established and content is identified, tested and implemented. Specific discussion of instructional and administrative strategies for detailed development, implementation, and evaluation of programs is dealt with in following sections.

SUMMARY

The preceding sections were intended to provide a framework for better understanding of the many dimensions which affect development of occupational programs. Specific attention was directed toward providing answers to the following questions:

1. What are the characteristics of occupational programs organized and structured according to analyses of the business system?

Such programs create general understanding and acceptable attitudes rather than specified technical knowledge and manipulative work skills. Supporters of this approach hold that understandings of the total business system and resultant occupations and careers are as essential as understandings of the technical segments of society, especially if young people are to make intelligent occupational choices. All productive activities should be analyzed and described in a manner which will provide students with a clear and concise picture of the occupational scene.

2. How does a program planner conceptualize a structure of business system operational units as a basis for selection of activities and experiences for occupational education endeavors?

Educators charged with the responsibility of identifying content and organizing instruction which depicts the entire spectrum of business activity, have many appropriate structures from which to choose. Prevailing educational thought will provide direction and guidance for the design of a taxonomy based upon one or a combination of analyses according to (a) functions, (b) activity, (c) product, (d) ownership, (e) size, or (f) level of technology.

3. How does a program planner test the adequacy of a given taxonomy for application to unique and specific educational environs?

Educators may test the adequacy of a taxonomy against three basic criteria: (1) A classification scheme must include all aspects and activities of the entire business system; (2) It must contain mutually exclusive subcategories; and (3) It must be appropriate for purposes of occupational simulation.

ACTIVITIES

1. Secure detailed information on one of the following programs and write a summarization of the pedagogical structure and content of the program.

    American Industry
    Enterprise: Man & Technology
    Functions of Industry
    Industriology

2. Select one of the business system analysis techniques discussed within this chapter and write your own rationale for its use as a basis for selection and organization of content for purposes of occupational program development.

3. Select one of the following business system characteristics which you feel might best be used to conceptualize a structure for development of occupational programs, and develop a written justification for its use and a classification scheme of its component parts.

    cost structure in industry   life cycle of industry
    degree of competition   marketing methods
    degree of concentration   number of firms
    economic importance   scale of production
    geographic location   total number of employees
    kinds of competition   value of industry products

4. Test the following taxonomy for its appropriateness to occupational education in terms of its universality, exclusive subcategories, and appropriateness.

"Exploration of industry can best be accomplished through study of:"

communication	procurement
energy	production
finance	property
management	relationships
marketing	research
materials	transportation
processes	

5. Develop a rationale and structure for an occupational education program based upon analysis of a business system characteristic of your choice. Use the developmental checklist as your guide in preparation of program. Include a written:

   a. classification scheme
   b. evaluation of structure and content
   c. statement of program objectives
   d. statement of your philosophy

6. Use the "Principle of Functional Emergence" and determine functions of a selected segment of the business system, i.e., functions of the food processing industry. The results of your analysis should include written statements of:

   a. business growth and specialization
   b. common objectives
   c. comparisons of growth and new employees
   d. like characteristics
   e. similar obstacles

7. Develop a rationale and structure content for an occupational program based upon the fundamentals of departmentation. Categorize work activities according to one or more of the following methods:

   a. customer
   b. functional
   c. process or equipment
   d. product or service
   e. regional

8. Investigations within the insurance industry suggest that major functional areas are sales, claims, and finance. Conduct your own functional analysis of the insurance industry and test the authenticity of the preceding statement. Report your findings in writing.

9. Develop a rationale and structure content for an occupational program having as its basis the assumption that business system units either engage in primary or secondary endeavors.

10. Develop a written structure of manufacturing establishments classified according to analytical, synthetic, processing, integrated, fabrication, and construction industries.

11. Prepare a written justification and structure for an occupational program organized around the product classification scheme of the *Standard Commodity Index Classification*.

12. Develop a written rationale and structure for instructional content which has as its basis different forms of ownership. A minimal list should include sole proprietorship, partnership, corporation, holding company, cooperatives, and mutual companies.

13. Construct an occupational program outline that describes the important dimensions of institutional size, from the small news stand operated by the owner to the large conglomerate which employs thousands of workers.

14. Prepare a written justification and organizational pattern for an occupational program organized around the underlying level of technology employed by the business system. Operational units might be structured according to six levels of technology: manual, semi-mechanized, mass-production, automation, and cybernation.

DISCUSSION QUESTIONS

1. Which characteristics best describe an occupational program organized according to an analysis of the entire spectrum of business activity?

2. Through which pedagogical structure might exploration of the whole of business system effort be best accomplished? Defend your choice.

3. How can understandings of the total business system provide youth and ill-fitted adults with a clear and concise picture of the occupational scene?

4. Contrast and compare technology vs. business system-oriented programs in terms of their ability to facilitate awareness and understanding of contemporary productive society and its impact on man's respective occupational role?

5. A great number of classification schemes have been proposed as a means by which content might be organized for purposes of occupational simulation. Which of these schemes best serves to describe the productive sector and subsequent work roles? Be prepared to defend your point of view.

6. What relationship should exist between preparation of business system programs and that of the total K-adult occupational education development effort?
7. Discuss the effects of functional differentiation, departmentation, and divisionalization on program development effort.
8. Several simplified taxonomical structures have been derived through use of functional integration. What drawbacks do you see in utilization of this technique?
9. Differentiate between functional and activity analysis.
10. How does an occupational program organized according to product analysis differ from one structured along the lines of material-processes?
11. What problems do you anticipate in attempting to draw up a program based upon identification and analysis of underlying levels of business system technology?
12. A simplified taxonomy which describes the many dimensions of the business world according to organizational size suggests operational units fall into three distinct categories: small, medium, and large. Discuss the pros and cons of this proposition.
13. Describe what you feel to be the greatest barriers to effectively categorizing the many dimensions of the business world.

BIBLIOGRAPHY

Amber, George. *Anatomy of Automation.* Englewood Cliffs, N.J.: Prentice-Hall, 1962.

American Assembly. *Automation and Technological Change.* Englewood Cliffs, N.J.: Prentice-Hall, 1962.

Ashley, William R. *An Introduction to Cybernetics,* New York: Wiley, 1956.

Bateson, W. M., and Stern, J. *"The Functions of Industry as the Basis for Industrial Education Programs."* Journal of Industrial Teacher Education 1:3-16. 1963.

Bateson, W. M., and Stern, J. *"Functions of Industry: Bases for Vocational Guidance."* School Shop 21:7, 20, 1962.

Buckingham, Walter S. *Automation: Its Impact on Business and People.* New York: Harper, 1961.

Bureau of the Census, *Census of Manufacturers.* Washington, D.C.: U.S. Dept. of Commerce, 1971.

Bureau of the Budget. *Standard Industrial Classification Manual.* Washington, D.C.: Office of Statistical Standards, 1967.

Carrel, Joseph J. *"Industriology: the Study of Industry."* American Vocational Journal 40: 26-7, 1965.

Cochran, Leslie H. *Innovative Programs in Industrial Education.* Bloomington, Ill.: McKnight, 1970.

Einzig, Paul. *The Economic Consequences of Automation.* New York: Norton, 1957.

Face, Wesley and Flug, Eugene. *"A Conceptual Approach to the Study of American Industry."* American Vocational Journal 40:15-17, 1965.

Fanning, Leonard M. *Fathers of Industries.* New York: Lippincott, 1962.

Fox, William. *The Management Process.* Homewood, Ill.: Irwin, 1968.

George, F. H. *Automation Cybernetics and Society.* New York: Philosophical Library, 1959.

Haney, Lewis H. *Business Organization & Combination.* New York: Macmillan, 1934.

Jucius, Michael J. and Terry, George R. *Introduction to Business.* Homewood, Ill.: Irwin, 1961.

Larson, Egon. *Men Who Shaped the Future.* London, N.Y.: Phoenix, 1960.

Moody's Industrial Manual. New York: Moody's Investors Service, 1971.

Moray, Neville. *Cybernetics.* New York: Hawthorn, 1963.

Olson, D. W., and Face, W. L., Flug, R. F., Maley, D. *"New Concepts and Where They Lead."* Industrial Arts & Vocational Education 55:24-28, 66. 1965.

Petersen, Elmore and Grosvenor, Plowman. *Bussiness Organization & Management.* Homewood, Ill.: Irwin, 1953.

Rusinoff, Samuel. *Automation in Practice.* Chicago: The American Technical Society, 1957.

Shilt, Bernard and Wilson, Harmon. *Business Principles and Management.* Cincinnati: South-Western, 1961.

Spriegal, Wm. R. *Principles of Business Organization and Operation.* Englewood, N.J.: Prentice-Hall, 1960.

Wheeler, Bayard. *Business: An Introductory Analysis.* New York: Harper, 1962.

Withers, Wm. *Business in Society.* New York: Appleton-Century Crofts, 1966.

Yoho, Lewis. *"Snap Maps of Educational Responsibility in Industrial Education."* Industrial Arts & Vocational Education. 54:34-35, 86. 1965.

Ziel, H. R. *"Interpreting the World of Work in the Industrial Arts Program."* Industrial Arts and Vocational Education, 51:26-27. 1962.

Chapter Seven

The Integrated Curriculum

INTRODUCTION

In recent years, administrators and curriculum researchers have emphasized the integrated curriculum. This chapter answers the following:

- What is an "integrated curriculum"?
- Are terms such as "core," "multidisciplinary," and "fusion" related to the integrated curriculum?
- What kinds of problems must be resolved when a totally integrated program is developed?

There are many definitions of integrated curriculum. Many books have been written about it. The terms *core, fusion, multi- and interdisciplinary,* and *integrated* have been used by various writers in a multitude of ways to describe essentially the same process. Conversely, many writers have spent considerable time differentiating between the various terms.

The purpose of this chapter is to discuss the concept of a total, integrated curriculum based on a central theme. Whereas the concept of a curriculum core or central theme is not new, the theme described here is new and very much different from earlier approaches. The writers utilize the term *integrated curriculum* to describe a career goal-directed curriculum system which effectively combines individual needs and abilities with functional area content. The attempt is to integrate the best of both worlds, i.e., the development of the whole individual with respect to career goals and development (Fig. 7-1).

The integrated curriculum is the essential concept underlying the articulated K-adult program. In effect, this approach provides for a horizontally articulated career offering as well as a vertical continuum. In-school vertical mobility is assured via articulated offerings only if all levels of the curriculum are aimed at the same goal. Articulation can exist only within a framework which provides a common weal at all

213

THE INTEGRATED CURRICULUM

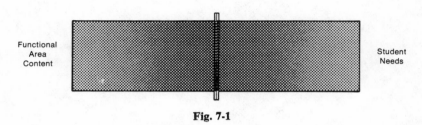

Fig. 7-1

levels. The integrated curricular offering provides the common weal of student life goals. Thus, career education must be central in the curriculum.

RATIONALE

In the development of this chapter, much discussion was given to the title. Trying to provide a one- or two-word description for a concept is sometimes difficult. Because much of curriculum commentary is mere tautology, literature review was a relatively fruitless resource for meaningful nomenclature for this curriculum concept. Considerable confusion exists regarding several terms which may be related to or synonomous with the integrated curriculum approach.

The integrated curriculum combines features of the more common curricular concepts such as core, fusion, and multidisciplinary. Curricula are integrated insofar as they are focused on the individual and the popular humanistic concept of psychology.

From the once-popular core curriculum, the integrated approach draws the idea of utilizing a central theme around which to fuse old and new learning experiences. However, unlike the core approach, the integrated curriculum utilizes a dual central theme. It must focus on self-development and career orientation. Like the original use of the term *integration,* it seeks to assist the child to understand and develop self as an entity. In keeping with the modern humanistic approach, it focuses on the learner, not on the instructional process.

Such a curriculum effort would most certainly indicate the beginning of the end of the classic general education concept. In fact, the title of the dirge played at its demise may well be "Career-Oriented Education." A systematic comparison of general education with career education may help to clarify this.

General education is comprised of selected "disciplines." Traditionally, these disciplines have been characterized as well-defined entities, general understanding of which is required of the "good" citizen. The major problem with this approach is that these well-defined entities do not exist in nature. Their existence can only be attributed to various performance standards in the real world. Hence, to structure all of learning around such intangibles is folly. The degree to which a youngster must possess "an appreciation for mathematics" is only relative to his life goals. The so-called disciplines are not entities in themselves. They exist only in the mind of the beholder. Thus, they are not a legitimate basis upon which to build relevant and meaningful systems of learning for youngsters.

If self and career development are the central theme of curriculum, functional areas (not disciplines) such as communication, mathematics, and research, become understandable to the learner because his quest for knowledge and skill is goal-directed. In the search for self-awareness and place in society, the youngster may explore and relate disciplines, professions and other specialties to his needs and aspirations. Because self and career goals are tangible realities, each person can define relationships between goals and learning experiences.

As concern to utilize performance-centered goals for education has grown, so has the number of educators who note the difficulty of stating behavioral objectives for the learning of traditional subject matter disciplines. "Appreciation of mathematics" is surely a worthy pursuit; however, this goal has been difficult to state in observable behavioral terms when mathematics is taught in the traditional subject matter-oriented curriculum. If the curriculum is oriented around the process of career development, the objective "appreciation of mathematics" is measurable. It is measurable because the degrees of mathematical understanding and ability can be assessed according to entry-level requirements of respective career goals and social responsibilities.

It must be remembered that the integrated curriculum is not designed to make traditional subject-matter courses more relevant. Rather, it is designed to replace the classical approach, which is content-oriented, with a learner-oriented curriculum. Many contemporaries in high places in government and education advocate an integrated curriculum, centered upon career development and understanding of self. By nature, such a curriculum provides humanistic educational experiences, selected according to each youngster's individual needs and self-perceptives. For the youngster, it answers the ever-present questions: "Who am I?" and "Where am I going?"

LEARNING ACTIVITIES AND THE INTEGRATED CURRICULUM

Any curriculum model must entail functional instructional activities. Learning activities and experiences are developed in two major ways.

They may be teacher-oriented or student-oriented. That is, learning experiences may be organized according to teacher or societal assessments of what should be learned or learning experiences may be organized according to more immediate student definitions of knowledge, skill, and attitude needs.

Traditionally, curriculum developers have focused on the teacher and responded to the educational establishment's assessment of the child's needs for so-called disciplines. When political groups and others have been successful in inserting content, it has usually been patched into courses which are already teacher-organized, e.g., sex education in biology, evils of alcohol in science, and flag display in social studies. Insofar as possible, educators have organized instructional materials and learning experiences according to preconceived notions re the organization of selected disciplines. Maslow described this type of learning experience in the *Harvard Educational Review.*

> . . . *extrinsic learning,* i.e., learning of the outside, learning of the impersonal, of arbitrary associations, of arbitrary (or at best, culturally determined) meanings and responses. In this kind of learning, most often it is not the person himself who decides, but rather a teacher or experimenter . . .[1]

The extrinsic learning approach has been the curriculum designer's primary tool. College preparatory and general curricula are almost completely extrinsic. As stated earlier, because the traditional general education curriculum is organized according to subject-matter disciplines, it relegates student needs to second-level importance. Such learning experiences stress "innate values of the content area," as contrasted to the basic and essential needs of the students, which they do not consider second-level in importance.

Instructional or learning experiences of this nature strive for such ephemeral objectives as "an appreciation of industry" or "an understanding of the American way." Certainly, an appreciation of industry, when studied out of context, means very little to the individual. It is extrinsic to him. However, this same goal can be quite meaningful and lasting when related to individual student needs, interests, and experiences. The inadequacy of learning experiences which are based on content is diagrammed in Fig. 7-2.

When referring to Skinner's *Walden Two,*[2] Maslow succinctly condemned the extrinsic learning process.

---

[1] Abraham Maslow, "Some Educational Implications of the Humanistic Psychologies," *Harvard Educational Review,* 38, No. 4 (Fall 1968), p. 691.

[2] B. F. Skinner, *Walden Two* (New York: The Macmillan Company, 1948).

This kind of learning too easily reflects the goals of the teacher and ignores the values and ends of the learner himself. It is also fair, therefore, to call such learning amoral.[3]

The antithesis to the external approach to learning experience development relates all formal instruction to the needs of the individual student. Learning experiences which are selected on the basis of goals and interests may more readily be conscious and meaningful experiences.

THE TRADITIONAL CURRICULUM COMPRISED OF SUBJECT MATTER DISCIPLINES

Classic Disciplines

Fig. 7-2

Harold Taylor, in *Students Without Teachers,* has written:

What is meant by a theory which says that education must be built around the student and that the student must be involved in planning it, making it, and doing it, is that knowledge is not a thing but a psychic state. Until the one who seeks it acts within his own consciousness and makes an idea or a fact or an experience part of his own psychic development, he has not gained knowledge.[4]

---

[3] Maslow, *op. cit.*
[4] Harold Taylor, *Students Without Teachers* (New York: McGraw-Hill, 1969), p. 196.

The structuring of student-oriented education begins at the basic instructional activity level. Books may be read, problems may be solved, current events may be analyzed, and careers may be explored only if student interests and abilities suggest points of departure. Other chapters in this book have discussed various means of utilizing this approach to organizing instructional activities. Without conscious, goal-directed experiences, the educational process is passive, rather than the dynamic experience it should be.

MASTER OF MY FATE

Humanistic psychology and its counterpart in education have encouraged public concern about the educational enterprise and its role in helping Dick and Jane develop into reliable citizens. Leaders in the future must be able to shape the society in which they live rather than (as many behaviorists would have) cope with that which already exists. Resourcefulness can only be fostered through educational experiences which emphasize the self as an innate being of worth with the ability to shape its own destiny.

This *sense of agency* as described by Tiedeman in *The Courage to Change* is already a very illusive concept for many inner-city and minority group youngsters; creativity and innovation are stifled by traditional educational experiences and the seemingly hopelessness of the real world.[5] Schooling tends to repress positive feelings relative to escape from what appears a hopeless situation. Many children take the view that their destinies are determined, i.e., that their lives are destined to consist of misery, depression, and unfulfilled dreams and aspirations.

As one very intelligent, black teenager from a ghetto area near Pittsburgh, Pennsylvania said, "Why should I dream? Why should I expect to be anything more than my old man and everyone else on our block? I can never be anything more or less than them. I'm trapped. When you live where I do, and you see what I've seen, it only takes a short while to learn that dreams and hopes that never come true hurt a darn sight more than accepting what you know will happen."

This type of response is typical. However, researchers and practitioners in the behavioral sciences are working to correct problems associated with the lack of upward mobility of the urban and rural disadvantaged. The same type of humanizing work and revision is essential in schools. Many millions of students are "trapped" in a different kind of ghetto—a ghetto bounded by out-of-date adherence to subject-matter disciplines.

[5] David V. Tiedeman, "The Agony of Choice: Guidance for Career Decisions," in *The Courage To Change*, ed. by Roman C. Pucinski and Sharlene Pearlman Hirsch Englewood Cliffs, N.J.: Prentice-Hall, Inc., 1971) p. 123-124.

Educators *must* accept the fact that self-understanding and career exploration are paramount to youngsters. The individual needs to be fully aware of his capabilities and limitations with regard to life goals. The integrated curriculum can alert the student to these factors and can provide avenues of learning which will enable him to see that he can achieve goals which are within his potential. This is possible because all learning is related to self and not to arbitrary content structures.

It is also important to note that lack of a sense of agency is not limited to minority group members. A majority of middle-class Americans limit the sense of agency of their own children by overemphasizing the benefits of collegiate education and the alleged disadvantages of earlier specialization. For too many, college becomes a terminal objective rather than a means to some end.

Many middle- and upper-class youngsters experience success in traditional elementary and secondary schooling. However, upon entry into college, many of these same youngsters are fraught with anxiety when confronted with the need to identify a major. At worst, these youngsters drop out and enter the labor market without salable skills. In a sense, they too are trapped. They are trapped insofar as they have not been provided opportunity for exploring their own drives and interests and defining appropriate educational and employment goals. Instead, they have been encouraged at every turn to satisfy the needs of their parents.

PERCEPTION AND THE INTEGRATED CURRICULUM

"Selective perception is a process by which individuals select and give attention to certain daily experiences."[6] This concept, described by Baer and Roeber, is an important part of the rationale of the integrated curriculum approach. Informational topics which are discussed, laboratory experiments which are conducted, and mathematical equations which are solved, are meaningful to the individual student only insofar as he attaches importance to them. The student himself determines the meaning of any experience in his own frame of reference. He selects those experiences which mean something to him and discards those which are meaningless.

Learning experiences which are extrinsic remain so. They mean little to the student. Those which are intrinsic, i.e., related to personal needs and drives, become meaningful, i.e., part and parcel of the youngster's data retrieval system. They can be retrieved and applied to real-life situations. From the idea that the student perceives experiences from

---

[6] Max F. Baer and Edward C. Roeber, *Occupational Information: The Dynamics of its Nature and Use* (Chicago: Science Research Associates, Inc., 1964), p. 2.

his own frame of reference, it allows that he should be provided experiences and knowledges which relate to him. To do otherwise is to waste student and instructor time.

SELLING THE INTEGRATED APPROACH

The integrated approach is beset by many obstacles. Obstacles cannot be overcome overnight. Averse faculty and administrators, community apathy or reaction, and student disorientation are the major barriers to integrated curricula. Implementing radical departures from traditional educational methods requires patience and perseverance. Because they have become acclimated to highly structured experiences, students at the junior and senior high levels will likely not be able to relate to the new approach. A drastically new approach to curriculum is best introduced progressively, beginning in the primary grades.

As classes progress through the curriculum, instructional methods, materials, and techniques must change accordingly. Broad features of each curriculum level must be designed well in advance so that learning experiences will be articulated. Community and faculty curriculum committees should develop broad and detailed guidelines. Curriculum consultants should be utilized to complement local expertise. Workshops should be conducted for and by teachers, guidance personnel, and administrators. Coordination of these and other activities related to the development of an integrated curriculum requires strong leadership and the highest possible degree of cooperation of several publics.

A picnic? Certainly not. However, the advancement of culture and, indeed, the well-being of individual citizens require a radical departure from tradition. Such change requires work. What greater work is there than to strive for individual happiness, well-being, and self-actualization?

SUMMARY

This chapter has dealt with a third approach to structuring learning experiences and business systems analysis. It answers three questions.

1. What is an "integrated curriculum"?

An integrated curriculum is a system which effectively combines individual needs and abilities with functional area content. Such a curricular system encourages the individual's self-realization by presenting subject matter in a context which clearly relates to his own personal career goals.

2. Are terms such as "core," "multidisciplinary," and "fusion" related to the integrated curriculum?

The integrated curriculum combines some features of these more common curricular concepts. However, these concepts become a part of the integrated curriculum only insofar as they concur with a central theme of self-development and career orientation.

3. What kinds of problems must be resolved when a totally integrated program is developed?

Problems with the faculty and administration, with the community, and with the students themselves must be resolved. Workshops should be conducted for faculty, guidance personnel, and administrators so that they may fully understand the importance of coordinating their efforts. The community should be consulted in order to dispel its fears or overcome its apathy, as well as to utilize local skills and knowledges. Students at the junior and senior high levels may be disoriented by an integrated approach because they have been conditioned to perform only in highly structured environments; therefore, a drastically new approach to curriculum is best introduced in the primary grades.

A gradual and progressive development of an integrated curriculum will avoid adverse faculty and community reactions and student disorientation and also allow time for development and utilization of all the positive contributions from faculty, community, and student sources.

ACTIVITIES

1. Develop a graphical model of a kindergarten-14 articulated and integrated curriculum.

    a. It must provide for self-awareness and career orientation as a central theme.
    b. It must illustrate vertical movement from kindergarten through the fourteenth year.
    c. It must be based on sound educational objectives.
    d. Each level must be so designed as to provide integrated experiences for all students.

2. Select members of the class to serve on teams that will debate the advantages and disadvantages of the integrated curriculum approach.
3. Prepare an outline that may be utilized by a school system curriculum coordinator in presenting a proposed integrated curriculum structure to the board of education.
4. Prepare a list of prominent educators and administrators at the local, state, and national levels who have supported or are propounding an education scheme such as the integrated curriculum.

5. Prepare a paper that explores such concepts as career development, sense of agency, self-actualization, the integrated curriculum, or humanistic education.

DISCUSSION QUESTIONS

1. What kind of evaluation techniques could be utilized in the integrated curriculum?
2. What would be some common learning experiences that could be shared by all students?
3. How would general objectives of an education system change as the result of adopting an integrated approach?
4. What problems would students have in such a learning environment?
5. What would be the parental response to an integrated approach to a curriculum?
6. Would the percentage of students entering a four-year college increase or decrease if they were provided such learning experiences? Why?
7. What would be the average instructor's major concern regarding his role in the integrated curriculum?
8. How would students be grouped in classes? What would be the basis of their grouping?

BIBLIOGRAPHY

Bronowski, J. "Science in the New Humanism." *Science Teacher,* Vol. 35 (May, 1968).

Cassidy, Harold G. *Knowledge Experience and Action.* New York: Teachers College Press, 1969.

Dow, Peter B. "Human Behavior," *Nation's Schools,* Vol. 88 (August, 1971).

Elam, Stanley. *Education and the Structure of Knowledge.* Chicago: Rand-McNally, 1964.

Fraenkel, Jack R. "Program Definition: Logic and Process," *The High School Journal,* Vol. 53, No. 7 (April, 1970).

Fuller, E. C. "Multidisciplinary Courses for Science Majors," *Journal of Chemical Education,* Vol. 45 (September, 1968).

Hackett, Donald F. "Industrial Arts Leads the Way," *Man/Society/Technology,* Vol. 31 (November, 1971).

Jenkins, David. "Cross-Fertile Teaching," *The Times Educational Supplement,* June 11, 1971.

Keochane, K. W. "Toward Integrated Teaching of the Sciences: Nuffield Begins Work on a Science Course Significant to the Average Student," *Science Teacher,* Vol. 35 (December, 1968).

Kuhn, Alfred. *The Study of Society: A Unified Approach.* Homewood, Ill.: Irwin and The Dorsey Press, 1963.

MacDonald, James B. "Myths About Instruction: The Myth of the Structures of the Disciplines," *Educational Leadership*, Vol. 22 (May, 1965).

Mitchell, M. P. "Patterns in the Humanities: An Innovation Program," *NCEA Bulletin*, Vol. 65 (April, 1968).

Pilder, W. F. "Curriculum Design and the Knowledge Situation," *Educational Leadership*, Vol. 26 (March, 1969).

Taylor, Harold. "Inside Buckminster Fuller's Universe," *Saturday Review*, (May 2, 1970).

Vars, G. F. "Core Curriculum: Lively Corpse," *Clearing House*, Vol. 42 (May, 1968).

Section Three

Developing Learning Experiences

After an educational enterprise is committed to learning goals, couched in terms of student self-actualization, and a learning experience structure(s), learning experiences must be developed so that they may be available to learners at appropriate times.

Curriculum developers answer questions such as:

- How can a variety of resources be utilized in a systems approach to instructional planning?
- What analysis procedures are useful with the several methods of structuring experiences and with aspects of the world which should be viewed for educational implications?
- What are the characteristics of good instructional strategies?

These and other questions are treated in three chapters:

Chapter 8. Planning for Instruction

Chapter 9. Analysis Procedures

Chapter 10. Organizing an Instructional Strategy

Chapter Eight

Planning For Instruction

INTRODUCTION

Thorough and systematic planning is at the base of good instruction. The planning process must be thoroughly understood if instructors in occupational education are to be effective and students are to accomplish the stated objectives of their programs. This chapter answers the following questions.

- How important is the planning function as it relates to instruction?
- Who should be involved in the instructional planning process?
- How can the effectiveness of instructional planning be evaluated?

Instructional planning may be defined as the process of accumulating data, analyzing and synthesizing it, and making decisions regarding curricular direction. From this definition, it follows that the planning process is composed of several functions and events which must be performed in logical and systematic sequence. The process itself is a fairly natural procedure. The most common weakness in the planning process is the lack of sufficient data and the development of effective alternatives.

For example, everyone has planned a hunting trip, fishing expedition, or family picnic. These outings often have trying moments because of various factors. How often has rain ruined the family picnic, high water the fishing expedition, and cold feet the hunting trip? Generally speaking, such activities fail because of things called unforeseen circumstances. Yet many of the unforeseen circumstances may have affected planning of the event if available information had been used.

A rained-out picnic may be partially successful if adequate shelter is included with the picnic basket. A fishing trip could be rescheduled if weather information from the area is available. And the hunting trip might have been successful if the planner had more thorough knowledge of several variables.

Similar planning errors are made by instructional personnel. Lack of sufficient information regarding student abilities and interests, condition of equipment, local manpower needs, position of organized labor, and budget allocations have ruined many an instructional plan. Likewise, the lack of alternative instructional plans has left many instructors helpless in various classroom situations.

THE SYSTEMS APPROACH TO PLANNING

The planning process must be systematic and closely coordinated. Not only must information and data sources be coordinated, but also must all levels of planning be related. That is, instructional planning at the specific course level must be based on total curriculum planning, which must, in turn, be based on total program planning (Fig. 8-1).

ALL LEVELS OF PLANNING ARE CLOSELY RELATED

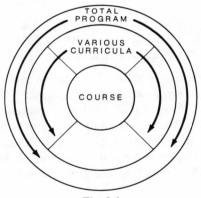

Fig. 8-1

In the picnic example, specific plans were only part of a plan for a particular day of a particular week, of a particular month, and so on. Hence, the first instructional planning theorem:

Specific instructional planning is based on a larger curriculum planning effort, which in turn is based on a total program plan.

Instructional planning is a process leading to decision making regarding effective instruction and learning. Hence, sound instructional goals must exist. Again, specific instructional goals must be based on larger curricular and program goals. Instructional planning must have direction. Direction should be provided, in part, by student and community needs. It is the function of specific courses, curricula and total educational programs to fulfill such needs. This important planning concept is diagrammed in Fig. 8-2.

The directional nature of instructional planning suggests the second theorem:

> *Instructional planning must have direction. Direction is based on student and community needs and operates in concert with the larger curricular and program goals.*

Because instructional planning leads to decision points, sufficient data must be available during the decision-making process. It is of extreme importance that sufficient instructional information be available to the planner. This information comes from many sources.

External data sources such as state employment agencies, advisory groups, state divisions of occupational education, and others must be utilized. Likewise, internal data regarding student wants and needs, school policy, budget allocations, and similar items must be available. Decision making and information systems will be discussed at greater length later in this chapter. The essentials of the decision-making aspect of instructional planning are shown in Fig. 8-3.

The importance of decision making in the planning process suggests the third theorem:

> *The importance of decision making in the planning process dictates a need for valid and accurate information from external and internal sources.*

INSTRUCTIONAL PLANNING REQUIRES DIRECTION

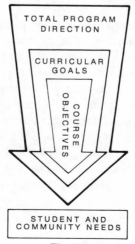

TOTAL PROGRAM DIRECTION

CURRICULAR GOALS

COURSE OBJECTIVES

STUDENT AND COMMUNITY NEEDS

Fig. 8-2

**DECISION-MAKING IS BASED ON INTERNAL AND EXTERNAL
INFORMATION SUCCESS**

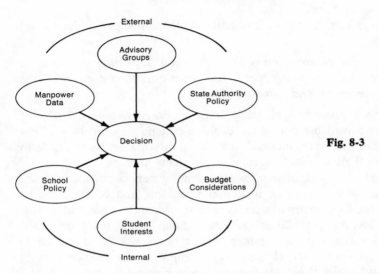

Fig. 8-3

The instructional process requires that alternative plans and procedures be readily available in the event that primary procedures become ineffective or inappropriate. The procedures utilized in developing alternative plans of action are much the same as those utilized in planning the primary thrust. However, because of the nature of the input, i.e., unforeseen circumstances, alternate procedures cannot be as well defined as the primary approach. They may also be affected by factors such as financial considerations, efficiency in given time allocations, and faculty competencies.

For example, a hunter may foresee the possibility of an early snowfall. But, because of weight limitations, he may have to decide to take either insulated boots or snowshoes. If he has elected to take the insulated boots and there is a deep snow, he may have a very frustrating hunt. On the other hand, he may carry the snowshoes, find them useless in a light snow, and suffer from cold. Alternative decisions are at best educated guesses. Of course, the experienced professional will make better guesses. Oftentimes they will make the difference between satisfactory and unsatisfactory learning. The need for alternative plans to achieve learning goals is illustrated in Fig. 8-4.

The fourth instructional planning theorem justifies alternative plans and decisions:

Alternative plans and decisions must be a part of any total planning effort.

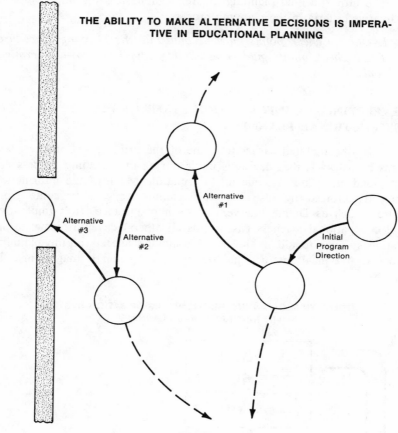

**THE ABILITY TO MAKE ALTERNATIVE DECISIONS IS IMPERA-
TIVE IN EDUCATIONAL PLANNING**

Alternative
#1

Alternative
#3

Alternative
#2

Initial
Program
Direction

Fig. 8-4

Finally, the planning process must have integral evaluative criteria. These criteria are generally called measuring points. At any point during the planning process or during the implementation of the plan, the instructional planner must be able to evaluate progress toward stated goals and directives. A system of built-in checks allows the planner to determine whether or not alternative procedures should be initiated. For example, if a data-processing instructor sees that his students do not understand fundamentals of Fortran programming, he must be able to switch to alternate instructional strategies to avoid additional waste of time and resources.

The importance of evaluative check points also is indicated in Fig. 8-5. When the instructional system is off target, an alternative method must be selected.

The fifth and final planning theorem emphasizes the importance of evaluative criteria in the planning process:

Evaluative check points must be built into the planning procedure. These check points guide the learning experience toward terminal goals.

DEVELOPING AN INFORMATION SYSTEM FOR INSTRUCTIONAL PLANNING

It has been stated earlier that one of the primary reasons best-laid plans go astray is that decisions made during the planning process are not based on sound or sufficient information. Much of the information currently utilized by instructional personnel appears to come from sources such as Divine intervention or happenstance. It is imperative that occupational teachers (as well as all others) develop formal information systems to aid in the decision-making aspects of the planning process. A typical Instructional Information System is diagrammed in Fig. 8-6.

UTILIZATION OF AN INSTRUCTIONAL INFORMATION SYSTEM IN INSTRUCTIONAL PLANNING

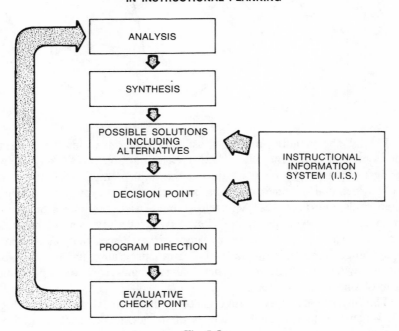

Fig. 8-5

What is known of information systems and concepts has come primarily from management research and experience. The concept of a central information system, usually implemented via data-processing procedures, is fundamental to *Management Information Systems*. While this type of formal information gathering and distribution system is essential to the classroom teacher, computer-assisted retrieval is not. In reality, the Instructional Information System (I.I.S.) can be contained in a file cabinet and can be accessible by telephone.

The effectiveness of any educational institution greatly depends upon information collection and transfer. A variety of informational 'inputs and outputs' are associated with each facet of the educational process. Many may be classified as routine, such as attendance and grade reporting; others, such as parent and teacher expectations, are highly subjective, yet equally important in judging the benefits of education. The term *information system* describes the full range of processes, methods, and techniques through which educational data are collected, permuted, and dispersed.[1]

INTERNAL STRUCTURE OF AN INSTRUCTIONAL INFORMATION SYSTEM (I.I.S.)

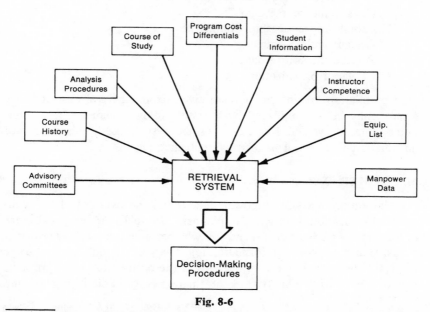

Fig. 8-6

[1] F. W. Blackwell, et al., *Educational Information System Design: A Conceptual Framework* (Santa Monica, California: The Rand Corporation, August, 1970), p. 1.

The information sources described in Fig. 8-6 are only representative samples of the types of pertinent data that must be made available in a formal I.I.S. Other sources may be added at the discretion of the instructor. An analysis of each of the illustrated sources follows.

ADVISORY COMMITTEES

Volumes have been written regarding the use of advisory committees for occupational curriculum planning. The single most important theme associated with this material is that *they must be used.* All advisory committee input must be recorded and included in the information system.

Riendeau has defined three types of advisory groups. These groups may serve as the primary organizational procedure used in maintaining advisory group information. The filing system or computer coding system may look like this:[2]

I. General Advisory Committees
   A. community data
   B. program data
II. Occupational Advisory Committee
   A. program data
   B. curriculum data
   C. specific course data
III. Joint Apprenticeship Committees
   A. curriculum data
   B. specific course data
   C. labor organization data

Compilation of information received from the various advisory groups may be accomplished by a simple filing system or by a computer-centered system. Regardless of the system used, this source of information is essential in instructional planning.

MANPOWER DATA

The importance of manpower data cannot be overlooked by occupational education instructional planners. In fact, the very existence of a course of study often depends on whether or not a manpower deficit exists. Hence, sources of information regarding job openings, average age of present personnel, and future trends in the occupational area must be part of a total I.I.S. This type of information is available from state and

---

[2] Albert J. Riendeau, *The Role of the Advisory Committee in Occupational Education in the Junior College* (Washington, D.C.: American Association of Junior Colleges, 1967), p. 26.

local employment services, community surveys, chambers of commerce, and advisory committees. It is evident that much information stored in the I.I.S. must be crosslisted.

PROGRAM COST DIFFERENTIALS

Costs of offering various courses are variable. It is therefore important that course cost data be available to instructional personnel. For example, the funds left in a commodities account during the Spring quarter will not cover the variable costs incurred in offering a particular course. If twenty students are expected to enroll in a tool and die course in which students produce numerous machined assemblies, there may be insufficient funds to pay for the raw materials. A course in tool design may be more feasible during that period because few consumable supplies are required.

The difficulty with cost differential data is that in many cases, they are simply not available. Very few secondary schools and junior colleges have formal cost differential information on a course basis. However, the trend is to determine cost differentials by programs and by courses.

STUDENT INFORMATION

Most schools have this information readily available. One major problem however is that instructional personnel seldom use this data. Cumulative record data includes information regarding past performance, attitude measures, interest inventories, personal problems, and similar information. Even when they assess entering abilities of students, instructional personnel seldom use such data. Often instructors discover that instructional methods used during the previous offering of a course are ineffective for the current offering. In many cases, this could be foreseen if student information had been analyzed.

Most states provide additional reimbursement to occupational programs which provide additional services to disadvantaged and handicapped youngsters. Many faculties, because of a lack of information, cannot identify such youngsters in their classes. Then compensation cannot be maximized.

INSTRUCTOR COMPETENCIES

The planning of instructional activities must be compatible with instructor competencies. This problem is not encountered frequently at the secondary level, but is rather common in postsecondary occupational programs, especially in programs which are scientifically and technologically based. Much like student information data, information about instructor competencies should be available to the curriculum planner.

COURSE HISTORY

What has been done before? This question is quite common when applied to developing course content. The history of specific curricular offerings is extremely important. Information such as old courses of study, enrollment data, cost data, and student achievement would be appropriately filed or keyed in this category.

ANALYSIS PROCEDURES

Occupational course content is often based on occupational, job, or other types of analyses. (See related chapters.) It is important that this material be available to the instructional planner.

COURSES OF STUDY

The value of having courses of study available has been previously discussed. No matter whether they are filed under "Courses of Study" or "Course History" or some other category, they provide valuable information for decision making.

EQUIPMENT LIST

Data regarding equipment and facilities are also imperative to decisions regarding instruction. For example, introductory courses for Licensed Practical Nurses may be taught in a Health Care Aide facility if scheduling considerations permit. Obviously, an advanced course in Medical Laboratory Technology cannot be taught in a machine shop. Whereas these and other extremes are obvious, the instructional planner needs stored information to maximize the match of facilities and resources with instructional needs.

The informational categories which have been discussed above are but a few of the types of information which must be included in an I.I.S. Characteristics of local programs suggest different information components for programs and even courses. Blackwell, et al, have said, "An information system cannot be designed in the abstract, that is, without reference to the particular educational environment under scrutiny."[3]

State and Federal agencies have long acclaimed the need for centralized occupational education information systems. These would certainly be appropriate for decision making at state and national levels. But they would, at best, assist the local instructional planner in decision making.

THE DECISION-MAKING PROCESS

As previously stated, the planning process leads to a series of decision points. For example, the data collection and information system development phase of the instructional planning procedure requires decisions regarding comprehensiveness of data collected, information storage systems, etc. Hence, occupational educators must analyze decision-making procedures to understand the implicit and/or overt aspects of this daily function.

The interrelatedness of decision-making theory and planning theory causes authors and researchers to utilize the terms synonomously. The relationship between the two is indicated in Fig. 8-5. Decision making is a function of the larger process, i.e., planning. By far the greatest amount of decision making is done intuitively. Most educators make instructional decisions informally. That is, they use their own experience as the data base and make decisions with little concern for a formal system, based on several kinds of information and logical processes.

Often the instructor, whose class does not appear to be achieving instructional goals as rapidly as it should, decides simply that more visuals should be utilized or that increased emphasis should be placed on the in-class activities of a classroom/laboratory situation. Oftentimes, this decision is the correct or an acceptable alternative method of achieving the desired outcomes. However, oftentimes such decisions are incorrect. How often do instructors say, "I just can't get through to those kids no matter what I try."? Instructors who make such statements do not base decisions on sound data.

INFORMAL DECISIONS

The occupational instructor described above utilized an informal approach to reaching decisions regarding instructional planning. The informal approach is characterized by the selection of alternative plans of action, without careful attention to the procedures utilized in the

---

[3] Blackwell, op. cit., p. 2.

selection process. For example, consider the task of driving to work. If upon leaving home one discovers that excessive traffic has slowed the freeway to a crawl, it is a simple matter to take the first exit and proceed on alternate highways and avenues. That is, it is a simple matter if one is familiar with the area in which he is driving.

Instructional personnel may make analogous decisions many times during a working day. If the machine tool instructor is having students acquire competency in drill press operation but finds that bottlenecks are occurring at work stations, he may have several students practice drilling operations on the vertical milling machine. Information about the operation of the two types of machines and analysis of objectives result in the decision to use both the drill presses and the milling machines. (Of course, the machine tool instructor could have arrived at different alternatives if there was no available milling machine or if any number of features of the situation were different.)

FORMAL DECISION STRUCTURE

Formal decision making occurs when plans of action are selected via the conscious effort of relating available data to alternative routes to a given goal(s). The machine shop instructor would have been involved in formal decision making if he had systematically analyzed the functions of both the drill and mill and related these on a formal basis to student needs. In other words, formal decision making takes place in a formal setting and utilizes conscious decision-making procedures. The decision maker knows he is in the process of making a decision.

RELATIONSHIP OF FORMAL AND INFORMAL DECISION STRUCTURES

Formal and informal are not mutually exclusive categories of decisions. Decisions which require formal procedures for one instructor may only be informal judgments for another instructor. And a major decision may involve both formal and informal subcomponents.

Decision making is a skill. It is learned best through experience, but it can be improved by analysis and training. Instructional planning decisions which require beginning instructors to use formal procedures may involve only simple and informal judgments of experienced teachers. This is usually evident in the lesson-planning procedures. In most cases, the beginning teacher prepares very careful and extensive lesson plans. However, as his experience increases, his plans become less structured and lengthy. He develops the necessary skills to make decisions in an increasingly informal manner.

INSTRUCTIONAL PLANNING TECHNIQUES

Thus far this chapter has been concerned with concepts which underlie instructional planning and decision making. There are several levels and types of planning procedures with which instructional personnel must be familiar.

PROGRAM PLANNING

From the instructional personnel standpoint, program planning (total occupational offerings) is considered a long-range effort. Program plans are generally formulated several years in advance of anticipated program changes. While the local program director generally accepts responsibility for total program planning, instructional personnel are also involved.

Data drawn from state agencies, school administration, general advisory committees, and community sources is used in the decision-making process at this level.

CURRICULUM PLANNING

Instructional personnel have more input to curriculum planning than to program planning. This planning is intermediate in nature. Curriculum planning is usually for a one- or two-year period. Again, state agencies and school administrators play an important part in decision making. But, more emphasis is placed on instructional personnel, occupational advisory committees, local business and industry personnel (consumers of the educational product) and students.

COURSE PLANNING

Course planning is the essence of instructional planning. At this point, the instructor is responsible for the planning effort. Occupational analysis, advisory committee inputs, labor organization feedback, co-operating instructor assistance, student input, and many other sources of information are used by the planner in realistic decision making regarding course direction, content, and evaluative procedures.

UNIT PLANNING

Unit planning and the unit system of organizing course content is not generally associated with occupational education. Unit planning originated as an attempt to make meaningful instruction out of bits and pieces of information which were not previously related. Occupational educators utilize unit planning in the development and organization of courses. For example, utilization of the task-oriented system to determine instructional content is a kind of unit planning.

WEEKLY PLANNING

This level of instructional planning has grown out of the desire of building principles to have common planning and reporting procedures followed by all instructors. Weekly planning is more nearly a reporting function than a planning procedure. The weekly plan is a valuable means of orienting new teachers and substitute teachers to the instructional activities of the school.

DAILY PLANNING

Daily planning is done by all occupational (and nonoccupational) program instructional personnel. It is very short range in nature and often based on the more comprehensive unit and course plan. For most instructional personnel, daily planning is done on an informal basis. It is generally supplemented by a written procedure for the day's activities.

SUMMARY

Instructional planning has been defined as the process of accumulating data, analyzing and synthesizing it, and making decisions regarding curricular direction. It may also be defined as a process for utilizing effective data inputs and decision-making skills to answer various instructional questions.

This chapter answered three major questions.

1. How important is the planning function as it relates to instruction?

Sound planning is the essence of good instruction. Without efficient planning procedures, many of the instructional activities of occupational teachers are misdirected. Planning is the basis of instruction. Student and community needs, availability of facilities and equipment, and personnel competencies must be analyzed in relation to the stated objectives of an occupational program.

2. Who should be involved in the instructional planning process?

Instructional planning can only be of value if accurate data is available to the planner. Several kinds of professional and lay citizens should be involved in instructional planning. General and occupational advisory groups, administrative and instructional staff, local and state employment agencies, business and industrial personnel, and state education agencies are some of the groups which should be involved in the planning process.

3. How can the effectiveness of instructional planning be evaluated?

Measuring or check points must be established as evaluative means in the planning process. Evaluation is critical to effective planning. The selection of alternative courses of action must be based on assessment of program direction as indicated by program planning. Chapter 11 further develops the evaluation function with respect to instructional planning.

ACTIVITIES

1. Select an educational system of your interest (secondary school, area vocational center, junior college, private training school, etc.). Develop an information system model. Include categories under which various data inputs may be stored. Determine who would manage such an information system. How would it be updated?
2. Prepare a written analysis of a formal instructional planning system that may be utilized in the above-mentioned situation. Identify the various levels at which different types of planning are done.
3. Develop a course outline that might be used at the teacher-training level to help prepare teachers as competent instructional planners.
4. Develop a packet of materials (sample letters, meeting agenda, etc.) that may be utilized by instructional personnel to assist in the establishment and utilization of advisory committees.

DISCUSSION QUESTIONS

1. Define the instructional planning process.
2. What is an information system? How can it be utilized in instructional planning?
3. What are the three major types of advisory committees? Define the role of each.
4. Explain what is meant by "the systems approach to planning."
5. What is an evaluative check point as it is related to instructional planning?

6. What types of people should be involved in the planning process?
7. List and explain the five basic theorems that relate to instructional planning. Can you formulate others?
8. List several common planning techniques.

BIBLIOGRAPHY

Ayres, Robert V. *Technological Forecasting and Long-range Planning.* New York: McGraw-Hill, 1969.

Caldwell, Michael S. "An Approach to the Assessment of Educational Planning," *Educational Technology,* Oct. 15, 1968.

Cleland, David I., and King, William R. *Systems Analysis and Project Management.* New York: McGraw-Hill, 1968.

Cox, Lanier, and Harrell, Lester. *The Impact of Federal Programs on State Planning and Coordination of Higher Education.* Atlanta, Georgia: Southern Regional Education Board, 1969.

Glenny, Lyman A. "State Systems and Plans for Higher Education," in Logan Wilson, Ed., *Emerging Patterns in American Higher Education.* Washington, D.C.: American Council on Education, 1965.

Halstead, Kent. *Handbook for State-wide Planning in Higher Education.* Washington, D.C.: U.S. Office of Education, 1971.

Kopkind, Andrew. "The Future Planners," *New Republic,* Feb. 25, 1967.

Palola, Ernest G., Lehmann, Timothy, and Blischke, William R. *Higher Education by Design: The Sociology of Planning.* Berkeley, California: Center for Research and Development in Higher Education, University of California, 1970.

Smiddy, Harold F. "Planning, Anticipating and Managing," *Management Technology,* Vol. 4 (Dec., 1964).

——————————— "State Planning and Coordination of Public and Private Higher Education," *Educational Record,* Vol. XLVII (Fall, 1966).

Ward, E. Peter. *The Dynamics of Planning.* Oxford: Pergamon Press, 1970.

Warren, E. Kirby. *Long-range Planning: The Executive Viewpoint.* Englewood Cliffs, New Jersey: Prentice-Hall, 1966.

Chapter Nine

Analysis
Procedures

INTRODUCTION

To organize and structure continuous, preschool-through-adult career education experiences, a planner must have answers to the following questions:

- How can analyses be coordinated at every level of the career continuum?
- How can the world of work be analyzed into components for application to a career program?
- How can information, derived by career analysis, be converted into a form suitable for instruction purposes?

This chapter presents alternate methods by which many aspects of the world of work may be converted to a form suitable for application to program development. The separate and interrelated aspects of developmental analysis, the traditional occupational, content, concept, job/trade, and task analyses, and instructional analysis will be discussed in detail.

Effective utilization of these analysis procedures will result only if they are carried out in concert with one another. Just as elementary school language arts, junior high English, and high school typing should be interrelated, so also should components of a career-education program be interdependent. Failure to utilize these analysis procedures or to plan in concert will weaken and undermine the entire career-development effort.

A coordinated curriculum can only be achieved through utilization of a systems approach to analysis. Individual analyses must be done in relationship to one another and adjusted and controlled to maximize total program effectiveness. A systems approach to career program development utilizing analysis procedures in program modification is outlined in Fig. 9-1.

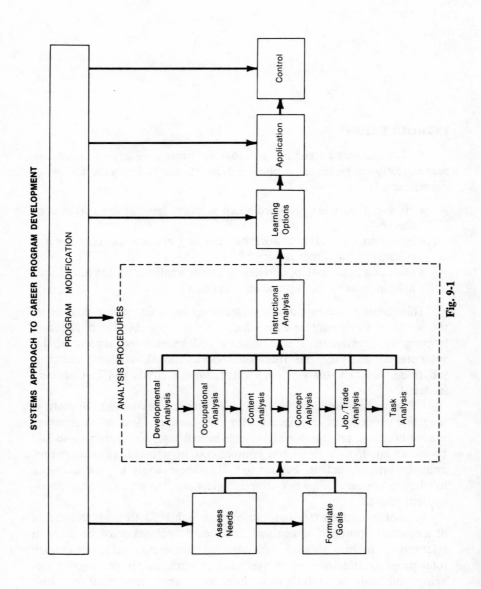

SYSTEMS APPROACH TO CAREER PROGRAM DEVELOPMENT

Fig. 9-1

SYSTEMS APPROACH

Derived from successful application to problem solving for defense, manufacturing, business, medicine, and space exploration, the systems approach holds great promise for career development. Application of the systems approach allows the planner to develop an effective program through a sequence of correlated, flexible, and controlled learning experiences. The systems approach involves the processes of analysis, synthesis, and control. These assure effective combination of key educational components, i.e., subsystems. Systems analysis seeks to increase developmental effectiveness through precise specification of expected outcomes. Expected outcomes are determined through consideration of the whole learning environment, i.e., all systems which influence the program: societal needs, resources, etc. Each system is analyzed for its impact upon other operating systems. The interrelationships and interdependence of each system is further examined for impact upon total career program effort. Briefly stated, a systems approach follows this procedure:

A. Define societal needs (Assess Needs)
B. State career program objectives (Formulate Goals)
C. Delimit constraints or restrictions (Analysis Procedures & Program Modification)
D. Develop alternate subsystems (Instructional Analysis)
E. Select alternates (Learning Options)
F. Implement selected alternate (Application)
G. Provide for feedback of results (Control)
H. Evaluate performance (Program Modification)
I. Modify program (Program Modification)

Previous chapters have discussed those systems which deal with assessment of societal needs and statement of career program goals. The remainder of this chapter will be devoted to clarification of those analysis techniques appropriate for application to career program development. Systems which serve to represent content organization (Learning Options), implementation (Application), and management (Control) will be presented in subsequent chapters.

DEVELOPMENTAL ANALYSIS

Traditionally, career (vocational-occupational) learning activity has been determined primarily through the use of occupational, content, concept, job/trade, task, and instructional analysis. With the advent of continuous preschool-through-adult career education, however, such analysis procedures fail to adequately describe activity which is appropriate for *all* levels of development. Traditional trade analyses still serve in developing programs at the career levels of emphasis and specialization (i.e., they describe the technological requirements of occupational clusters and specific jobs). However, they are inadequate to develop programs which satisfy the other (earlier) career levels in the human developmental process.

Current thought suggests that designing activity which is applicable to all levels can be accomplished by examining the human career development process. Career development is regarded as a process, a maturation process, consisting of stages through which learners progress. Thus, learning experiences should be based upon analysis of identified stages of student maturation. Called developmental analysis, this procedure holds great promise as a basic method for organizing and structuring learning activity for *all* levels of the career continuum. It may well provide the means by which technological activities, derived from occupational or trade analysis, can be coordinated with neglected human developmental needs. A successful marriage of traditional trade analyses with developmental analysis might well be the combination which maximizes the learner's chances to achieve desirable work attitudes, self-realization, and salable job competencies.

Analysis of the human developmental process is a logical first step in the systems approach to creation of a total career program. Applicable to all career continuum levels, developmental analysis provides insight and understanding into the *process* of career development, something which has been neglected in the formulation of traditional vocational education programs. Developmental analysis serves to describe the interaction between a person's behavioral patterns and the requisites of a productive environment. This technique examines career or "vocational" development "as an orderly and patterned process, ongoing, continuous, generally irreversible, and dynamic, involving interaction of the behavioral repertoire, vocational developmental tasks, and other factors."[1]

The entire process has been described by Buehler according to a series of Vocational Life Stages. While subject to limitation, the five life stages of growth, exploration, establishment, maintenance, and decline represent a vehicle for formulating a rationale and structure for the development of a total career program. Planners should familiarize themselves with the characteristic behaviors of each stage, and with the fact that behaviors evidenced at any given level are dependent upon the degree of potential developed in the preceding stages. It is a continuous

---

[1] Donald Super, *et al.*, *Vocational Development: A Framework for Research* (N.Y.: Columbia University Teachers College, 1957), p. 45.

process of emerging behavioral patterns which culminate in a set of career behaviors. Once basic career behaviors have been formulated, thrust and movement toward those ends are usually fixed and without alternatives. The direction, or patterning, of behavior is determined by the extent to which an individual achieves success in mastering many

VOCATIONAL LIFE STAGES

1. *Growth Stage* (Birth–14)
   Self-concept develops through identification with key figures in family and in school; needs and fantasy are dominant early in this stage; interest and capacity become more important in this stage with increasing social participation and reality-testing. Substages of the growth stage are:
   FANTASY (4–10). Needs are dominant; role-playing in fantasy is important.
   INTEREST (11–12). Likes are major determinant of aspirations and activities.
   CAPACITY (13–14). Abilities are given more weight, and job requirements (including training) are considered.

2. *Exploration Stage* (Age 15–24)
   Self-examination, role tryouts, and occupational exploration take place in school, leisure activities, and part-time work. Substages of the exploration stage are:
   TENTATIVE (15–17). Needs, interests, capacities, values, and opportunities are all considered. Tentative choices are made and tried out in fantasy, discussion, courses, work, etc.
   TRANSITION (18–21). Reality considerations are given more weight as the youth enters labor market or professional training and attempts to implement a self-concept.
   TRIAL (22–24). A seemingly appropriate field having been located, a beginning job in it is found and is tried out as a life work.

3. *Establishment Stage* (Age 25–44)
   Having found an appropriate field, effort is put forth to make a permanent place in it. There may be some trial early in this stage, with consequent shifting, but establishment may begin without trial, especially in the professions. Substages of the establishment stage are:
   TRIAL (25–30). The field of work presumed to be suitable may prove unsatisfactory, resulting in one or two changes before the life work is found or before it becomes clear that the life work will be a succession of unrelated jobs.
   STABILIZATION (31–44). As the career pattern becomes clear, effort is put forth to stabilize, to make a secure place, in the world of work. For most persons these are the creative years.

4. *Maintenance Stage* (Age 45–64)
   Having made a place in the world of work, the concern is now to hold it. Little new ground is broken, but there is continuation along established lines.

5. *Decline Stage* (Age 65-on)

As physical and mental powers decline, work activity changes and in due course ceases. New roles must be developed; first that of selective participant and then that of observer rather than participant. Substages of this stage are:

DECELERATION (65–70). Sometimes at the time of official retirement, sometimes late in the maintenance stage, the pace of work slackens, duties are shifted, or the nature of the work is changed to suit declining capacities. Many men find part-time jobs to replace their full-time occupations

RETIREMENT (71-on). As with all the specified age limits, there are great variations from person to person. But, complete cessation of occupation comes for all in due course, to some easily and pleasantly, to others with difficulty and disappointment, and to some only with death.

Reprinted by permission of the publisher from Donald E. Super, *et al, Vocational Development: A Framework for Research.* (New York: Teachers College Press, 1957; © 1957 by Teachers College, Columbia University), p. 40-41.

OUTLINE OF VOCATIONAL DEVELOPMENTAL TASKS IN CHRONOLOGICAL ORDER*

Preschool Child

1. Increasing ability for self-help
2. Identification with like-sexed parent
3. Increasing ability for self-direction

Elementary School Child

1. Ability to undertake cooperative enterprises
2. Choice of activities suited to one's abilities
3. Assumption of responsibility for one's acts
4. Performance of chores around the house

High School Adolescent

1. Further development of abilities and talents
2. Choice of high school or work
3. Choice of high school curriculum
4. Development of independence

Young Adult

1. Choice of college or work
2. Choice of college curriculum
3. Choice of suitable job
4. Development of skills on the job

Mature Adult

1. Stabilization in an occupation
2. Providing for future security
3. Finding appropriate avenues of advancement

Older Person

1. Gradual retirement
2. Finding suitable activities for skills to occupy time
3. Maintaining self-sufficiency insofar as possible

* Adapted from Stratemeyer, Forkner, and McKim (137).

and varied tasks which arise during his lifetime. Successful achievement of elementary tasks (called developmental tasks) allows one to move on to bigger and better tasks. Failure to master developmental tasks will cause frustration and dissatisfaction, and eventually it will cause problems in mastering higher order tasks. Hence, selection and ordering of tasks for any given career-education level must be made with extreme caution so as not to create insurmountable barriers to learning.

Those entrusted with the creation of a program must remember to treat career development as a process. Acquisition of patterns of behavior is not a static occurrence, but rather a dynamic, ongoing phenomenon which evolves with the passage of time. Hence, selection and organization of learning experiences must evolve from an analysis of career-vocational developmental tasks according to stages of maturation. A representative Outline of Vocational Developmental Tasks in Chronological Order illustrates six stages and subsequent developmental tasks for each.

The planner seeking to identify career-related activity for preschool and elementary children should be cognizant of the fact that, at these levels, nearly all developmental tasks have no direct relationship to occupations. Selection of activity must be made with this thought in mind; for example, experiences appropriate for awareness and/or exploratory levels could include:

A. Study importance of the home in developing good work habits.
B. Study the effect each family member's work has upon the home life.
C. Examine the relationships between an individual's occupation and his family, avocational, and citizen life roles.
D. Perform role-playing activities wherein students assume the parts of family members.

Learning activities for successive stages of development should increasingly provide for experiences which are more directly related to the world of work. Throughout adolescence and into early adulthood, individuals should be *selectively* exposed to experiences which reflect the responsibilities and rewards of productive effort. Exemplary learning experiences include:

Table 9-1. An Integrated Approach to the Process of Vocational Development

VOCATIONAL DEVELOPMENT PROCESS

Developmental Stages	Cultural Variables	Intra- and Inter-Personal Variables		Vocational Developmental Tasks	Vocational Developmental Opportunities
		Traits and Factors	Personality Development		
Preschool	Father's job income Parental attitudes values expectations residence social status	Sex Constitutional factors Intelligence Early interests Early aptitudes Physical appearance	Constitutional factors Early psychosexual development Position in family Parental handling and need satisfaction Identifications	To learn: Dependency Independence Social interaction Industriousness Goal setting Persistence	Opportunity to: React to parental handling and attitudes Explore environment Develop peer relations Develop authority relationships
Elementary School	Urban-rural Religion Class affiliations School	Scholastic aptitude Emerging personality patterns Developing interests and attitudes Physical capacities	Parental relations Peer relations Authority relations Emerging identity or self-concept Success-failure reactions	Socialization Coping with school Dealing with family attitudes and values Developing own attitudes and values Passing school subjects	Opportunity to: Learn about world of work Develop attitudes toward school and school subjects Have afterschool work experiences

Table 9-1. An Integrated Approach to the Process of Vocational Development (continued)

High School	Family associates Family behavior Class values Peer values Teacher values	Special aptitudes and abilities Crystallization of interests Emergence of values	Heterosexual relationships Psychosexual development Adult role playing Clarification of self-concept Methods of need satisfaction	Choosing curriculum Developing study habits Making tentative educational-vocational choices Implementing self-concept	Opportunity for: Academic exploration Occupational exploration Social role exploration
Young Adulthood	Courtship patterns Marriage patterns Family finances Educational patterns Military service Labor market Occupational requirements	Crystallization of values, attitudes, and personality Motivation and drive at peak Intellectual and physical capacities at peak	Success-failure reactions Changes in identity or self-concept Changes in role Crystallization of self-concept	Evaluation of need gratifications: marriage college job Specification of goals Launching of career	Opportunity for: Choice of educational major, minor Further exploration in study and work Change of curriculum or occupation Return to student or beginner status in new field

Table 9-1. An Integrated Approach to the Process of Vocational Development (continued)

Developmental Stages	Cultural Variables	Intra- and Inter-Personal Variables		Vocational Developmental Tasks	Vocational Developmental Opportunities
		Traits and Factors	Personality Development		
Mature Adulthood	Family status Economic responsibilities Realities of the marketplace: war, depression, prosperity, technological change	Aptitudes on developmental plateau Gradual narrowing of interests	Role acceptance or rejection	Vocational establishment and advancement Resolution of conflicts	Opportunity for: Change of job or occupation Promotion In-service training

Reprinted by permission of the publisher from Donald E. Super and Paul B. Bachrach, *Scientific Careers and Vocational Development Theory.* (New York: Teachers College Press, 1957; © 1957 by Teachers College, Columbia University), p. 114-117.

A. Write letter of application or inquiry about jobs.
B. Use tools, materials, and equipment which are representative of selected occupations.
C. Engage in cooperative work experiences.
D. Compare/contrast the local or state economy with the national picture.

Finally, description of learning experiences for application to the adult stages of establishment, maintenance, and retirement might include the following:

A. Acquire salable skills.
B. Perfect job skills for advancement.
C. Alter work experiences.
D. Retrain for alternate career.
E. Develop avocational skills.

A valuable aid in the selection of appropriate developmental activities for the different life stages appears in An Integrated Approach to the Process of Vocational Development (Table 9-1). It is a summation of the key intra- and inter-personal variables which occur throughout the career (vocational) development process. Personnel who formulate learning activities should become thoroughly familiar with this outline.

Analysis of the human developmental process is further facilitated through the use of the Example of Completed Developmental Analysis Form (Fig. 9-2). It helps to identify and organize effort according to program level, life stage, developmental task, and learning activity. The first step is the identification of the career level for which the learning activity is to be designed. A program level designation of awareness, exploration, emphasis, or specialization is entered in column 1. The second step requires the planner to write out the life stage(s) for which he is developing the program activity (column 2). Life-stage developmental tasks which are representative of this period are identified and listed in column 3. Finally, appropriate learning activities are isolated and entered in the last column. See the Example of Completed Developmental Analysis Form in Fig. 9-2. Completion of this analysis will provide a framework within which to carry out successive phases of career program development.

OCCUPATIONAL ANALYSIS

Occupational analysis serves to gather, synthesize, and classify information on occupations and related employment situations. It is a first step in deriving order from the vast array of environments which

EXAMPLE OF COMPLETED DEVELOPMENTAL ANALYSIS FORM

DIRECTIONS:

Complete this form in the following order.

1. State career level(s) for which activities are to be developed. (Column 1)
2. State appropriate life stage(s).(Column 2)
3. List developmental tasks normally associated with this life stage. (Column 3)
4. Identify appropriate learning activities. (Column 4)

		Column	
1 Career Level	2 Life Stages	3 Developmental Tasks	4 Appropriate Activities
Awareness	Growth–Birth to 14	Participation in group work	Role playing activities
		Selection of activity appropriate for individual ability	Field trips Group enterprises
		Increasing ability to assume responsibility	Guest speakers Individual readings
		Carry out household responsibilities	Individual projects
			Individual and/or group observation of employee at work

Fig. 9-2

constitute the world of work. The process seeks to delimit manageable areas of work through which jobs can be identified and subsequently analyzed through content, concept, job/trade, or task analyses.

Occupational analysis synthesizes and classifies work according to a number of alternate schemes, such as occupational families, technological foundations, enterprises, and applied disciplines. Generally, schemes move from the general to the specific. The list of occupational classification schemes is endless. The individual curriculum planner should select one with which he can work comfortably.

Identification of a classification scheme will enable the planner to isolate primary occupational areas. For example, using the categorization scheme of the *Dictionary of Occupational Titles, Vol. I* (Fig. 9-3) a planner can group agricultural occupations into manageable

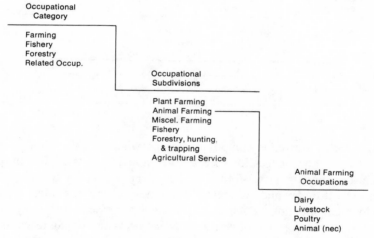

OCCUPATIONAL ANALYSIS CATEGORIZATION SCHEME

Fig. 9-3

categories. Moving from general to specific, the planner will find a broad occupational category which includes farming, fishery, forestry, and related occupations. Upon closer examination of this category, he will find seven occupational subdivisions: plant farming; animal farming; miscellaneous farming; fishery; forestry, hunting, and trapping; and agricultural service occupations. Selection of just one occupational subdivision, such as animal farming occupations, results in the identification of four animal farming occupational groups, i.e., dairy, poultry, livestock, and animal farming, which are not classified elsewhere. Such categorization gives order and structure to agricultural occupations. It facilitates identification of key occupations and, in turn, expedites job/ trade analysis.

To further illustrate the process of occupational analysis, note in Fig. 9-4 that related jobs are grouped into an occupational family or

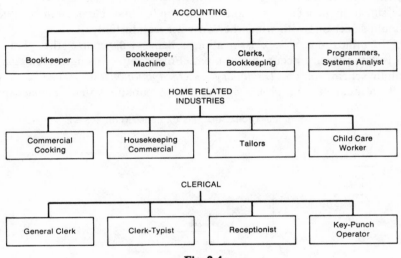

OCCUPATIONAL CLUSTERS ANALYSIS

Fig. 9-4

cluster. Each cluster is composed of jobs which require similar types of skills and knowledges for successful completion of task. The purpose of cluster activity is two-fold. First, it identifies within the total productive sector. Second, it creates awareness of relationships between employment situations. Such understandings are essential to the planner who would develop a program which represents the dynamic nature of the nation's workplace.

Occupational analysis serves to delimit specific employment situations from the total productive arena. It examines broad occupational areas, then classifies them according to an acceptable scheme, and finally identifies and describes key occupations. The entire process sets the stage for subsequent steps of content, concept, job/trade, task, and instructional analyses.

CONTENT ANALYSIS

Those levels of a career program which have as their goals development of occupational awareness and/or exploration might well utilize content analysis to describe significant aspects of the productive arena. Content analysis enables the planner to examine, in varying detail, those broad areas of employment identified through analysis of occupational clusters, business system units, technological foundations, and contributing disciplines. A selected area is analyzed for unique characteristics which set it apart from other productive sectors of the economy. Resulting descriptors serve as sources of content for development of learning experiences which will enhance career awareness and/or provide opportunities for occupational exploration.

For example, levels of technology employed by various business system enterprises might be classified according to a hierarchy consisting of manual, semi-mechanized, mechanized, mass-production, automated, and cybernated stages. Each level may be examined in depth, according to unique characteristics. For instance, business system agencies employing automation would be described as: those enterprises which employ integrated units utilizing self-regulated control and decision-making devices, generally represented by those agencies who manufacture or distribute electricity, petroleum, and chemicals.

The analyst needs to identify and describe the elements which comprise automated systems employed by these enterprises. A representative listing included the historic, economic, social, psychological, technological, and organizational aspects of automation. Each of the above is a reservoir of content for a career program. All traditional subject matter areas can draw upon these sources of content. To illustrate, let us examine the technological aspects of automation. Investigation of this classification reveals a vast amount of content pertaining to careers related to electricity and electronics. Electronic devices serve to (a) control industrial processes, (b) monitor product quality, (c) correct machine deviations, (d) compute material requisites, and (e) regulate material flow.

Content derived from these five areas alone is enough to structure untold numbers of learning experiences in mathematics, science, electronics, and economics with career awareness and exploration as the core. The career-development level for which the program is to be designed will determine the extent and depth to which a selected area is analyzed. In other words, analysis of "automation," for career emphasis and specialization activities, requires a greater level of specificity than does analysis for awareness and exploration. Specific program goals should guide analysis.

Another example illustrates how content can be derived for a career program through analysis of business system functional categories. Through examination and review of various classification schemes, the analyst can select one scheme which suits his needs. For example, he might select a classification which categorizes institutional effort according to five divisions: (a) sales, (b) production, (c) personnel, (d) finance, and (e) standards and records. Each of these must, in turn, be examined and detailed for component characteristics. Representative functions of the "personnel" division follow.

Education and Training	Employment
Employee Relations	Research and Standards
Employee Services	Safety

Each of these functions needs to be analyzed, in turn, for its constituent characteristics. To illustrate, observe the breakdown for the employment function.

Change of status	Merit rating
Counseling	Placement
Employment records	Recruiting
Induction	Separation interviews
Interviewing	Testing

Such functions represent content areas which provide excellent opportunities for integration of English, mathematics, business, psychology, sociology, and like learning experiences with a central core of career activities.

Hence, content analysis is a process which facilitates development of a rationale and structure for a career program, based upon investigation of the characteristics which comprise both the human and technological aspects of work. The process requires that the analyst complete the following:

A. Analyze various schemes	D. Break down each division
B. Select one scheme	E. List the identified areas
C. List the major divisions	

The areas may be listed without regard to order because sequencing techniques will be covered under instructional analysis.

CONCEPT ANALYSIS

Concept analysis is an alternate method of categorizing human and technological aspects of work for purposes of career program development. It is usually used below the specialization level. That is, it has primary application to awareness, exploratory, and emphasis levels. The process provides a basis for program development through analysis of concepts which represent man and technology in efficient combination. Some representative concepts are:

Business procedures   Industrial material-process
Economic   Production-consumption
Human relations

Analysis of industrial materials and processes illustrates this technique.

Step 1. Identify and list major concepts which describe all industrial material-processes:

    A. Material removal
    B. Combination and assembly of materials
    C. Materials

Step 2. Identify and list subconcepts:

    A. Material Removal

        boring   planing
        drilling   separating
        etching   shaping
        heat cutting   shearing
        mechanical cutting   turning
        milling

    B. Combination & Assembly of Materials

        classifying   laminating
        coating   mixing
        fastening   positioning

    C. Materials

        forming   identification
        heat treatment   measurement

The major concepts and subconcepts serve as a basis for decision making regarding development of career programs. Here, as in content analysis, excellent opportunities arise for integration of effort with science, mathematics, business, industrial arts, and similar areas. All activity needs to be organized around a common core of activities which deal with occupational situations that involve materials and processes of industry.

Another example of the conceptual analysis process illustrates how basic business system procedures can be conceptualized for application to career program planning effort.

Major Concepts

    A. Common Industrial Procedures

Subconcepts

        1. products
        2. sales

    B. Organic Business Procedures

        1. sales
        2. production
        3. financial

    C. Managerial Procedures

        1. planning
        2. organizing
        3. controlling

The result of this analysis is an outline for a career program which has great potential for integrating all manner of learning activity around a common core of career experiences. Home economics, business education, mathematics, science, and industrial education can provide expertise in the areas of consumer economics, distribution, production, planning, and fiscal affairs. All of these can foster self-awareness and intelligibility of the world of work.

Concept analysis requires the planner to carry out the following steps:

    A. Conceptualize elements of the economy into manageable and universal groupings.
    B. List the concepts identified (no specific order).
    C. Break these concepts down into subconcepts.
    D. List the subconcepts.
    E. Evaluate and revise to meet needs.

Concept analysis is based on the idea that certain aspects of the world are of significance to career development. Selected concepts describe the many facets of productive society in a manner which allows the analyst to derive structure and content for a career program.

JOB OR TRADE ANALYSIS

Job and trade analysis mean essentially the same thing. Trade analysis represents the same procedure as does job analysis, with the exception that the process is limited to specific trades, i.e., plumbing, electricity, carpentry, etc. Since job analysis is a more inclusive term, it is used hereafter.

Job analysis is an extension of occupational analysis. It involves the review of jobs or trades, identification of specific on-the-job performance conditions, and preparation of job descriptions. Results of job analyses provide frameworks for career programs. Representative job descriptions are:

* Salesman, metals (wholesale tr.) Sells nonfabricated metals, such as brass, copper, iron, and steel, utilizing knowledge of metallurgy and applications of various metals. Performs other duties as described under Salesman.[2]

* Yardman, Used Building Materials (ret. tr.) Salvages and stores used building materials: Stacks cleaned lumber according to size and condition. Sorts and stores used millwork, plumbing fixtures, heating equipment, and structural steel. Cuts lumber to customer's specifications, using power saw. Fills yardmaster's order and loads materials on car or truck.[3]

* Cook, Mess (any ind.) cook, boat; cook, ship. Cooks and serves meals to crew on passenger ship: Cleans, cuts, and cooks meat, fish, and poultry. Serves food to crew members. Washes dishes and cleans galley and galley equipment. Requisitions supplies. Compiles cost records of food used.[4]

* Farmhand, Dairy (agric.) I. dairy-field man; dairy hand; dairy helper; hired hand, dairy. Works on dairy farm, performing duties requiring knowledge of dairy cattle: Weighs and mixes specified feed and feed supplements, fills feed troughs with grain and roughage, and fills water troughs. Drives cows from stalls into pasture for grazing. Examines cows to detect mastitis . . . and injuries, such as cuts and bruises. . . . May maintain farm buildings and equipment, plant, cultivate, and harvest feed for stock, and maintain breeding and cost records.[5]

* Stenotype Operator (clerical) stenotype-machine operator; steno-typist. Takes dictation of correspondence, reports, and other matter on machine that writes contractions or symbols for full words on paper roll. Transcribes stenotype notes on typewriter or dictates notes into recording machine for typist to transcribe.[6]

---

[2] U.S. Department of Labor, *Dictionary of Occupational Titles*, 3rd ed., (Washington, D.C.: U.S. Government Printing Office, 1965), Vol. I, p. 618.

[3] *Ibid.*, p. 806.

[4] *Ibid.*, p. 165.

[5] *Ibid.*, p. 265.

[6] *Ibid.*, p. 692.

Job analysis enables the planner to look at critical components of a given job, deriving a list of significant operations, processes, equipment and tools, and essential information. These answer three important questions: (a) What gets done? (b) How does it get done? and (c) Why is it done? Answers to these questions provide an excellent outline for learning units. The outline provides the framework for identifying and analyzing tasks for direct application to learning situations.

TASK ANALYSIS

Task analysis is a process whereby required work of an occupation is identified, synthesized, and detailed for application to learning situations. It consists of blocking duties, listing tasks, and then detailing subsequent performance steps. See Task Analysis Process (Fig. 9-5). A planner first must examine the results of job analysis, especially the job description, and determine what must be done in order to list the duties of the job in question. A job may consist of just one duty or it may involve many and varied duties. A duty is defined as a major division of work with unique and distinct characteristics. Jobs which consist of one major work division are ordinarily referred to as single-block occupations. Jobs which involve more than one major work division are called multiblock occupations. The jobs of window washer, keypunch operator,

---

TASK ANALYSIS PROCESS

STEP 1 — BLOCK JOB DUTIES

 • Examine job description

 • Identify major work divisions (blocks)

 • List divisions (blocks) as duties

STEP 2 — LIST TASKS

 • Submit duties to competent evaluators

 • List resultant tasks for each duty

 • Determine frequency of performance, importance, and learning difficulty of each task

STEP 3 — DETAIL TASK PERFORMANCE STEPS

 • List steps required in performance of each task

Fig. 9-5

and coat checker are examples of single-block occupations. Representative multiblock occupations are: electronic technician, photographer, journalist, teacher, and secretary. The major blocks or divisions of the occupation secretary are:

A. Performing office procedures.
B. Taking dictation.
C. Transcribing dictation.
D. Performing clerical duties.
E. Performing typing activities.
F. Performing receptionist activities.

The actions within each of these blocks are called tasks. The planner should carefully examine the identified blocks or divisions of work for a list of tasks. Tasks may be determined by consulting a variety of individuals and agencies. Competent sources include printed materials, employees in the occupation, and employers. Information from several sources should be collated into a list of tasks representing a consensus of expert opinion. This procedure is known as task inventory. Initially, tasks for each of the blocks are listed as they are identified, without regard for order. The following is a listing of tasks in the secretarial duty of "performing stenographic activities."

Secretarial Science Task Inventory

Duty: Performing Receptionist Activities

Tasks:

A. Handle grievances.
B. Keep an appointment book.
C. Utilize telephone.
D. Organize office records.
E. Greet customers.

The process of task analysis is demonstrated by the various treatments of the tasks of a Short Order Cook (Fig. 9-6).[7]

After tasks have been identified and verified as being essential to the successful completion of a work duty or block, they should be arranged in logical sequence. For example, the planner must decide what tasks are essential to job entry and, therefore, need to be taught first. Such decisions are made easy by careful analysis of each task in terms of several variables. Some authorities, exemplified by Fryklund, choose

---

[7] Oregon Board of Education, *Food Service Occupations: Occupational Cluster Guide* (Salem, Oregon: The Board, 1970).

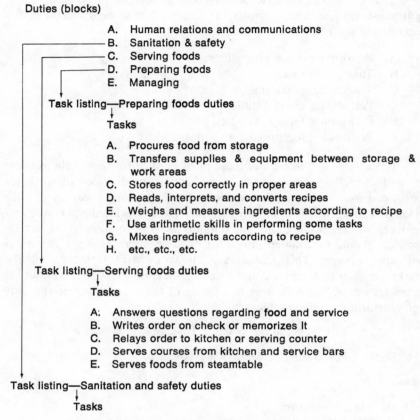

SHORT ORDER COOK

Duties (blocks)

A. Human relations and communications
B. Sanitation & safety
C. Serving foods
D. Preparing foods
E. Managing

Task listing—Preparing foods duties

Tasks

A. Procures food from storage
B. Transfers supplies & equipment between storage & work areas
C. Stores food correctly in proper areas
D. Reads, interprets, and converts recipes
E. Weighs and measures ingredients according to recipe
F. Use arithmetic skills in performing some tasks
G. Mixes ingredients according to recipe
H. etc., etc., etc.

Task listing—Serving foods duties

Tasks

A: Answers questions regarding food and service
B. Writes order on check or memorizes it
C. Relays order to kitchen or serving counter
D. Serves courses from kitchen and service bars
E. Serves foods from steamtable

Task listing—Sanitation and safety duties

Tasks

A. Handles food and equipment in safe and sanitary manner
B. Cleans work areas, equipment, and utensils

Fig. 9-6

to consider only performance frequency.[8] Others, exemplified by Mager, prefer analysis of task performance and learning difficulty, as well as frequency.[9] Note the three rating scales for the tasks of a Hostess, with regard to: Performance Frequency (Fig. 9-7), Importance of Task (Fig. 9-8), and Learning Difficulty (Fig. 9-9). Observe that each rating technique yields a different order.

[8] Verne C. Fryklund, *Occupational Analysis: Techniques & Procedures* (N.Y.: Bruce, 1970), p. 101-102.

[9] Robert F. Mager & Kenneth M. Beach, *Developing Vocational Instruction* (Palo Alto, Calif.: Fearon, 1967), p. 10-14.

Rating Scale PERFORMANCE FREQUENCY					
Occupation: Hostess **Duty (Work Block):** Serving Foods **Tasks**	**How often task is performed**				
	Seldom				Often
	1	2	3	4	5
Welcomes patrons to establishment					✔
Seats patrons					✔
Presents menu					✔
Makes suggestions re: food & service			✔		
Answers questions re: food & service		✔			
Serves ice water	✔				
Fills beverage cups & glasses			✔		
Fulfills diners requests			✔		
Assists in adjusting complaints		✔			

Fig. 9-7

Order derived from rating frequency of performance:

Most often done   1. Welcomes patrons to establishment
                    2. Seats patrons
                    3. Presents menu
                    4. Makes suggestions re food and service
                    5. Fills beverage cups and glasses
                    6. Fulfills diners' requests
                    7. Answers questions re food and service
                    8. Assists in adjusting complaints
Least often done   9. Serves ice water

Order derived from rating importance:

Most important   1. Welcomes patrons to establishment
                    2. Seats patrons
                    3. Answers questions re food and service
                    4. Fulfills diners' requests
                    5. Assists in adjusting complaints
                    6. Presents menu
                    7. Makes suggestions re food and service

8. Fills beverage cups and glasses

Least important   9. Serves ice water

Rating Scale					
TASK IMPORTANCE					
Occupation: Hostess **Duty (Work Block):** Serving Foods	**How Important is Task?**				
	Little Import				Extreme Import
Tasks	**1**	**2**	**3**	**4**	**5**
Welcomes patrons to establishment					✔
Seats patrons					✔
Presents menu			✔		
Makes suggestions re: food & service			✔		
Answers questions re: food & service					✔
Serves ice water	✔				
Fills beverage cups & glasses		✔			
Fulfills diners requests					✔
Assists in adjusting complaints					✔

Fig. 9-8

Order derived from rating learning difficulty:

Hardest to learn   1. Fulfills diners' requests
2. Assists in adjusting complaints
3. Answers questions re food and service
4. Welcomes patrons to establishment
5. Makes suggestions re food and service
6. Presents menu
7. Seats patrons
8. Serves ice water
Easiest to learn   9. Fills beverage cups and glasses

The several arrangements are not necessarily confusing or conflicting. Rather, they should serve as alternate methods for deciding a sequence of tasks.

To sequence tasks according to performance frequency (see Fig. 9-7), one determines how often the task is performed in normal work assignments. It is often helpful to convert the frequency with which a

Rating Scale LEARNING DIFFICULTY					
Occupation: Hostess **Duty (Work Block):** Serving Foods	How difficult is task to learn?				
	Easy				Very Hard
Tasks	1	2	3	4	5
Welcomes patrons to establishment			✔		
Seats patrons	✔				
Presents menu		✔			
Makes suggestions re: food & service			✔		
Answers questions re: food & service				✔	
Serves ice water	✔				
Fills beverage cups & glasses	✔				
Fulfills diners requests					✔
Assists in adjusting complaints					✔

Fig. 9-9

task occurs into a numerical quantity. Whereas a rating scale of 1 to 5 is illustrated, any range can be used. Likewise, the scale-frequency descriptors (seldom-often) can be altered to fit different situations. The nature of the job and work performed determine words best suited to serve as rating-scale descriptors. Some alternate descriptors of frequency are:

Daily	Hourly
Hourly	Every minute
Infrequently	Frequently
Biweekly	Twice daily

When rating the importance of a task (see Fig. 9-8), one defines significance to successful completion of the job under normal operating conditions. Again, a numerical rating scale with interchangeable descriptors lends objectivity to analysis. To meet varying levels of importance, the rating scale may be altered to employ values such as:

1-2-3
1-2-3-4-5
1-2-3-4-5-6-7-8-9-10

When attempting to rate learning difficulty of given tasks (see Fig. 9-9), one must be conscious of the developmental level of students. Learning difficulty must be predicted from the learner's viewpoint. What seems simple and easy to professionals may have been learned slowly and with great difficulty. Again, use of an appropriate rating scale provides a degree of objectivity not available through other means.

The planner may use frequency of performance, task importance, and learning difficulty individually or collectively to order tasks for students. A degree of objectivity is achieved if a rating scale is employed to assess tasks each of the three ways. All judgments made by the planner should be tempered and verified by individuals and/or groups who possess expertise in the work unit under consideration.

A final phase of the task analysis process involves detailing of steps required for performance of each task. Task detailing describes what a worker must do under normal employment circumstances to satisfy given work assignments. This procedure provides bases for identifying major presentations and bases for identifying related technical, general, and career information. Each performance step is listed in terms of what is *done* by the worker. Steps are *not* listed according to what an employee must know. Observe the following analysis of task details.

Appliance Repairman

Task: Soldering
Performance Steps:

1. Clean work
2. Select proper soldering device
3. Tin joint to be soldered
4. Apply proper heat
5. Apply flux and solder
6. Check joint

A listing of the major steps required for completion of specific work tasks paves the way for subsequent development of demonstration, lesson, and discussion outlines.

The following are additional examples of performance step details:

Machinist

Task: Holding work in the universal vise
Performance steps:

1. Clean sharp burrs and edges from part
2. Place angle plate on surface plate
3. Clamp part to be measured to angle plate

    4. Measure angle with proper instrument
    5. Check measured angle with blueprint

Photographer

    Task: Loading a camera
    Performance steps:

    1. Open camera back in subdued light
    2. Remove exposed film role
    3. Insert unexposed film role
    4. Thread leader onto take-up spool
    5. Advance film several frames
    6. Close camera back
    7. Advance film several frames

INSTRUCTIONAL ANALYSIS

Instructional analysis is a process by which curriculum planners organize material which results from developmental, content, concept, occupational, job, or task analyses into sequential learning experiences. The respective analyses result in abundances of material which is not directly applicable to instructional settings. Much of it cannot be communicated in an instructional setting. Some is too elementary, and some is inappropriate for specific career program level objectives.

Instructional analysis entails review and synthesis of an array of material into a manageable instructional package. Priorities are established and certain bits of information and/or tasks are discarded, while others are retained. It is a weeding-out process. The planner selects and orders material which is applicable to given career outlines. The process consists of:

    A. Specifying outcomes.
    B. Grouping items into units.
    C. Organizing informational topics.
    D. Structuring learning activities.
    E. Specifying learning sequences.

SPECIFYING OUTCOMES

The first step involves specification of total program goals. Usually formulated during earlier planning stages, the goals should be reexamined in view of changing human and technological needs. They should be written in terms of observable competencies which pupils should possess upon completion of the career program. With overall goals firmly in mind, the analyst can identify and/or write objectives, specifying terminal behaviors related to the career level (awareness, exploratory, emphasis, or specialization) for which he is responsible. Moving from long-range to short-term outcomes, the process seeks to maintain continuity and coordination of effort in every learning environment and at every career level. Essential to successful specialization of outcomes is strict adherence to the following procedure:

    a. Specify long-range, total program goals.
    b. List appropriate career level objectives.
    c. List student performance objectives for specific learning experiences.

Prior analyses have identified relevant content, concepts, skills, etc., which represent selected aspects of the world of work. However, mere identification, as pointed out earlier, does not provide ready-made learning packages. In order to convert such data into usable form, the analyst must develop instructional units. These are major subdivisons of experiences. Units consist of like items, concepts, or competencies, and may utilize a knowledge, concept, skill, or similar organizational base. Several examples will illustrate.

Knowledge Base

(Understanding Community Occupations)

Unit Titles

Health care occupations
Secretarial occupations
Marketing occupations
Forestry occupations
Food service occupations
Agricultural occupations
Government service occupations

Concept Base

(Electronic Systems)

Unit Titles

Orientation to electronic systems, subsystems, and
    components
Input subsystems

Control subsystems
Output subsystems
Components

Skill Base

(Waiter-Waitress)

Unit Titles[10]

Orientation
Mechanics of service
Table-clearing services
Menu and order service
Preparation and presentation of guest check
Business arithmetic
Basic English
Safety and sanitation
Duties and working relations

GROUPING ITEMS INTO UNITS

Units of instruction should be formulated in terms of three levels of terminal behavior: specific learning outcomes, career level objectives, and long-term overall program goals. Analysis and classification according to these three levels will serve to identify irrelevant items and designate important learning areas.

Consultation with experts regarding choice of units will assure proper direction. Input from workers and employers can suggest deletion, revision, and/or addition of learning units. Once major instructional units have been identified and verified as essential to the three levels of terminal behavior, one can proceed to identify informational topics, learning activities, and an instructional order.

ORGANIZING INFORMATIONAL TOPICS

Instructional units should entail related information. Maximum benefit of related information is realized if it is analyzed and categorized according to technical, general, and career characteristics. Organizing related information into these three categories assures that relevant topics are included. Related technical information consists of those topics which are essential to successful completion of a job duty or task. For example,

[10] U.S. Department of Health, Education & Welfare, *A Guide for a Training Course: Waiter-Waitress* (Washington, D.C.: U.S. Government Printing Office, 1970), OE 87046.

related technical informational topics for an electronics technician program include:

Technical Information Topics
(Electronic Technician)

I. Electrical Terminology
   A. Ampere
   B. Ohm
   C. Volt
   D. Watt

II. Formulas
   A. Ohm's law
   B. Kirchoff's law
   C. Watt's law

Related general information is that which is good for the individual to know, but not absolutely necessary for successful completion of a job duty or task. An example follows:

General Information Topics
(Body & Fender Repairman)

I. Paint chemistry
II. Paint manufacture
III. Physical characteristics of sheet metal
IV. Properties of body repair compounds
V. Properties of abrasive compounds

Related career information topics are those which help the learner to identify self and work roles. In an articulated career program, the teacher assumes guidance and counseling functions. Thus, the planner of instructional units must assure that appropriate career information topics are included in instructional outlines for each career continuum level. An example of related career informational topics follows:

Career Information Topics

(Careers in Health Occupations)

Unit Titles

Admitting clerk	Mail clerk
Ambulance aide	Medical cashier
Central supply aide	Medical clerk

File clerk
Food service worker
Housekeeping aide
Kitchen aide

Medical laboratory aide
Messenger clerk
Medical receptionist

Properly organized informational topics give direction and thrust to instructional effort at all levels of the career program. An instructional analysis cannot be considered complete until the technical, general, and career-related informational topics have been reviewed and listed for all appropriate units. With instructional units and their respective related informational topics defined and listed, the analyst may proceed to the fourth step of the instructional analysis process.

STRUCTURING LEARNING ACTIVITIES

The fourth step requires identification and selection of instructional activities for effecting desired behavioral changes. Such activities are numerous and can variously be accomplished in the classroom, laboratory, business establishment, clinic, factory, governmental agency, or home. The classroom must often be abandoned in favor of more meaningful learning environments. Learning activities and the environment wherein they occur are dependent upon desired performance and knowledge. Previously stated objectives, i.e., behaviors which the learner is supposed to demonstrate at the end of the learning experience should dictate specific experiences. Specific learning activities for each unit can be derived from a synthesis of expected pupil behaviors and related knowledge, as in the form for Instructional Analysis for typewriting (Fig. 9-10).

SPECIFYING LEARNING SEQUENCES

The remaining step is to place the instructional units along with their informational topics and learning activities into a logical sequence appropriate for educational purposes. The sequence in which events occur on the job or in the work place is not necessarily the best order to use for teaching career skills and knowledges. There are several alternate ways in which units can be arranged into a logical instructional order. They include sequencing according to frequency of performance, deductive reasoning, and career or occupational prerequisites. There is no general agreement regarding which technique is superior.

By recording the number of times a given task is performed in a given work situation, the analyst may determine which competencies are absolutely essential. There results a sequence of events and related

INSTRUCTIONAL ANALYSIS

Unit Title   Typewriting

K-Adult Long-Range Goals   Creation of desirable work attitudes, habits, & salable job skills

Career Level Objectives   Development of saleable job skills

Observable Behaviors	Information			Learning Activities
	Technical	General	Career	
The student will type on business forms inserting words and/or numbers according to acceptable business practice.	Typewriter operation	Kinds of typewriters	Job descriptions.	Type in required information on a variety of different business forms
	Kinds of forms	Kinds of papers	Worker requirements	Practice on both manual and electric typewriters
			Employment conditions	Drill on typing numbers
			Special aptitudes	Utilize activity where pupil must evaluate additions and extensions

Fig. 9-10

informational requirements proceeding from most often used to least often used. Those who advocate this method suggest that determination of frequency of performance is basic to all other forms of sequencing. They imply that this method sets all career and/or occupational prerequisites and provides an instructional order which proceeds from the simple to the complex. They also submit that units arranged according to performance frequency afford the greatest opportunity for learner advancement because they foster interest and mastery of a series of increasingly difficult tasks in a logical sequence.

An alternate method arranges instructional units into a learning sequence according to degree of specificity. It orders units from the general to the specific. In other words, the first instructional units provide the big picture of the world of work, career clusters, employment situations, etc. Subsequent units add specificity, e.g., cleaning teeth, mixing concrete, typing letters, planting shrubs. This method assumes that learners should become intelligible of total career opportunities and practices before mastering specific job tasks, and holds great promise for the sequencing of units for career programs at the levels of awareness, exploration, and emphasis, as well as at the level of specialization.

A final sequencing technique orders instructional units according to career or occupational prerequisites. Here instructional order is derived through analysis of practices and procedures required at each stage of career or occupational development. Competencies which are required for job entry are identified first. Then succeeding competency levels are determined. For example, certain principles of flight and aeronautics must be taught in ground school before the learner assumes control of an aircraft in flight. Likewise, the gas-welder must be able to correctly set up equipment, select and adjust a tip, and adjust the flame before he can successfully weld pipe and tubing.

The sequencing of instructional units can be achieved through utilization of one or a combination of these methods. Each should be evaluated for its appropriateness to a given career continuum level. The aspects of frequency, difficulty, prerequisites, learner motivation, and career competencies should be carefully weighed.

The Instructional Analysis form aids in planning. One instructional unit is placed on each form. Place the unit title in the appropriate space, leaving the unit number blank at this time. Proceed to fill in the long-range goals and career-level goals. Indicate specific unit objectives in terms of observable behaviors in the first column. Then list the general, technical, and career-related informational topics in the second column. List the activities required for effecting desired behavioral changes in the third column.

Repeat this process for each instructional unit. There will result a set of analysis forms equal in number to instructional units which comprise the entire career learning experience. Determine a logical instructional sequence for the units by examining each of the analysis forms according to one or a combination of alternate sequencing techniques. Make a tentative ordering of analysis forms by placing the forms in a pile with the number one unit on top. Reexamine the ordering and make revisions. Using a pencil, place the number which represents the instructional order of each unit in the appropriate blank. Submit numbered unit analysis forms to various competent personnel for criticism. Evaluate criticism and finalize the order of units.

SUMMARY

This chapter gives alternate solutions to the following questions:

1. How can analyses be coordinated at every level of the career continuum?

Such coordination can be achieved by adopting the systems approach to career program development. Systems analysis facilitates program development through consideration of the entire learning situation and effective combination of key educational subsystems.

2. How can the world of work be analyzed into components for application to a career program?

Those processes which delineate components of both human and technological aspects of the world of work are: developmental, occupational, content, concept, job, and task analyses.

3. How can information, derived by career analysis, be converted into a form suitable for instructional purposes?

Information regarding various characteristics of the world of work can be organized through the instructional analysis process. It serves to specify outcomes, organize units and informational topics, structure learning activities, and indicate learning sequences.

ACTIVITIES

1. Review relevant literature on systems analysis and report, in writing, some of the existing alternate approaches which can be used for career program development.
2. Select a specific human developmental stage and write out the associated developmental tasks and appropriate learning activities.

3. Select a broad occupational area and break it down into specific key employment situations.
4. Break down an occupational area into manageable parts, according to the content found to be essential for its very existence.
5. Identify a broad occupational area and list those concepts which serve to universally and exclusively describe the knowledges and skills required of personnel employed in that area.
6. Write a job description for an occupation of your choice.
7. Select a specific job and block the major work divisions, list its major tasks, and detail subsequent performance steps.
8. Contact practicing career-education personnel and determine which analysis techniques they employ to give structure and meaning to their programs.
9. Identify a list of tasks for a selected job and determine the sequence in which they occur. Contact competent personnel and ask them to place the tasks in order, according to:

    a. Frequency of performance.
    b. Importance.
    c. Learning difficulty.

    Compare the resultant ordering of tasks.
10. Perform an instructional analysis for a given career area of your choice. Submit your completed analysis to a practicing career educator for his evaluation.
11. Arrange to visit an educational institution which employs systems analysis procedures for purposes of program development. Report on your findings in writing.

DISCUSSION QUESTIONS

1. Discuss the characteristics of traditional analysis techniques in terms of their ability to adequately describe both the human and technological aspects of work.
2. Comment to the effect that systems analysis will, in fact, provide a viable means by which various career program elements can be coordinated for more efficient operation.
3. Discuss the pros and cons of systems analysis for application to career program development.
4. Discuss the concept of the vocational developmental process and draw some implications for career program development.
5. Comment on the statement that analysis of the human developmental process serves as a general guide for the conduct of succes-

sive stages of occupational content, concept, job, task, and instructional analysis.

6. How might planners best gather, synthesize, and classify information on occupations and employment opportunities?
7. Compare and contrast content versus concept analysis.
8. Compare and contrast job and trade analysis.
9. Describe what you feel to be the major shortcomings of the task analysis process.
10. Discuss the pros and cons of determining task sequence according to:

    a. Frequency of performance.
    b. Importance.
    c. Learning difficulty.

11. In your opinion, which method of unit organization (knowledge, concept, or skill) provides the best means for organizing a program? Why? Justify your choice.
12. What factors should influence your choice of instructional activities for selected units?
13. Compare and contrast the alternate ways in which instructional units can be arranged into a logical teaching order.

BIBLIOGRAPHY

Bollinger, Elroy W., and Weaver, Gilbert G. *Trade Analysis and Course Organization.* New York: Pitman, 1955.

Cox, R. C. *Item Selection Techniques and Evaluation of Instructional Objectives.* Pittsburgh: University of Pittsburgh Learning Research Center, 1965.

Cross, Aleene A. "Searching Out the Common Concepts . . . ," *American Vocational Journal,* 42:35-36, January, 1967.

Friese, John F. *Course Making in Industrial Education.* Peoria, Ill.: Bennett, 1958.

Fryklund, Verne C. *Occupational Analysis.* Milwaukee: Bruce, 1958.

Gagne, R. M. *The Conditions of Learning.* New York: Holt, 1965.

Giachino, J. W., and Gallington, Ralph O. *Course Construction in Industrial Arts, Vocational, and Technical Education.* Chicago: American Technical Society, 1967.

Kirchner, Wayne K., and Lucas, Jane A. "Using Factor Analysis to Explore Employee Attitudes," *Personnel Journal,* 49:492-494.

Larson, Milton E. *Review and Synthesis of Research: Analysis for Curriculum Development in Vocational Education.* Research Series No. 46, Columbus, Ohio: Center for Vocational and Technical Education, Ohio State University, 1969.

Mager, Robert F. *Developing Vocational Instruction.* Palo Alto, Calif.: Fearon, 1967.

McCormick, E. J. *The Development, Analysis, and Experimental Application of Worker-Oriented Job Variables.* Lafayette, Ind.: Occupational Research Center, Purdue University, 1964.

Miller, Robert B. "Task Description and Analysis," *Psychological Principles in System Development,* edited by R. M. Gagne. New York: Holt, 1962.

Morgan, R. M. and Bushnell, D. S. *Designing an Organic Curriculum.* Washington, D.C.: Bureau of Research, United States Office of Education, November, 1966. (mimeographed)

Optner, L. O. *Systems Analysis for Business and Industrial Problem Solving.* Englewood Cliffs, N.J.: Prentice-Hall, 1965.

Palmer, G. J., Jr., and McCormick, E. J. "A Factor Analysis of Job Activities," *Journal of Applied Psychology,* 45:289-94, 1961.

Selvidge, R. W., and Fryklund, V. C. *Principles of Trade and Industrial Teaching,* Peoria, Ill.: Bennett, 1946.

Selvidge, Robert W. *How to Teach a Trade.* Peoria, Ill.: Bennett, 1929.

Silvius, G. H., and Bohn, R. C. *Organizing Course Materials.* Bloomington, Ill.: McKnight, 1961.

Sjorgen, Douglas, and Sahl, Robert. *Review of Research on Common Job Behaviors.* Interim Report, Office of Education, Bureau of Research, United States Department of Health, Education and Welfare, Contract Number OE-6-85-073, December, 1966.

Smith, Brandon B., and Moss, Jerome. *Process and Techniques of Vocational Curriculum Development.* Minneapolis, Minnesota: Research Coordinating Unit for Vocational Education, 1970.

Studdiford, W. S. "A Functional System of Occupational Classification," *Occupations,* 30:37-42, 1951.

Super, Donald E., and Bachrach, P. *Scientific Careers and Vocational Development Theory.* New York: Teachers College, Columbia University, 1957.

Super, Donald E., et al. *Vocational Development,* New York: Teachers College, Columbia University, 1957.

Chapter Ten

Organizing an Instructional Strategy

INTRODUCTION

Those who are responsible for development of instructional strategies for career programs must have answers to the following questions:

- How can a program be planned and organized to allow maximum flexibility for meeting changing needs of a dynamic society?
- What items make up an overall instructional strategy?
- What kinds of information should be included in specific teaching plans?

An instructional strategy is fitted into a total plan in Fig. 10-1. The overall planning process is a deductive one, involving screening and/or sorting of data. The world of work is examined for content for established categories. These categories are in turn subjected to a variety of analysis procedures which further delimit selected occupational areas, concepts, jobs, or tasks. At this point an occupation(s) is said to have been completely analyzed into its essential human and technological characteristics.

The next step is instructional analysis. Content is synthesized for selected learning situations. The result of instructional analysis is major instructional units and selected student activities which are relevant to the needs of learners at varying developmental levels. Data about and from occupations are converted to forms which are appropriate for learning situations. A strategy or roadmap or guideline facilitates movement toward short- and long-term career program goals. The instructional plan must be structured in a manner which encourages pupil entry, progression, and termination at rates commensurate with individual experience, ability, and interest. It includes (a) major learning units, (b) primary student activities, (c) appropriate teaching methods, (d) essential human and material resources, (e) critical assessment procedures, and (f) necessary instructional timing. All these precede development of in-

Fig. 10-1

dividual lesson plans. Thus, this chapter is concerned with presenting and discussing techniques for achieving a practical instructional plan for career learning experiences.

CONTENTS OF AN INSTRUCTIONAL PLAN

The process by which an instructional plan is developed involves the following steps:

A. Subdivide major instructional units.
B. Select student activities
C. Choose appropriate teaching methods
D. Develop assessment procedures.
F. Identify critical time intervals.

In the first step, major units are broken down into subunits, subconcepts, or competencies. What the units are called does not matter. The major learning units must be divided into manageable learning subcategories. For example, some major instructional units and subcategories for a program designed to prepare "building custodians" follows:

Major Unit I. General Housekeeping

    Subunits   A. Responsibility
                  B. Sweeping
                  C. Dusting
                  D. Polishing and waxing

Major Unit II. Sanitation

    Subunits   A. Cleanliness and maintenance
                  B. Pest control

Major Unit III. Maintenance Buildings and Grounds

    Subunits   A. Maintenance assignments
                  B. Interior maintenance
                  C. Exterior maintenance
                  D. Mechanical maintenance
                  E. Maintenance standards

One of the easiest ways to identify subtopics is to utilize the topical outline format illustrated above.

A written topical outline, containing major learning units and contributing subdivisions, enables the planner to identify and list student activities, resources, assessment procedures, and time requirements. It is imperative that decisions regarding each of these be made in light of characteristics and desired terminal behaviors. Student activities, teaching methods, and assessment procedures must be selected with total awareness and practical understanding of learner characteristics which can be described according to developmental stages, attitudes, interests, educational background, physical attributes, and socioeconomic levels. It is usually best to write out a brief description of generalized learner characteristics before attempting to select activities, methods, and procedures. Desired terminal behaviors are equally important to this stage of planning. For instance, examine the following objective:

Objective:
Using the proper equipment and supplies, troubleshoot an electric circuit and diagnose malfunctions.

Student activities, teaching methods, and human and material resources should be chosen and listed insofar as they will maximize opportunity for mastery of electrical circuit troubleshooting and diagnostic procedures. In this case, learner activities should center about hands-on exercises with live circuits. Appropriate methods might include live demonstration of how to troubleshoot and diagnose a circuit, readings, motion pictures, and individualized instruction packets. Necessary resources may include electrical test instruments, circuit components, manuals, filmstrips, videotapes, and a laboratory assistant.

Selection of student activities and determination of teaching methods should be governed in part by what is known about human development. There is evidence to suggest that pupils learn best by working directly on or with the topic, object, product, or task in question. Learners gain most from concrete and real experiences. The more abstract an experience, the more complex learning becomes. Therefore, every possible effort should be made to select student activities, teaching methods, and aids which enable the learner to work directly with the real stuff.

If we wish to teach rough framing to beginning building-construction students, the best technique is to put the pupil out on the job with tools in hand. In this environment he can experience the real sights, sounds, smells, joys, and hardships of the occupation. But, if there are 20 to 24 students in each of three classes, it is a physical impossibility to provide such experiences. There simply are not enough on-the-job learning stations available. Therefore, alternate experiences must be provided. Though not as desirable as on-the-job activity, a more practical method is to have pupils build full-size wall sections and similar projects in the school laboratory or on adjacent grounds. This allows each learner to use tools and knowledges employed by tradesmen. However, it lacks some of the sights, sounds, smells, and pressures of the real world of work.

Practical considerations of space, tools, materials, and finances may render full-size framing impractical, and require another alternative to real work. A workable solution may be pupil-constructed scale models of a soft wood or styrofoam. If this is impractical, a still greater level of abstraction might be appropriate. Students could merely draw wall sections, footings, etc. This experience could be augmented by films of workmen performing rough framing operations.

Additional examples of student activities, teaching methods, and resources for selected learning objectives follow:

Objective:
Given appropriate resources regarding occupations in public services, the learner will list and describe the major duties of five jobs which interest him. Descriptions will be compared to those found in the *D.O.T.*

Student Activity:
View film on public service occupations.
Visit and observe people employed in public service occupations.
Read Occupations in Public Services, *D.O.T.*
Observe visiting lecturer.

Teaching Method:
Team lecture-discussion
Film
Field trip

Resources:
Film, projection equipment
Field trip centers
Career library
Travel expense account
Speakers bureau

Objective:
Identify, test, and write out descriptions of plant material which are representative of each type of reproductive process. Evaluation will be based upon inclusion of at least one reproductive process example.

Student Activity:
Visit seed testing laboratory
Collect plant materials

Submit plant cells to microscopic inspection
Conduct growth process experiments
View film
Write a technical report of activities
Read text

Teaching Method:
Lecture-discussion
Laboratory interaction
Individualized learning package
Field trip

Resources:
Field trip centers
Travel budget
Laboratory equipment (microscopes)
Greenhouse
Audiovisual equipment
Library

Objective:
Given access to narratives about the growth and subsequent development of corporations, businesses, and agencies which have played roles in the formation of society, the learner will write an autobiography of a prominent American enterpriser. Evaluation will be based upon authenticity of the report as checked by the instructor using the biographical guide, *Who's Who in American Enterprise.*

Student Activity:
View films on famous enterprisers
Read biographical sketches
Observe visiting lecturer
Write biography

Teaching Method:
Lecture-discussion team
Audiovisual aids
Resource people

Resources:
AV equipment
Film budget or library
Career library
Speakers bureau

Other examples of student activities which may be appropriate for specific objectives include:

A. Construct a project out of plastic, metal, and wood.
B. Perform several experiments using selected chemicals.
C. Engage in full- or part-time work experiences.
D. Read references on the industrial revolution.
E. Fill out a job application form.
F. Interview individuals currently employed in a job which interests you.
G. Write a job description.

The planner should provide for alternate learning experiences which may be matched to learner needs as they arise.
Methods which should be considered include:

A.	Demonstration	I.	Question-answer
B.	Lecture	J.	Recitation
C.	Lecture-demonstration	K.	Observation
D.	Class discussion	L.	Testing
E.	Individualized, one-to-one	M.	Conference
F.	Trial and error	N.	Written instructions
G.	Experimentation	O.	Illustrations
H.	Imitation		

To maximize opportunity for learning, the planner must consider all alternate teaching methods and select those which fit learner needs and instructional objectives.

Resources also must be selected on the basis of desired terminal pupil behaviors. While these are not always available or appropriate, each should be considered. Resources are either human or material. Representative human resources are:

Learners	Clerical help
Teachers	Administrators
Guidance personnel	Resource people
Parents	Speakers bureau
Technicians	Union leaders
Aides	Management personnel

Representative material resources are:

Audiovisual equipment	Donations
Cooperative work-experience	Equipment
centers	Film libraries

Finances	School plant
Grants	Supplies
Laboratories	Tools
Material resource centers	Transportation

Whenever practical, selection of activities, methods, and resources should enable the learners to interact with real work situations. These should be tempered with experiences which foster awareness and understanding of financial, technical, and other features of components of the world of work.

In order to maximize student involvement at varying levels of abstraction, the program planner should specify a number of alternate learning options. These should range from concrete to abstract. Then students who learn effectively at different levels of abstraction can be served equally well.

An instructional strategy or plan must also provide for a continuous program of pupil assessment. The planner should list procedures which will be used to assess entering pupil characteristics, monitor individual progress, and evaluate terminal behaviors. Representative assessment techniques which need be listed in the instructional plan include:

A. Pretests to ascertain possessed competencies.
B. Check tests to measure varying levels of competency development.
C. Scholastic aptitude tests to measure general intelligence.
D. Special aptitude tests to determine unique and specific abilities of the individual.
E. Interest inventories to ascertain areas of special interest.
F. Character or personality instruments to assist with special problems.
G. Post-tests to determine individual terminal competency levels.
H. Follow-up instruments to determine or assess program graduate success.

Some features of an assessment program require close working relationships between personnel who possess expertise in the administration and interpretation of special instruments and teachers. Classroom teachers assume ever greater responsibility for measuring variables which affect learning. Teachers not only are purveyors of information but also are counselors who plan, organize, coordinate, direct, and control individual learner progress. Thus, it is imperative that within the overall instructional plan, adequate space be devoted to a listing of assessment procedures which will be used to measure learning at several stages in the program.

Written competency-based objectives should serve as a guide for listing critical instructional intervals. These are intervals where learners must have knowledge of results before going on to new material. This is not to imply that all pupils must complete learning experiences at the same rate. Rather, identification of initial intervals provides learners and instructional personnel with a flexible schedule which can be adjusted to suit individual needs, abilities, and learning rates.

Various learning situations require different levels of time specificity. That is, mastery of unit or subunit competencies can be described for periods of a year, a semester or quarter, a week, a day, or a given number of minutes.

Teachers must budget instructional time if career program objectives are to be achieved in an economic and effective manner.

Computer-assisted flexible modular scheduling makes more critical the need for well-planned and organized instructional plans. Computerized flexible scheduling is a means by which times, spaces, and numbers are arranged in a manner which maximizes interaction of human and material resources. Flexible scheduling is achieved through utilization of a man-machine system composed of teachers, learners, programmers, technicians, administrators, and electronic-automated technology.

The overall responsibility for planning flexible schedules rests with administrative and supervisory units of an educational enterprise. Responsibility may be delegated to computer department personnel. Such specialists can convert significant instructional data into forms suitable for application to electronic data-processing equipment. Only instructional personnel can provide computer specialists with necessary data regarding courses of study, criterial intervals, etc.

Instructional personnel must provide written course and specific objectives, detailed descriptions of learning options, and student requisites. Instructional objectives must be stated in observable behavioral terms. Likewise, both required and alternate learning options must be described according to explicit unit competencies, student activities, teaching methods, resources, and estimated time requirements. Learner characteristics, such as interest, also should be listed.

Failure to provide supervisors and programmers with accurate, specific written descriptions of instructional plans will result in schedules which are educationally and technologically unmanageable. A schedule derived from a computer programmed with inaccurate and/or incomplete instructional data will lock learners and teachers alike into inflexible schedules. Modular schedules are as flexible as inputs are complete and accurate. Attention to detail at scheduling stages alleviates hardships and misgivings.

Table 10-1. Scope and Sequence

CAREER LEARNING EXPERIENCE   Orientation to Careers   NUMBER OF WEEKS: 10
                                      (title)

UNIT	UNIT TITLE	WEEKS PER UNIT	TOPICS	ACTIVITIES
1	Orientation to careers	½ week	All	2.32 3.42 5.12 6.22
2	Hunting, fishing, forest, and grazing occupations	1 week	2.1 2.2 2.3 2.4	2.11 2.21, 2.22 2.31 2.41, 2.42 quiz
3	Agricultural occupations	1 week	3.1 3.2 3.3 3.4 3.5	3.11 3.21 3.31, 3.32 3.41 3.51, 3.52
4	Mining occupations	1 week	4.1 4.2	4.11, 4.12 4.21, 4.22 quiz
5	Manufacturing occupations	1½ weeks	5.1 5.2 5.3	5.11 5.21, 5.22 5.31, 5.32
6	Transportation occupations	2 weeks	6.1 6.2 6.3	6.11 6.21 6.31, 6.32 quiz
7	Trade and Service occupations	2½ weeks	7.1 7.2 7.3 7.4	7.11 7.21 7.31 7.41
8	Review	½ week	All	Examination

ORGANIZING THE INSTRUCTIONAL PLAN (SOME ALTERNATE FORMATS)

Major subunits, student activities, teaching methods, assessment procedures, and time intervals form the core of an instructional plan. These components must be organized in a format which teachers and students can understand. Several formats result in manageability. Four representative organizational formats will be described. These range from the general to specific and are: (a) unit scope and sequence, (b) weekly instructional plan, (c) daily/weekly instructional plan, and (d) competency-based instructional plan. Each format organizes the same information, but in a different way.

The major aspects of an instructional plan can be arranged on a "scope and sequence" form (Table 10-1). This form provides a convenient means for listing instructional units, time intervals, topics, and activities on one page. An observer can understand the range and order of instruction for a given period of time at a glance. An overall picture of the career learning experience and unit title and number, time allocation, topic, and student activities are described in the appropriate columns. This form serves as a cover page for other forms which detail instructional units, topics, and activities. One disadvantage of this method is that the professional must refer to the cover sheet while using the more detailed sheets.

Another method of organizing instructional data is shown in Table 10-2. The weekly instructional plan serves the same purpose as the "scope and sequence." However, it presents all necessary information on a single sheet, eliminating cumbersome coding and referencing of supplementary sheets. Time requisites, student activities, methods, resources, and assessment procedures are instantly observable. This form does not, however, allow for as much detail for each item as does the "scope and sequence."

Instructional plans may also be organized according to a format which details weekly and daily strategies. This format is provided in Table 10-3. This organization requires the program planner to specify instructional effort by the week and then by the day. Each week's instructional plan is described in detail, according to daily informational topics, student activity, teaching method, necessary resources, and assessment procedures. This form is especially helpful to beginning teachers, substitutes, and others who need well-organized day-to-day instructional guides.

Precise specification of weekly and daily instructional experiences need not unduly limit program flexibility. Concise statements of strategy give direction to instructional effort and abet regular assessment of movement toward program goals. Daily movement toward objectives can be recorded on the instructional plan. The teacher can pencil notations on the form regarding the success or failure of various activities, methods, resources, pupil progress, and estimated time requisites. Such anecdotal records are an invaluable source of data for subsequent revision of career learning experiences.

Table 10-2. Weekly Instructional Plan

CAREER LEARNING EXPERIENCE: <u>Baby and Child Care</u>
                              (title)

UNIT NO.	UNIT TITLE	WEEK	ACTIVITY	TECHNIQUES	RESOURCES HUMAN & MATERIAL	ASSESSMENT
1	First aid	1	Treat patient for cuts and burns Dislodge swallowed objects	Lecture-discussion Demonstration Film	Guest speaker (Dr.) First-aid supplies Childrens' ward Dolls AV equipment	Administer first-aid treatment to child in front of instructor
2	Detecting and dealing with illness	2, 3	Take oral and rectal temperatures Give prescribed medicines Give enemas	Lecture Film Demonstration Discussion	Thermometers Babies Children Medicines AV equipment	Before the instructor take temperatures, give medicines and enemas
3	Bottle feeding	4	Prepare a formula terminal method aseptic method	Lecture Demonstration	Formula Bottles and related Babies	Administer formula to baby
4	Prepares foods and meals	5, 6	Prepare: milk, meats, fish, eggs, vegetables, fruits, cereals, frozen foods	Film Lecture Demonstration Discussion	Required foods and utensils Kitchen facilities AV equipment	Administer prepared foods to babies and children under supervision of the instructor

Table 10-3. Daily/Weekly Instructional Plan

CAREER LEARNING EXPERIENCE: Floristry (Flower Arranging)
(title)

WEEK	ITEMS	MONDAY	TUESDAY	WEDNESDAY	THURSDAY	FRIDAY
1	Topic	Orientation to flower arranging	Aids to flower arranging	Mechanical equipment	Choosing vases and containers	Review
	Activity	View film	Assist instructor in demonstration	Selection of equipment	Selection of proper containers	Class discussion
	Demo-Lect.	Lecture-Discussion	Demonstration	Prepare for field trip to florist shop	Lecture	Discussion
	Resources	Film, AV equipment, flower arrangement	Arrangement aids, flowers, etc.		Flowers, containers	
	Assessment					Check test
2	Topic	Arranging flowers				
	Activity	View film	Arrange flowers	Arrange flowers	Arrange flowers	Class critique of arrangements
	Demo-Lect.	Demonstration				
	Resources	Film, AV equipment, flowers, container	Flowers, container	Flowers, container	Flowers, container	Check list
	Assessment		Visual inspection	Visual inspection	Visual inspection	Written evaluation of each arrangement
3	Topic	Shells, rocks, and wood in arranging				
	Activity	Use same	Arrange flowers with shells, rocks, and wood	On-the-job training	On-the-job training	Review work experience
	Demo-Lect.	Demonstration Film				Discussion
	Resources	Shells, rocks, wood, film, AV equipment		Job station	Job station	
	Assessment		Visual inspection			Student self-check test

Table 10-4. Competency-Based Instructional Plan

CAREER LEARNING EXPERIENCE: Bartending
                                (title)

STARTING DATE	COMPETENCY NO.	ACTIVITY	DEMONSTRATION LECTURE, ETC.	RESOURCES HUMAN & MATERIAL	ASSESSMENT	COMPLETION DATE
	1. Mix Cocktails A. B. C. D. E. F. G. H. I.	Prepare: brandy cocktail gin cocktail rum cocktail sloe gin cocktail vodka cocktail wine cocktail whiskey cocktail liqueur and cordial miscellaneous cocktails	Teacher Demonstration	Bar facilities mixes liquor liqueurs wines instruction sheets	Submit cocktails to instructor for taste test	
	2. Mix Collins A. B. C. D. E.	Prepare: brandy collins John collins rum collins Tom collins whiskey collins	Teacher Demonstration Lecture		Submit collins to instructor for taste test	
	3. Mix Fizzes A. B. C. D.	Prepare: Alabama fizz Albemarle fizz Amer. Picon fizz Aziz fizz	Teacher Demonstration		Submit fizzes to instructor for taste test	

Still another viable organizational format structures instructional effort around identified competencies. A competency-based instructional plan is displayed in Table 10-4. Competencies which contribute to specific learning objectives are listed in an early planning step. Derived from prior occupational, task, and instructional analyses, competencies are the basis of instructional experiences. Competencies, activities, methods, resources, and assessment procedures are listed without regard to specific time intervals.

The learner must be provided with a copy of the competency-based instructional plan before he attempts to master competencies. In Table 10-4, the extreme left- and right-hand columns are entitled starting date and completion date. Having satisfied one competency assessment, the student undergoes experiences which prepare him for the next assessment. The learner enters the date in the column marked "starting date" and proceeds to necessary activities, methods, and resources.

When a learner has experienced the various elements leading to mastery of a selected competency, he seeks out the instructor and submits to a supervised evaluation against the new competency criteria. Successful performances are recorded in the last column, "completion date." If he fails to exhibit an appropriate level of competence, the student returns to relevant activities and later challenges the competency test again. Within reason, a learner may challenge and rechallenge a competency any number of times.

The competency-based plan provides student and teacher alike with a continuous record of achievement. Complete articulation of instructional effort can result from such a plan. If a learner is provided with a competency-based plan, starting at kindergarten and expanded as he progresses through developmental stages, he will possess a permanent record of achievements. If cumulative records accompany learners wherever they go, both students and teachers will be better able to plan, organize, direct, and control variables which aid and abet subsequent learning.

Four alternate organizational formats have been presented. Each has characteristics which set it apart from the others. Professionals should select formats which serve peculiar needs of specific instructional experiences. Without a written plan, learners and teachers are without a road map which guides movement toward personal and program goals.

DEVELOPING SPECIFIC TEACHING (LESSON) PLANS

Preparation of instructional plans according to sequences of critical intervals or significant competencies fosters development of specific written teaching or lesson plans. There are numerous good teaching or lesson plan formats. (See examples at the end of this chapter.) Lesson plan formats are not sacred. Most provide for preparation, presentation, application, summary, and testing.

The value of preparing written teaching or lesson plans cannot be overemphasized. Regardless of how experienced he might be, the teacher cannot hope to remember all significant components of a unit of content when performing before a group of learners. Teachers who contend that they do not need written teaching plans are not totally honest and overrate their abilities. Failure to prepare written teaching plans fosters slovenly instructional habits. Teaching off the "top of one's head" results in poorly stated learning objectives; lack of necessary tools, materials, and instructional apparatus; poor content organization; unintentional elimination of key points; omission of career guidance information; inadequate provision for pupil interaction; and informal assessment procedures. Teaching "off the cuff" compounds poor communication habits. The teacher's task is so broad and encompasses such a diversity of competencies and knowledges that it is impossible to commit to memory even a single lesson.

In the first stage of lesson planning, the teacher should identify steps which are essential to preparation of human and material instructional resources. The preparation stage entails development of the following elements:

A. Learning-experience title and career level,
B. General purpose and location of lesson,
C. Specific performance objectives,
D. Materials and human resources,
E. Procedures and arrangements for pupil readiness.

The planner should state the title of the learning experience and identify the career level for which the lesson is intended. Then the general purpose of the lesson and the place where it will be given can be stated. Emphasis upon learning in real work environments requires special consideration of transportation and scheduling problems during identification of location. Work environments, such as hospital laboratories, emergency rooms, florist shops, greenhouses, machine shops, courthouses, and banks should be considered.

Specific objectives for which the lesson is to be designed must be written out in observable terms. Lesson objectives should spell out *in certain terms* observable behaviors which the learner will be expected to exhibit upon completion of the learning experience. Objectives must likewise pinpoint exact conditions under which students will be expected to exhibit these behaviors and the level of competence which must be attained by the learner (see sample Lesson Plan Formats).

Preparation also entails listing of instructional materials, lesson procedure, and learner preparation items. It is helpful to write out estimates of times which will be required to prepare (1) materials and (2) learners for the presentation. These times should not be hard and fast but should serve as guidelines for more detailed planning. As lessons are prepared and presented, i.e., as experience is gained with given individuals, timing and other features of lesson development can become more precise. Many teachers make pencil notations of successes and failures in achieving lesson objectives and in using techniques in different parts of the lesson. Such notations provide for revision and updating instructional effort.

Instructional materials must be listed. Audiovisuals, published materials, teacher-developed materials—all hardware and software items must be listed on the lesson plan. Materials, equipment, and supplies essential to the lesson must be collected before the presentation. This is better done with a list. Projectors, screens, films, slides, filmstrips, tapes, recorders, transparencies, television monitors, etc., cannot be secured in advance if the teacher trusts to memory. Furthermore, a variety of textbooks, learning packages, laboratory manuals, government documents, pamphlets, bulletins and teacher-prepared materials such as information, instruction, job, operation, and assignment of activity sheets, will not be used unless they are listed during the preparation step.

Listing the procedure or sequence of major points in the lesson is the most important step in the preparation stage. The planner should outline the steps he will take to implement the lesson. For example, a teacher might list the following:

A. Prior to lesson assign readings No. 2, 3, and 4.
B. Administer pretest No. 5.
C. Introduce unit and film.
D. Show film.
E. Discuss film.
F. Demonstrate technique.
G. Question learners.
H. Assign individual laboratory exercises.
I. Assign reading No. 5 for the next unit.
J. Evaluate learner progress.

An integral part of the presentation is the task of preparing the learner for forthcoming lessons. Effort must be made to stimulate learner interest; motivational techniques must be utilized. Representative motivational techniques include: guest speakers, student-prepared bulletin boards, visits to industry and business, on-the-job work experience, displays, videotapes, and pretest instruments. If they are used in the proper manner, pretesting activities can serve as motivational tools. Proper use entails sessions with individuals to fully interpret pretest scores. Clear and concise understanding of where one stands with respect to the educational process is very conducive to morale and efficiency.

Key instructional points should be written in great detail during the preparation step. Key points describe significant tasks, concepts, and content, as well as related technical, general, and career guidance information. A topical outline of such items is usually adequate for instructional purposes. Many teachers find it well to make estimates of times required for the several parts of the lesson. After a lesson has been presented, it is well to correct the time estimates and other features of the lesson plan.

The third phase of lesson development requires detailed specification of activities in which learners will be required to participate either during or immediately following the presentation. Representative activities are: adjust a carburetor, change a dressing, bake a cake, type a letter, prune a tree, arrange flowers, load a pistol, make change, mix concrete. Performance-based activities must be accompanied by written instructions which give direction to immediate and future student effort. Immediate applications are essential to learner understanding and to mastery of increasingly difficult competencies. Again, estimated times are helpful to the classroom-laboratory teacher.

The fourth phase of lesson development is a summary or review of the key points. This may be merely a list of the significant points of the presentation. Some authors incorporate the summary steps as part of the presentation step. It is described as a separate step here to emphasize its importance. The summary is the clincher and is omitted all too often. Lesson planning also must provide for assessment or testing. The lesson planner should list appropriate techniques for assessing pupil mastery of material presented. The techniques include manipulative performance tests which can measure such things as ability to adjust water pressure, paint a room, mix chemicals, plant bushes, and balance a checkbook. They also can include written examinations, oral questioning and discussion, and student-teacher conferences. The assessment step not only informs learners of their progress but also provides feedback for teachers to use in lesson redesign.

Elapsed time between the presentation, summation and assessment may vary from minutes or hours to days or weeks. But it should be held to the minimum. The period of time required for completion of student activities will depend on the competency level of the learners and complexity of assigned tasks. But when application takes longer than several days, intermediate assessments should be made. Lessons involve five steps: (a) preparation, (b) presentation, (c) application (d) summary, and (e) assessment. Each of these must be planned carefully. Each should be detailed according to unique and specific instructional requirements.

SUMMARY

This chapter has answered the following questions:

1. How can a program be planned and organized to allow maximum flexibility for meeting changing career needs of a dynamic society?

A flexible program can be achieved through development of an overall instructional strategy which provides the teacher with guidelines for the preparation of specific teaching plans.

2. What items make up an overall instructional strategy?

An instructional strategy is composed of elements which identify, describe, and organize major learning units, primary student activities, required teaching techniques, essential human and material resources, appropriate assessment procedures, and critical time intervals.

3. What kinds of information should be included in specific teaching plans?

Teaching plans are composed of items which specifically state what is required for the preparation, presentation, application, summary, and assessment of selected learning situations (Figs. 10-2 through 10-6).

ACTIVITIES

1. Visit a selected career-program teacher and ask to read his instructional plans. Write out the major headings and organizational format used.
2. Visit a career program at another institution and gather the same information.
3. Compare/contrast the two instructional plans observed in Activities 1 and 2.
4. Interview a career-program director and secure a copy of overall program objectives and the plan by which he hopes to achieve these goals.

LESSON PLAN FORMAT

COURSE TITLE: _Commercial Diving_   LESSON NO. 9

PREPARED BY _Howard Deterick_

CAREER LEVEL (check one) ___Awareness, ___Exploratory, ___Emphasis, _X_ Specialization

PURPOSE OF LESSON   To develop the ability to don and ditch diving gear –

LESSON LOCATION _Pool or tank_

PERFORMANCE OBJECTIVES   With the instructor observing the learner will don and ditch diving gear after reaching the bottom of the tank. Upon reaching the bottom all equipment will be taken off and the diver will, in no way, be connected to the equipment. He will put the gear back on and surface. Gear will be functioning properly.

PREPARATION (time estimate ___)

REQUIRED RESOURCES _10 minutes_

PRESENTATION (time estimate ___)
40 minutes

(Human)	Material)	CONTENT	PROCEDURE
Instructor learners	Tank and backpack Weight belt Fins Mask Tank Manual	A. equipment B. breathing C. water characteristics D. regulators E. descent precautions F. safety regulations G. surfacing H. stowing gear	1. demonstrate don and ditch procedure at tank side a. remove fins, weight belt, and mask b. remove tank and backpack

TEACHING METHODS

Demonstration

c. hold breath
d. turn off air
e. turn on air
f. put on equipment
g. surface

2. demonstrate don and ditch in tank
   a. "
   g. "

SAFETY PRECAUTIONS

check health of learners
have safety ring available
post guards around tank

ASSIGNMENTS (time estimate _____)

Read diving manual, p. 15-50
Observe demonstration
Practice dives   2 days prior

APPLICATION (time estimate _____)

Don and ditch gear (each learner) 10 minutes per.

SUMMARY

don and ditch procedures
Question-answer

ASSESSMENT PROCEDURES (time estimate _____)

Observe each learner as he dons and ditches gear (10 minutes per learner)

10-2

LESSON PLAN FORMAT

Student_____Date_____

Subject_____Period_____Grade Level_____

Unit_____Est. Time_____Actual Time_____

Topic_____

Method_____

Specific Objectives_____

_____

_____

_____

Safety Points_____

_____

Introduction:

Content: What am I going to teach	Procedure: How shall I teach it

Fig.

Summary:

Application of Learning:

Evaluation of Learning:

References:

Tools and/or Materials:

10-3

LESSON PLAN OUTLINE

Purpose:

Objectives: Stated in Behavioral Terms

References: Texts, Other Books, and Handouts

Materials Needed for Lesson:

Procedure: Sequence of Events to Present
              Complete Unit or Lesson

Preparation: 1. Of Students for Lesson

                2. Of Material for Lesson for Day

Presentation:

          Steps   Key points

Application: Have Students Do It

Summary or Review:

Assignment:

Testing:

Summary:

Evaluation: Tests; Demonstrate Ability

Fig. 10-4

LESSON PLAN

METHOD OF INSTRUCTION	COURSE TITLE	LESSON NO.

TOPIC

OBJECTIVE

TOOLS, EQUIPMENT, AND MATERIALS	PROCEDURE
TEACHING AIDS AND DEVICES	
TECHNIQUES	
SAFETY	

ASSIGNMENT	REFERENCE

SUMMARY

QUESTIONS AND PROBLEMS

Fig. 10-5

LESSON PLAN FORMAT

Career Experience Title_____

Prepared by:_____

Lesson Objectives:_____

_____

_____

_____

_____

	TIME	LEARNER ACTIVITIES	TEACHER ACTIVITIES	MATERIALS NEEDED
Introduction				
Sequence of activities in main body of lesson				
Conclusion				

Fig. 10-6

5. Observe several career-program teachers who employ different student activities to get learners involved in the educational process (exercises, projects, experiments, work experience, etc.). Write out your observations in terms of your estimation of each activity's effectiveness in reaching stated goals.

6. Observe teaching methods of several different teachers. Write out your estimation of each instructor's effectiveness in reaching objectives through his selected method.

7. Visit an instructional materials resource center in an educational institution. Consult the center director or librarian regarding available resources for your specific instructional area; i.e., law enforcement, health, home economics; and make a list of such materials.

8. Arrange to obtain copies of specific lesson plans from several different career-program teachers. Compare/contrast the various plans for their format and content.

9. Secure several different assessment instruments from practicing teachers. Compare/contrast the form and format of each instrument.

10. Present a short lesson to your classmates without the aid of a lesson plan or any prior preparation.

11. Now present a short lesson to your classmates with the aid of a previously prepared lesson outline.

12. Visit a school which is on computerized modular scheduling. Interview the individual(s) in charge of scheduling, several teachers, and several students. Write out their comments regarding the pros and cons of this technique.

13. Interview different teachers at various institutions and record their views on the necessity to plan their courses and lessons in accordance with established written guidelines.

14. Observe and/or collect various instructional plans from different institutions and determine the extent to which each provides for articulated career-program effort.

DISCUSSION QUESTIONS

1. Discuss the kinds of information which should be included in an overall instructional plan.

2. Discuss the entire analysis process which serves to describe the world of work through occupational, job, content, concept, and task analysis.

3. Compare/contrast occupational versus instructional analysis.

4. Describe the many variables which should serve to effect choice of student activities and teaching methods.

5. Discuss the need for and implication of preassessment techniques in facilitating flexible career-program activity.
6. Discuss the implications which computerized flexible modular scheduling hold for career education.
7. Define and discuss the teacher's role in modular scheduling.
8. Discuss the pros and cons of the competency-based instructional plan.
9. In your opinion, which instructional organization format best facilitates flexible career-program activity? Justify your stand.
10. React to the following statement: "Specification of critical instructional time limitations leads to an inflexible career program."
11. Discuss the advantages and disadvantages of using adequately prepared lesson plans.
12. What impact will a detailed written instructional strategy have upon career-program direction and effectiveness?
13. How must learning activities for pupils be determined?
14. What factors should influence an instructor's choice of teaching methods?
15. Discuss the factors influencing choice of instructional material resources for a given teaching task.
16. Describe what you feel to be the greatest barriers to effective instruction.

BIBLIOGRAPHY

Ashton, Warner, Sylvia. *Teacher*. New York: Simon and Schuster, 1963.

Butler, Frank A. *The Improvement of Teaching in Secondary Schools*. Chicago: University of Chicago Press, 1954.

Cenci, Louis, and Weaver, Gilbert G. *Teaching Occupational Skills*. New York: Pitman, 1968.

Clapp, Elsie Ripley. *The Use of Resources in Education*. New York: Harper, 1952.

DeGrazia, Alfred. *Revolution in Teaching: New Theory, Technology, and Curricula*. New York: Bantam, 1964.

Heathers, Glen. *Organizing Schools Through the Dual Progress Plan: Tryouts of a New Plan for Elementary and Middle Schools*. Danville, Ill.: Interstate, 1967.

Jarvis, Oscar T. *The Transitional Elementary School and Its Curriculum*. Dubuque, Iowa: W. C. Brown, 1966.

Inlow, G. M. *The Emergent in Curriculum*. New York: Wiley, 1971.

Keith, Lowell G. *Contemporary Curriculum in the Elementary School*. New York: Harper, 1968.

Mallery, David. *New Approaches in Education: A study of Experimental Programs in Independent Schools*. Boston: National Council of Independent Schools, 1961.

Massialas, B. G., and Zevin, J. *Creative Encounters in the Classroom.* New York: Wiley, 1971.

Miles, Matthew B. *Innovation in Education.* New York: Bureau of Publication, Teachers College, Columbia University, 1964.

Mortensen, D. G., and Schmuller, A. M. *Guidance in Today's School.* New York: Wiley, 1971.

Pautler, Albert J. *Teaching Shop and Laboratory Subjects.* Columbus, Ohio: Merrill, 1971.

Peter, Lawrence J., and Tracy, John. *Prescriptive Teaching System: Volume I, Individual Instruction.* New York: McGraw-Hill, 1972.

Stones, E. *Learning and Teaching: A Programmed Introduction.* New York: Wiley, 1971.

Risk, Thomas. *Principles and Practices of Teaching in Secondary Schools.* New York: American Book, 1968.

Silvius, G. Harold, and Curry, Estell H. *Teaching Successfully in Industrial Education.* Bloomington, Ill.: McKnight, 1967.

Section Four

Assessing, Staffing, and Managing Career Programs

The best-laid plans of educational planners and curriculum developers can only be eventualized by well-organized professionals who are benefited by regular information from several kinds of external assessments and by classroom and laboratory management systems which expedite learning. This section answers questions such as:

1. What may be expected of assessments conducted by regional and professional accrediting agencies and other bodies who accredit, certify, or recognize educational enterprises?
2. What are the essential features of staffing models which maximize economics and learning?
3. How can safety, inventories, behavior rules, and similar areas of concern be incorporated into instructional and conduct schemes for mutual benefit of students, staff, and establishment?

These are treated in:

313

Chapter Eleven

Assessment
of
the
Program

INTRODUCTION

This chapter deals with one of the three parts of educational endeavor: objectives, curriculum, and *evaluation*. It answers the following questions.

- How does the process of assessment relate to the process of planning?
- What is the difference between instructional assessment and instructional evaluation?
- What is the value of a continuous process of program assessment?

It is virtually impossible to treat the evaluation aspect of educational programs as a separate entity. Placement, follow-up, manpower needs, community services, curricular content, and many other factors contribute to the success or failure of occupational programs in the public and private sectors. To define evaluation or assessment without relating it to all aspects of a program is folly.

Many texts treat instructional program evaluation in a separate section or chapter entitled "Tests and Measurements," "Evaluation," or "Evaluating Student Progress." Because the concern here is to analyze the total process of the instructional program, the term *assessment* is utilized throughout this section. It is hoped that this will eliminate any confusion which might exist regarding the differences between the "tests and measurements" types of evaluation and instructional program assessment.

Assessment may be defined as the systematic *process* of continually analyzing instructional program direction in relation to stated, measurable goals as outlined in the short, intermediate, and long-range plans of the institution. It is clear then, that assessment cannot be effective if sound planning procedures are not utilized. An example from a classroom situation illustrates this idea.

The best-constructed written test, combined with an oral examination and a psychomotor performance measure, can be totally useless for evaluating how well a student understands and operates an engine lathe if operation of the lathe was not a stated objective of the course. Likewise, an American history examination will do little to assess the effectiveness of a new instructional tool utilized in a health-care aide curriculum.

The instructional program assessment process involves not only periodic student evaluation, but also (1) analysis of regional manpower needs, (2) specific course cost differential data, (3) follow-up studies, (4) guidance services, including occupational orientation and graduate placement, (5) community services to the school and by the school, (6) instructional and administrative staff functions, (7) etc.

The specific instructional quality of any course can be enhanced through community-wide acceptance of the total occupational program if the administrator in charge is dedicated to a sound public relations program. Conversely, poor guidance services can adversely affect a specific instructional program if students show little interest in an occupational area but are, nevertheless, forced to attend classes related to the occupation.

Just as every good teacher knows that effective testing of students must be done frequently and on a continuing basis, every teacher should appreciate that instructional program assessment must take place systematically and on a continuing basis. If five-year follow-up data is the only information available regarding the relevancy of certain course or unit offerings, far too many students may be adversely affected by misdirected content or irrelevant information before sufficient data is obtained to verify program weaknesses. Hence, a multitude of assessment techniques must be in continual utilization, if the instructional program assessment process is to be effective.

PROGRAM ELEMENT ANALYSIS

Just as occupation or job analysis is the basis for the development of occupational courses of study, program element analysis is the basis for the development of a systematic assessment procedure. In order for this procedure to be developed, all facets of the total instructional system must be identified. This requires close working relationships among occupational area instructors, administrators in charge of occupational programs, guidance personnel, and advisory committee members. All must work together to define the basic elements of the total instructional program at the unit, course, program, and school levels.

A short digression at this point will be useful. It is extremely important that all staff members in any type of instructional enterprise understand that each aspect, each function, of the enterprise is interrelated with all other functions. Even such nonacademic considerations as the condition of the school's front lawn may be related to the success of the football team, to the personal life of the staff, and to the effectiveness of the instructional offering. It is often difficult for instructional personnel to appreciate that everything that goes on within the school and surrounding community affects the quality of the student output. It is therefore important that element analysis entail *all* aspects of the school. The student is a product of the total school, not just of one curricular offering.

Several research studies and national accrediting agencies have endeavored to develop lists of evaluative criteria, based on instructional program element identification. The following is a brief analysis of several such studies and programs. The elements identified represent attempts to analyze various factors contributing to total school effectiveness. It should be noted that occupational or career education is not considered a central school theme in any of the following examples. However, a later section of this chapter will describe a system for total assessment, based on career choice as the major objective of the school system.

National Study of School Evaluation

In 1933, the National Study of School Education (formerly called the Cooperative Study of Secondary School Standards) began work on the development of "an effective evaluation instrument for secondary schools."[1] NSSE is composed of a General Committee whose members are appointed by six Regional Accrediting Associations. They are:

1. New England Association of Colleges and Secondary Schools, Inc.
2. Middle States Association of Colleges and Secondary Schools
3. Southern Association of Colleges and Schools
4. North Central Association of Colleges and Secondary Schools
5. Northwest Association of Secondary and Higher Schools
6. Western Association of Schools and Colleges

The National Study of School Evaluation utilizes an eleven-section evaluative instrument in its assessment procedure. The elements identified as areas of evaluative concern are:

---

[1] National Study of School Evaluation, *Evaluative Criteria*, 4th ed., (Washington, D.C.: National Study of School Evaluation, 1969), p. vi.

1   Manual (a guide to the evaluation procedure)
2   School and Community
3   Philosophy and Objectives
4   Curriculum
     4- 1   Agriculture
     4- 2   Art
     4- 3   Business Education
     4- 4   Distributive Education
     4- 5   Driver and Traffic Safety Education
     4- 6   Languages
     4- 7   Foreign Languages
     4- 8   Health Education
     4- 9   Home Economics
     4-10   Industrial Arts
     4-11   Mathematics
     4-12   Music
     4-13   Physical Education
     4-14   Religion
     4-15   Science
     4-16   Social Studies
     4-17   Special Education
     4-18   Trade, Technical, and Industrial Education
5   Student Activities Program
6   Educational Media Services—Library and Audio-Visual
7   Guidance Services
8   School Facilities
9   School Staff and Administration
10   Individual Staff Member
11   Summary of the Self-Evaluation

Several samples of the instruments utilized by the National Study of School Evaluation follow.*

* Reprinted by permission of the National Study of School Evaluation.

EXPLANATIONS

Evaluation of secondary schools, as developed by the National Study of School Evaluation, is based partly on the extent to which the needs of students enrolled, or those who should be enrolled, in the school are being met. Since these needs are related to resources and opportunities in the environment, it is necessary that the community as well as the student body be described. This section is prepared to permit such descriptions to be made systematically and with a minimum of effort.

Much of the information called for is not easily available in some communities. Those responsible for preparing this section will have to decide whether to seek accurate information through detailed research procedures or to take what is readily available and indicate the inadequacies of the description. The school committee responsible for filling in this blank should not hesitate to extend tables or questions that seem incomplete and omit those that are inappropriate with respect to the school or community. The goal is to give the most complete description possible of the student body, the community or group served by the school, the opportunities for youth, and the hopes of their parents and friends. Perhaps the question should be, "What is important to know about the young people and the community supporting this school in order to know whether the school is meeting the needs of the community?" The purpose of this section is to help find the answer to that question. Because, among schools, the staff, time, and other resources available for completing this section will vary; the completeness and adequacy of the description will also vary somewhat.

All schools—public and nonpublic—have an important obligation to know the nature and needs of their patrons. They should also be concerned about the activities and agencies of the community in which they are located. All schools should present, in the best available form (statistical or descriptive or both), data and information equivalent to what is called for in this section. A nonpublic school which serves as a general secondary school for a community should be able to demonstrate that it provides adequately for the needs of that community.

DEFINITIONS

The *students* of a *public school* are the young people enrolled in the school. Those responsible for the public school should have considerable knowledge about the youth of school age in the district supporting the school, not only those attending, but also those who for any reason are not in attendance, in order to determine how well the school is meeting its responsibility. If a school is serving only part of a community, an attempt should be made to report the special characteristics of this part either in a general statement or in a detailed statement.

The *students* of a *nonpublic school* are the students enrolled in the school.

The *school community* for a *public school* is the area and population of the district that is legally repsonsible for the support and control of the school.

The *school community* for a *nonpublic school* is primarily the parents of the students who are enrolled, except that there are usually important resources in the vicinity which should be known and used to supplement the resources of the school.

I. BASIC DATA REGARDING STUDENTS*

A. ENROLLED STUDENTS AND GRADUATES

1. In the space below enter data for current year (as of October 1) in the last group of three columns, and for the preceding years in the preceding groups of columns, the three columns at the left being for the earliest year. Enter data only for the grades in the school as organized—three-year, four-year, five-year, or six-year unit. If necessary, change designation of the school grades to conform to actual organization of school. If the school is ungraded or for other reasons the organization does not lend itself to this table, modify or replace it so that the enrollment of the school is accurately described.

Classification	19__-19__			19__-19__			19__-19__			19__-19__			19__-19__		
	Boys	Girls	Total	Boys	Girls	Total	Boys	Girls	Total	Boys	Girls	Total	Boys	Girls	Total
Enrollment: Regular:															
Twelfth grade															
Eleventh grade															
Tenth grade															
Ninth grade															
Eighth grade															
Seventh grade															
Postgraduate and Special															
Total															
Graduates: Number during year															

* Reprinted by permission of the National Study of School Evaluation.

2. Describe any studies that have been made regarding the progress of a group of students who entered the lowest grade at the same time (attach sheet).

3. Indicate the significance of these data to the objectives and programs of the school.

IV. DIRECTION OF LEARNING

A. INSTRUCTIONAL STAFF

Checklist

For data on preparation of teachers, see Section 10, "Individual Staff Member"

The vocational agriculture staff members:

1. Are certified to teach the courses to which they have been assigned. .... na 1 2 3 4

2. Have had occupational experience, including operational and managerial responsibilities. .... na 1 2 3 4

3. Have preparation in basic biological sciences. ...... na 1 2 3 4

4. Have preparation in basic physical sciences. .... na 1 2 3 4

5. Have preparation in basic earth sciences. .... na 1 2 3 4

6. Have preparation in such applied plant sciences as field crops, forage crops, and horticultural crops... na 1 2 3 4

7. Have preparation in such applied animal sciences as animal husbandry, dairying, and poultry. .... na 1 2 3 4

8. Have preparation in the problems of plant and animal diseases. .... na 1 2 3 4

9. Have preparation in rural social sciences—agricultural economics, farm management, and rural sociology. .... na 1 2 3 4

10. Have preparation in soils and conservation. .... na 1 2 3 4

11. Have preparation in agricultural mechanics, including power and machinery, structures, electricity, agricultural mechanics shop, and soil, water, and natural resources conservation. .... na 1 2 3 4

12. Have preparation in general and professional education, including general and special methods of teaching agriculture. .... na 1 2 3 4

13. Have preparation in the area of public relations. .. na 1 2 3 4

14. Have knowledge of laws and regulations affecting agriculture and agricultural education. .... na 1 2 3 4

15. Have had experience in conducting Future Farmers of America activities and working with youth and adult groups. .... na 1 2 3 4

16. Continue in-service education through formal study and other professional activities. .... na 1 2 3 4

Reprinted by permission of the National Study of School Evaluation.

17. Maintain an active interest in professional advancement, including participation in educational organizations. ....   na 1 2 3 4

18. Participate in deciding upon agriculture courses and planning their content. ....   na 1 2 3 4

19. Are currently informed about occupational needs and are personally acquainted with farmers and agricultural businessmen in the community. ....   na 1 2 3 4

20.   na 1 2 3 4

Supplementary Data

1. Indicate the number of professional staff found in each of the following categories (do not count the same individual more than once in *a, b, c, d* respectively):

a) Educational level:

Less than bachelor's degree	_____
Bachelor's degree	_____
Master's degree	_____
Sixth-year program	_____
Doctor's degree	_____

b) Semester hours (approximate) of preparation in agriculture:

0–11	_____
12–23	_____
24–48	_____
More than 48	_____

c) Years since last formal study in agriculture:

0–3	_____
4–7	_____
8–12	_____
More than 12	_____

d) Previous experience in years:

0–2	_____
3–5	_____
6–15	_____
More than 15	_____

2. List areas of concentration in agriculture of each staff member (attach sheets, if necessary).

Evaluations

a) How adequate is the preparation *of the staff?* ....   na 1 2 3 4

b) How adequate is the agricultural experience *of the staff?* ....   na 1 2 3 4

Comments

B. INSTRUCTIONAL ACTIVITIES

Checklist

1. Instruction for the *high school* group is directed toward clearly formulated objectives that are appropriate for this group. .... na 1 2 3 4
2. Instruction for *out-of-school youth and adults* is directed toward clearly formulated objectives that are appropriate for these groups. .... na 1 2 3 4
3. Careful planning and scheduling for both class instruction and applied activities are evident. .... na 1 2 3 4
4. Planned instruction is available during each month of the calendar year. .... na 1 2 3 4
5. Students are provided opportunities to participate in planning their activities within the framework of established procedure. .... na 1 2 3 4
6. Instruction is correlated with agricultural experiences of students. .... na 1 2 3 4
7. Opportunities are provided for a variety of experimental and testing activities. .... na 1 2 3 4
8. Audio-visual aids, field trips, and demonstrations and other instructional aids are used appropriately. na 1 2 3 4
9. Students enrolled in high school vocational agriculture have an opportunity to participate in the student activities program. .... na 1 2 3 4
10. Students with aptitude for agriculture have counseling available about possibilities of continuing in advanced agriculture courses in high school. .... na 1 2 3 4
11. Students with aptitude for agriculture have counseling available about possibilities of continuing postsecondary agriculture study. .... na 1 2 3 4
12. Cooperative occupational experience supervised by teacher is available to students to supplement classroom instruction. .... na 1 2 3 4
13. Classroom, shop, greenhouse, nursery, and other laboratory activities reflect current problems of the occupations in which students are being placed for experience. .... na 1 2 3 4
14. na 1 2 3 4

Evaluations

a) *How adequately have the instructional activities been planned?* .... na 1 2 3 4
b) *How well are instructional activities adapted to the needs of individual students?* .... na 1 2 3 4

Comments

Reprinted by permission of the National Study of School Evaluation.

C. INSTRUCTIONAL MATERIALS

Checklist

1. Current agricultural reference books and materials are provided in a wide range of difficulty and variety. .... na 1 2 3 4

2. U.S. Government and state agricultural publications, as well as materials issued by commercial publishers, are provided. .... na 1 2 3 4

3. Periodicals, catalogues, and pamphlets are accessible to students. .... na 1 2 3 4

4. Teaching units, resource units, and study guides are available for use in instruction. .... na 1 2 3 4

5. Farm planning, budgeting, record-keeping, and analysis materials are available for the experience programs of high school and adult students and out-of-school youth on enterprise and whole-farm basis. .... na 1 2 3 4

6. Tackboards are used for display of a variety of materials that are current and appropriate. .... na 1 2 3 4

7. A variety of suitable specimens and agricultural exhibit materials are available. .... na 1 2 3 4

8. The instructional materials contain information and suggestions regarding practical work experiences. .... na 1 2 3 4

9. Materials for instruction are organized efficiently... na 1 2 3 4

10. There is a plan for replacing materials, tools, and equipment which are used for instruction in classroom, laboratory, and agricultural shops. .... na 1 2 3 4

11. Audio and visual aids to instruction are available... na 1 2 3 4

12. na 1 2 3 4

Evaluations

a) *How adequate is the* variety *of instructional materials?* .... na 1 2 3 4

b) *How adequate is the* quality *of instructional materials?* .... na 1 2 3 4

c) *How adequate is the* quantity *of instructional materials?* .... na 1 2 3 4

Comments

Reprinted by permission of the National Study of School Evaluation.

V. GENERAL NATURE AND ORGANIZATION
A. GENERAL NATURE OF THE PROGRAM

Checklist

The student activities program:

1. Is integrated with and supplementary to the program of studies. .... na 1 2 3 4

2. Provides opportunities for leadership and for experiences in cooperation. .... na 1 2 3 4

3. Gives students opportunities to exercise initiative and to assume responsibilities. .... na 1 2 3 4

4. Provides opportunities to coordinate some activities of the home, school, and community. .... na 1 2 3 4

5. Provides opportunities for students to assist in resolving school issues and problems. .... na 1 2 3 4

6. Seeks to develop desirable attitudes, ideals, and appreciation essential for the age in which we live. na 1 2 3 4

7. Fosters the development and perpetuation of desirable school traditions, such as standards of conduct, school festivals, and historical observances. na 1 2 3 4

8. Seeks to make every student and teacher feel accepted in the total life of the school. .... na 1 2 3 4

9. Seeks to make each member feel a sense of loyalty and responsibility to the school. .... na 1 2 3 4

10. Provides membership opportunities to all students on a democratic basis and helps to prevent the development of clannish tendencies and cliques. .... na 1 2 3 4

11. Receives active cooperation and support from members of the school staff. .... na 1 2 3 4

12. Receives cooperation and support from parents and other members of the community. .... na 1 2 3 4

13. Provides activities for the variety of interests and needs of individual students. .... na 1 2 3 4

14. Provides for activities to be organized, changed, or discontinued as student interests and needs change. .... na 1 2 3 4

15. Provides orientation for students new to the program. .... na 1 2 3 4

16. Avoids the exploitation of students. .... na 1 2 3 4

Reprinted by permission of the National Study of School Evaluation.

17. Is geared to the general economic levels of the school population. ....   na 1 2 3 4

18.   na 1 2 3 4

Supplementary Data

1. Describe membership and activities of any adult community groups which are associated with any part of the student activities program.

Evaluations

a) *How well does the student activities program complement and enrich classroom activities?* ....   na 1 2 3 4

b) *To what extent is the student activities program based on study and analyses of student interests and needs?* ....   na 1 2 3 4

c) *To what extent have policies been established to serve as guidelines and safeguards for the activities program?* ....   na 1 2 3 4

Comments

VI. SERVICES AND ACTIVITIES

Checklist

Members of the educational media materials staff:

1. Produce a written statement of policy concerning selection and use of educational media which involves the thinking of administrators, faculty, students, and board. .... na 1 2 3 4

2. Involve faculty and students in selection of materials. .... na 1 2 3 4

3. Organize all educational media for convenience, availability, and effective use. .... na 1 2 3 4

4. Keep chief school administrators informed of the needs of the program as well as of the services performed. .... na 1 2 3 4

5. Assure effective articulation and coordination of educational media services within the school system. .... na 1 2 3 4

6. With cooperation of teachers, keep collection functional by systematic weeding and maintenance. ...... na 1 2 3 4

7. Take annual inventory of educational media, wherever located. .... na 1 2 3 4

8. Maintain a clearinghouse of up-to-date information concerning community resources for instructional purposes. .... na 1 2 3 4

9. Maintain communication with students, faculty, and community. .... na 1 2 3 4

10. Participate in the activities of professional organizations. .... na 1 2 3 4

11. Contribute to knowledge through research and publication in the educational media field. .... na 1 2 3 4

12. Coordinate procurement of educational media and equipment purchased by individual departments. na 1 2 3 4

13. Develop an in-service training program for teachers as well as orientation for new faculty. .... na 1 2 3 4

14. Maintain an active interest in current developments in educational media. .... na 1 2 3 4

15. Share with teachers the indexes and published bibliographies of educational media and assist teachers in selecting printed and audio-visual materials for classroom planning and use. .... na 1 2 3 4

16. Systematically inform teachers of new materials and equipment that have been acquired. .... na 1 2 3 4

Reprinted by permission of the National Study of School Evaluation.

17. Assist in planning for effective use of educational media and equipment. .... na 1 2 3 4

18. Systematically inform teachers of student interests and needs as observed in the use of educational media. .... na 1 2 3 4

19. Assist teachers in the development of resource lists of available materials in special areas. .... na 1 2 3 4

20. Cooperate with teachers in providing materials and preparing exhibits for bulletin boards and other displays. .... na 1 2 3 4

21. Provide professional assistance in the production of educational media. .... na 1 2 3 4

22. Order and schedule the use of rented or borrowed educational material. .... na 1 2 3 4

23. Train projectionists to operate audiovisual equipment. .... na 1 2 3 4

24. Provide educational media for reserve collections or subcenters. .... na 1 2 3 4

25. Provide instruction and encouragement in the use of computer-assisted instruction, dial access, and data storage and retrieval. .... na 1 2 3 4

26. Assist in the production of radio and television presentations. .... na 1 2 3 4

27. Cooperate with other members of the staff in acquainting students with the proper and effective use of educational media. .... na 1 2 3 4

28. Guide students in their selection and use of educational media in terms of their abilities and interests. .... na 1 2 3 4

29. Assist students to develop discrimination in reading, viewing, and listening. .... na 1 2 3 4

30. Assist special-interest groups to use resources of the educational media center in the promotion of their projects. .... na 1 2 3 4

31. Develop research and reference skills in students. na 1 2 3 4

32. Acquaint students with the use of a network of libraries and information centers. .... na 1 2 3 4

33.   na 1 2 3 4

Supplementary Data

1. Describe ways in which the services are provided (including reports, utilization records, yearly acquisitions, and publicity releases).

NATIONAL EDUCATION ASSOCIATION—
PROFILES OF EXCELLENCE

Profiles of Excellence is designed to provide local professional associations, boards of education, and administrators with an instrument for comprehensive self-study and evaluation of their school system's operation. It embraces those readily observable aspects of school system operation which encourage and support excellence in educational service to children and youth. It was not designed to measure the quality of teaching that goes on in the classroom, nor does it deal exhaustively with the professional service rendered in the schools.

Profiles of Excellence is not intended to serve as an accrediting instrument, nor as a means of establishing comparative standards. It is intended as an aid to local school systems in analyzing and evaluating efforts to provide educational programs of high quality. If it proves helpful in identifying lines of approach to improving educational service, it will have served its purpose.[2]

The program elements defined by the National Education Association are:

I. The Educational Program
    1. Educational Objectives
    2. Scope of the Educational Program
    3. Pupil Growth and Development
    4. Curriculum Organization and Content
    5. Curriculum Study and Revision
    6. Strategy for Curriculum and Instructional Change
    7. Equality of Educational Opportunity
    8. Staff Preparation
    9. Staff Certification
    10. Staff Growth and Development
    11. Number of Professional Personnel per 1,000 Pupils
    12. Specialized Instructional Personnel in the Elementary Schools
    13. Health Services
    14. Special Services
    15. Special Education
    16. Libraries
    17. Instructional Materials and Equipment
    18. Grouping for Instruction

[2] National Education Association, *Profiles of Excellence: Recommended Criteria for Evaluating the Quality of a Local School System* (Washington, D.C.: National Education Association, 1966), p. 3.

19. Evaluating Pupil Progress
20. Guidance Program
21. Reporting to Parents
22. Cooperation in Teacher Preparation
23. Student Activities
24. Research, Experimentation, and Innovation

II. Administrative Operation

1. Policy Determination
2. The Superintendent of Schools
3. Central-Office Administrators and Supervisors
4. Administrative Staff for Individual Schools
5. Delegation of Responsibility to Individual Schools
6. Communication with Staff
7. Public Information Program
8. Data-Processing Service
9. Transportation Service
10. Food Service

III. The Board of Education

1. Selection of Board Members
2. Size and Composition
3. Orientation of New Members
4. Methods of Operation
5. Board Meetings
6. Responsiveness to the Community
7. Ethical Standards
8. Negotiation with the Staff

IV. Staff Personnel Policies and Procedures

1. Development of Policy
2. Written Policies
3. Job Descriptions
4. Recruitment
5. Selection
6. Contractual Agreement
7. Orientation
8. Initial Assignment
9. Transfer
10. Promotion
11. Evaluation
12. Paid Sick Leave
13. Paid Leaves for Personal Reasons

14. Paid Professional Leaves
15. Paid Sabbatical Leaves
16. Extended Leaves
17. Medical Examinations
18. Assessment of Staff Attitudes
19. Tenure and Separation—Probationary Personnel
20. Tenure and Separation—Permanent Personnel
21. Grievance Procedure
22. Retirement Information
23. Substitute Service
24. Personnel Records

V. Professional Compensation

A. Salaries
   1. Schedule and Implementation
   2. Development and Revision
   3. Single-Salary Schedule
   4. Professional Basis
   5. Minimum Salary
   6. Maximum Salary with Master's Degree or Five Years of Preparation
   7. Preparation Levels
   8. Number of Annual Increments
   9. Amounts of Annual Increments
   10. Experience Credit
   11. Merit Pay
   12. Supplementary Salaries
   13. Administrative-Supervisory Salaries

B. Fringe Benefits
   1. Group Health Insurance
   2. Group Life Insurance
   3. Liability Protection
   4. Payroll Deductions
   5. Other Benefits

VI. Conditions of Professional Service

1. Academic Freedom
2. Personal Freedom
3. Teaching Assignments
4. Work Load
5. Clerical and Nonprofessional Assistance
6. Lunch Period

    7. Policy on Class Interruptions
    8. Policy on Pupil Behavior
    9. Work Rooms and Faculty Lounges

VII. The School Plant
    1. Sites and Buildings
    2. Building Facilities
    3. General Purpose Classrooms
    4. Operation and Maintenance

VIII. District Organization, Finance, and Business Administration
    1. Size of the District
    2. Organization of the District
    3. Fiscal Authority of the District
    4. Current Expense per Pupil
    5. Budgetary Process
    6. Business Administration
    7. Local Tax Effort
    8. Administration of Property Tax
    9. Cooperation with Local Governmental Units
    10. State Support and Services
    11. Federal Support

IX. The Local Professional Association
    1. Program and Goals
    2. Recognition and Effectiveness
    3. Constitution and Bylaws
    4. Executive Function
    5. Leadership
    6. Member Identification
    7. Committees
    8. Meetings
    9. Communication
    10. Facilities
    11. Handbook
    12. Unity
    13. Membership
    14. Membership Campaign
    15. Budget and Finance
    16. Local Dues

Summary Profiles[3]

Several samples of the instruments utilized by the National Education Association follow.

[3] *Ibid.,* p. 1-2.

I. THE EDUCATIONAL PROGRAM

1. Educational Objectives

Inferior

The system has no statement of educational philosophy and aims; or has one that is obsolete and obscure, bearing little relationship to reality; or has one that has been devised by the administration and imposed upon the staff.

Superior

The system has a clearly worded, written statement of broad educational philosophy and aims which has been developed in close cooperation between school-board members and all levels of the professional staff. Included is a clear statement of specific educational priorities which lists objectives in some order of importance, which relates objectives to practice in the schools, and which gives direction to curriculum planning. The statement has been written or revised within the past five years, is well publicized among the staff and community at large, and is used consistently as one of the bases for curriculum planning and evaluation.

☐   ☐   ☐   ☐   ☐
Inferior   Below   Average   Above   Superior
                average   average

Action Needed To Close the Gap

_____

_____

_____

_____

_____

_____

_____

_____

_____

_____

_____

_____

_____

Reprinted by permission of the National Education Association.

2. Scope of the Educational Program

Inferior	Superior
Pre-kindergarten and kindergarten education are not part of the educational program, nor are opportunities available for grades 13 and 14. The total program comprises just 12 years of instruction, grades 1 through 12.	The basic educational program comprises pre-kindergarten and kindergarten education and grades 1-12. Publicly supported institutions are available for education in grades 13 and 14, as well as for credit and noncredit adult study.

☐   ☐   ☐   ☐   ☐

Inferior   Below   Average   Above   Superior
       average   average

Action Needed To Close the Gap

_____

_____

_____

_____

_____

_____

_____

_____

_____

_____

_____

_____

_____

_____

_____

_____

_____

_____

_____

_____

_____

_____

Reprinted by permission of the National Education Association.

3. Pupil Growth and Development

Inferior

Focus of the educational program is almost completely upon the acquisition of subject matter. No provision is made for responding to individual pupil needs, interests, or abilities. Factual content is stressed exclusively; no effort is made to develop or foster pupil creativity and problem-solving skills.

Superior

Focus of the educational program is upon the needs, interests, and abilities of pupils as well as upon subject matter. Pupil creativity and problem-solving skills are fostered and developed along with appropriate emphasis on factual content. Emphasis is placed upon developing physical, emotional, social, and intellectual competence, enabling pupils to develop their powers to learn to accept responsibility, to adjust to their natural environment, and to relate appropriately to their social environment. Stress is placed upon desirable changes in behavior and attitudes as well as upon the absorption of information.

□ Inferior   □ Below average   □ Average   □ Above average   □ Superior

Action Needed To Close the Gap

_____

_____

_____

_____

_____

_____

_____

_____

_____

_____

_____

_____

_____

_____

4. Curriculum Organization and Content

Inferior

Teachers are held closely to an inflexibly prescribed curriculum, or they are provided with no guidelines whatsoever and left completely on their own, in which case the textbooks or programmed materials in use control the curriculum organization and content. There is either great rigidity or great laxity in stated expectations for pupils.

Superior

The vertical organization in each curriculum area takes into account the logical structure of the subject, the difficulty of the material as related to the pupil's intellectual maturity, and the relation of the field to other fields. Content is organized in such a way that pupils may progress toward increasingly mature utilization and organization of their knowledge. Elementary and secondary curriculums are closely coordinated so as to avoid unnecessary duplication and to insure adequate coverage of subject matter.

☐   ☐   ☐   ☐   ☐
Inferior   Below   Average   Above   Superior
              average   average

Action Needed To Close the Gap

_____

_____

_____

_____

_____

_____

_____

_____

_____

_____

_____

_____

_____

_____

_____

_____

_____

Reprinted by permission of the National Education Association.

III. THE BOARD OF EDUCATION

1. Selection of Board Members

Inferior

Board members are appointed by the mayor, court judges, or some other governmental group, generally on the basis of partisan political considerations,

or

Board members are elected by means of partisan elections, with candidates running under the sponsorship of political organizations.

Superior

The method of selection results in securing board members who are representative of the entire community and not of special interest, and who are committed to the welfare of the public schools.

Board members are selected by means of nonpartisan elections held at special times,

or

If board members are appointed, machinery for selecting candidates includes a caucus committee or some other organized community plan for canvassing, screening, and nominating only the best qualified candidates.

☐	☐	☐	☐	☐
Inferior	Below average	Average	Above average	Superior

Action Needed To Close the Gap

_____

_____

_____

_____

_____

_____

_____

_____

_____

_____

_____

_____

2. Size and Composition

Inferior

The composition of the board changes frequently with complete or majority turnover at each election,

or

Average length of service on the school board is 12 or more years.

The board is too large for effective discussion or too small for adequate representation of the community. Members of the board frequently represent special interest goups in the community and seek to protect these interests to the detriment of the educational program.

Superior

The term of office for board members is from 4 to 6 years. The board has 5, 7, or 9 members. Less than a majority of the terms of office expire in any single year. Few board members serve for more than two terms. Board members are committed to public education, understand the importance of public schools and the school board's role in public education, and represent the community as a whole rather than segments of the population.

☐   ☐   ☐   ☐   ☐

Inferior   Below average   Average   Above average   Superior

Action Needed To Close the Gap

_____

_____

_____

_____

_____

_____

_____

_____

_____

_____

_____

_____

_____

_____

3. Orientation of New Members

Inferior	**Superior**
Little or nothing is done to introduce new board members to the responsibilities of board membership. Cliques in the board, community, and schools compete for the loyalty of new members.	A systematic, cooperative program conducted by the superintendent, experienced board members, and selected staff personnel is in operation to give new board members information basic to learning the duties and responsibilities of board membership. Resources from nearby universities, the state school boards association, and the state department of education are used. Pertinent printed materials, both those locally developed and those of more general applicability, are supplied; other professional publications including educational periodicals are made available to all board members.

☐   ☐   ☐   ☐   ☐

Inferior   Below   Average   Above   Superior

average   average

Action Needed To Close the Gap

_____

_____

_____

_____

_____

_____

_____

_____

_____

_____

_____

_____

_____

_____

_____

_____

4. Methods of Operation

Inferior

There are no written policies governing school-board operation. The board gives the superintendent little authority to carry out his responsibilities, sometimes barring him from board meetings. Standing committees generally carry out administrative functions. The board does not participate in activities of its regional, state, and national counterparts.

Policies, rules, and regulations governing the schools are not available in written form. Few meetings are open to the public.

Superior

There is a set of written bylaws governing all phases of school-board operation. The board clearly recognizes the superintendent as its chief executive officer, seeking and considering his recommendations on policy matters and delegating to him and his staff the responsibility for administering adopted policy. The board participates in activities of its regional, state, and national counterparts.

Current policies, rules, and regulations governing the schools are made widely available in all the schools throughout the community. All meetings except executive sessions are open to the public.

□   □   □   □   □

Inferior   Below   Average   Above   *Superior*

average   average

Action Needed To Close the Gap

_____

_____

_____

_____

_____

_____

_____

_____

_____

_____

_____

_____

_____

_____

_____

_____

5. Board Meetings

Inferior

Meetings are held too frequently or not frequently enough to accomplish board business properly. Meetings are poorly organized, with no written agendas and no accompanying reports upon which to base decisions. Minutes of the meetings are too sketchy to be of value, or too voluminous to be readable, and are not available in appropriate form.

Superior

Regular meetings are scheduled from 12 to 24 times annually, with special meetings as required—usually no more than 12 annually. Agendas are prepared by the superintendent and the board president and sent to board members, news media, and the local association president well in advance. Clearly stated procedures for inclusion of agenda items are specified in the board's rules. Board members receive pertinent written materials and recommendations along with the agendas. Comprehensive minutes of regular and special meetings are available to interested individuals.

☐ Inferior ☐ Below average ☐ Average ☐ Above average ☐ Superior

Action Needed To Close the Gap

_____

_____

_____

_____

_____

_____

_____

_____

_____

_____

_____

_____

_____

_____

_____

_____

Reprinted by permission of the National Education Association.

6. Responsiveness to the Community

Inferior

The board generally acts without reference to community thinking, but sometimes responds to the undesirable influences of pressure groups. Citizens committees are not appointed, and public hearings are not held unless required by law. Complaints and petitions concerning the schools are seldom answered, or, if answered, are dealt with in such a manner as to cause controversy. Budgets and bond issues are frequently turned down by the voters.

Superior

The board maintains contact, through its meetings and by the appointment of citizens committees when necessary and desirable, with the thinking of all segments of the community. Parent-teacher organizations in particular, and citizens in general, are encouraged to be actively interested in education and the improvement of the schools. Petitions and complaints are considered thoughtfully and with dispatch, and the staff and the community are promptly informed of resulting decisions. Reasons are always given when it is necessary to reject petitions from special-interest groups or recommendations of citizens committees. Public hearings are held before action is taken on matters of extreme public interest and importance.

☐   ☐   ☐   ☐   ☐
Inferior   Below average   Average   Above average   Superior

Action Needed To Close the Gap

_____

_____

_____

_____

_____

_____

_____

_____

_____

_____

_____

_____

_____

7. Ethical Standards

Inferior

Individual board members sometimes exploit their positions by such practices as nepotism in appointments, solicitation of business or patronage from school employees, personal profit from awarding construction or school supply bids, or seeking special consideration for some staff members or pupils. School-board business is sometimes conducted by individual members.

Superior

Official actions of board members concern only the welfare of the school system; no member uses his office for personal profit, advancement, or patronage. The board adheres to the codes of ethics of its regional, state, and national counterparts. Purchases in any substantial amount are always placed on bid, with contracts awarded to the lowest responsible bidder.

☐ Inferior ☐ Below average ☐ Average ☐ Above average ☐ Superior

Action Needed To Close the Gap

_____

8. Negotiation with the Staff

Inferior	Superior
There is no professional negotiation agreement. Policy decisions, unilaterally made by the board, usually come as a complete surprise to those concerned. Any staff suggestions, requests, or complaints are either ignored or considered evidence of "disloyalty" and dealt with severely. Frequent conflict arises, and harsh unilateral action on the part of the board is more the rule than the exception. The board does not recognize any organization as representing the staff. A general punitive approach is exercised in relations with the staff.	The board has formally adopted a written professional negotiation agreement which governs the development and revision of policies affecting staff welfare and the quality of the educational program. The superintendent is included in all negotiations. Specific provision is made for resolving, through educational channels, persistent disagreements that may arise during negotiations. The board recognizes as the negotiating representative the organization enrolling in its membership a majority of the professional staff employed by the school district, and negotiates in good faith with the designated organization.

☐   ☐   ☐   ☐   ☐

Inferior   Below   Average   Above   Superior

        average   average

Action Needed To Close the Gap

_____

_____

_____

_____

_____

_____

_____

_____

_____

_____

_____

_____

_____

_____

_____

_____

_____

Reprinted by permission of the National Education Association.

NATIONAL STUDY FOR ACCREDITATION OF VOCATIONAL/TECHNICAL EDUCATION

The American Vocational Association is currently field testing a total vocational/technical education assessment procedure called the National Study for Accreditation of Vocational/Technical Education. This assessment procedure and the one following are specifically designed for occupational programs.

In a memorandum to selected vocational educators, Lane C. Ash, Director of the National Study for Accreditation of Vocational/Technical Education spells out the unique features of the AVA's pilot evaluation program.[4] They are:

1. It holds schools accountable for preparing students for gainful employment. Traditional accreditation has held schools accountable for preparing students for further education.

2. Product and process factors are clearly differentiated. Emphasis is on evaluation in terms of outcomes.

3. Objectives are expected to be in measurable performance terms permitting evaluation of achievement.

4. The relationship between need, objectives, and outcomes is expressed and used as a basis for evaluation.

5. Two levels of objectives—institutional and program—are distinguished and form the basis of the two major instruments, neither complete in itself, each to be used in conjunction with the other. Institutional objectives, deriving from an analysis of population and labor market needs, express themselves in the choice of population groups served, occupations taught, and modes of delivering services. Program objectives, growing out of an analysis of occupational requirements and student abilities and interests, express themselves in the choice of learning experiences through which occupational proficiency develops.

6. The concept of external examination as audit is introduced. Evaluation is seen as the responsibility of the institution or program itself—an integral part of the continuous Planning-Implementing-Evaluating-Feedback process—with the self-evaluation verified ("audited") by competent external examiners as a basis for certification to the public (accreditation).

---

[4] Taken from a memo to selected vocational educators entitled: "Instruments and Procedures for the Evaluation of Vocational/Technical Education—12/71 Pilot Test Edition," by Lane C. Ash, Director, National Study for Accreditation of Vocational/Technical Education.

7. The role of documentation is clarified. Documentary evidence is called for to provide a basis for both self-evaluation and subsequent verification.

8. In keeping with accrediting practice, evaluation is in terms of each institution's or program's own stated objectives and circumstances. This differs from evaluation comparing one institution or program with others on the basis of externally derived objectives and assumed comparability of circumstances.

9. The concept of negative outcomes has been introduced. Institutions and programs are held accountable for negative as well as positive outcomes. They are expected to take note of negative outcomes and prevent them insofar as possible.

10. The need is emphasized for adequate resources and processes at all steps of the planning-implementing-evaluating-feedback cycle, at both institutional and program levels.

11. The instruments and procedures recognize that parts can be evaluated only in their relationship to the whole; and that to accommodate to innovation and all modes of delivery systems (home based, school-based, industry-based, residential-based) they must allow for a considerable degree of flexibility in means used to achieve outcomes, and of interchangeability of resources (human, material, financial), processes, and structures.

Note that item number 11 supports the author's claim that assessment must be based on the interrelationships of all program elements.

The AVA has identified the following elements of a vocational/technical education program. The NSAV/TE utilizes two evaluation forms. The *Institutional Form* is aimed at total institution assessment and the *Program Form* is aimed at specific occupational program assessment.

INSTITUTIONAL FORM[5]

Distinguishing Characteristics
> Distinguishing Characteristics
Objectives

[5] National Study for Accreditation of Vocational/Technical Education, *Instruments and Procedures for the Evaluation of Vocational/Technical Education Institutions and Programs* (Washington, D.C.: American Vocational Association, 1971). Developed under Project No. 9-0489 Grant No. OEG-0-9-180489-4672 (085) from the National Center for Research and Development, U.S. Office of Education, DHEW), pp. 29-85. This is a pilot test edition published and distributed solely for the purpose of field testing the instruments and procedures and to elicit comments and suggestions for improvement from a limited audience whose reactions were sought.

Philosophy and Objectives
The School Community: Matching Objectives to Need
Achievement of Objectives: Indicators of Success
Structure and Means
Delivery Systems
Management
    A. Organization; Governing Body
    B. Administration
    C. Staff
    D. Finance and Business Management
    E. General Advisory Committee
Planning
Research and Evaluation
Student Personnel Services
    A. Recruitment and Admissions
    B. Guidance and Counseling
    C. Placement and Follow-Up
    D. Student Educational Records
    E. Student Activities
Learning Resources
Physical Plant
Instructional Self-Evaluation Report

PROGRAM FORM[6]

Distinguishing Characteristics
    Distinguishing Characteristics
Objectives
    Philosophy and Objectives
    Matching Objectives to Need
    Achievement of Objectives: Indicators of Success
Structure and Means
    Organization and Management
    Occupational Advisory Committee
    Program Research and Evaluation
    The Teaching-Learning Process
    Curriculum
    Learning Resources
    Supplies and Equipment
    Instructional Space and Facilities

Samples of forms, still in the pilot test stage of development, are shown below.

---

[6] *Ibid.*, p. 98-122.

Pilot Test Edition 12-71
Institutional Form

DISTINGUISHING CHARACTERISTICS

Vocational/technical education is part of the total educational picture in the United States. Its function is enabling people to prepare for the work of their choice, or to improve their competency in their chosen occupation. Vocational/technical educators must be thoroughly familiar with the needs of the labor market and with the requirements of the occupations for which preparation is given. While they work within the framework established by labor market needs and occupational requirements, their emphasis is upon increasing the options open to people, and helping people to a fuller realization of individual potential.

Within the educational complex, vocational/technical education is clearly marked by certain identifying characteristics. It is distinguished not by content, but by intent; not by methodology, but by its practicality; not by its breadth, but by its ties with the working world.

If vocational/technical education is to *be* vocational/technical education—that is, if it is to perform its intended function as the link between man and work—these fundamental, distinguishing characteristics must be present. The user of this document must keep these characteristics in mind as underlying everything said in succeeding parts.

Characteristic

Evaluation:

> *The institution's vocational/technical education exhibits the characteristics that identify and distinguish vocational/technical education.*

_____

Guidelines

1. Vocational/technical education:

   a. Prepares peoples for initial employment; _____

   b. Retrains those in the process of changing occupations; and/or _____

   c. Provides training supplementary to the daily work of the employed. _____

2. Vocational/technical education is:

   a. *Specific.* It improves the efficiency of an individual in a specific occupation, either as preparation for employment or supplementary to employment. _____

b. *Selective.* It is directly related to actual occupational requirements. _____

c. *Practical.* The necessary skills and knowledge of a particular occupation are taught and learned in their practical and appropriate application to the work. _____

d. *Immediately applicable.* It is timed and organized so that the learner can apply it at the time it is learned to useful and productive work in a specific occupation. _____

3. Vocational/technical education is directly related to employment opportunities. _____

4. Vocational/technical education develops to a *marketable* degree *all* the abilities required by the occupation, such as technical knowledge and skills; manipulative skills; work habits; communication skills; human relations skills; and the ability to reason, to solve problems, to think independently, and to make judgments necessary for employment in the chosen occupation (Breadth and depth of instruction). _____

5. Vocational/technical education is planned around the student's occupational objectives. _____

6. Effective placement and follow-up of students who finish or leave is an integral and continuing part of vocational/technical education. _____

7. Continuous research and evaluation are integral parts of vocational/technical education, including surveys of clientele needs for occupational preparation, surveys of manpower needs (i.e. employment opportunities), occupational analyses, and student follow-up. _____

Clientele—Inclusive, Not Exclusive

8. Instruction is offered to all persons who need, desire, and can profit from it occupationally. _____

Programs Offered (Occupations Taught)

9. The choice of program offerings is based on surveys of population needs for occupational preparation and on surveys of job availability (manpower surveys). _____

Curriculums

10. The curriculum in each program is based on an analysis of the requirements of the occupation. _____

11. The content of courses is kept current with occupational practice by means of periodic analyses of the occupations for which the training is being given. _____

12. The courses for a specific occupation are developed, maintained, and evaluated with the advice and cooperation of representatives of the occupation, both employers and practitioners. _____

Methods of Instruction

13. Learning in vocational/technical education is based on direct experience rather than vicarious experience (participating and doing rather than hearing and reading about). _____

Facilities; Conditions

14. The facilities and equipment used in instruction are comparable to or compatible with those found in the particular occupation. _____

15. The conditions under which instruction is given duplicate as nearly as possible desirable conditions in the occupation itself. _____

16. The length of teaching periods and the total hours of instruction are determined by the requirements of the occupation and the needs of the students. _____

17. Day and evening classes are scheduled at hours and during seasons convenient to enrollees. _____

Instructor Qualifications

18. Instructors:
    a. Are competent and experienced in the occupation taught; and _____

    b. Have been recommended by leaders in the occupation. _____

Reprinted by permission of the American Vocational Association.

Pilot Test Edition 12-71
Institutional Form

STUDENT PERSONNEL SERVICES:
Placement and Follow-Up

Characteristic

Evaluation:

> *A formalized procedure, adequately funded and staffed, is in operation providing effective placement and follow-up services as an integral part of institutional operation.*

_____

Guidelines

1. The institution is successful in placing a high percentage of graduates in jobs related to the field of preparation.
2. The placement and follow-up functions are definitely assigned and adequately supported with sufficient staff and other resources to operate effectively.
3. Placement information and services are available for all students, graduates, temporary withdrawals, and other members of the school's clientele.
4. Placement activities are an integral part of both counseling and instruction.
5. The curriculum for each instructional program includes activities to help students seek and obtain employment.
6. The instructional staff is actively involved in placement and follow-up activities.
7. Placement records are kept current and include such information as: job opportunities, job placements, unsuccessful placements, follow-up activities.
8. Students with the ability to benefit from education beyond that given by their present school are encouraged and helped when necessary to continue at more advanced schools.
9. The constraints and limitations affecting student placement are clearly defined, and efforts are made to expand employment opportunities despite existing limitations.
10. Parents and students are made aware of placement services and occupational information available.
11. Regular communication is maintained with public and private sources of labor market and employment information.
12. The institution involves advisory committees, public and private agencies, business and industry, and

other groups in its placement and follow-up activities. _____

13. Students are referred to positions which they have a reasonable probability of filling successfully. _____

14. Students who need part-time employment in order to remain in school are assisted in securing work that will improve their occupational skills. _____

15. Follow-up surveys are used to determine the adequacy, appropriateness, and effectiveness of the institution's efforts in occupational preparation and placement. _____

16. Information is available on a program-by-program basis as to:
    a. Rate of student failure or withdrawal from the institution.
    b. Reasons for student failure or withdrawal.

17. Follow-up data are obtained from all former vocational/technical students and include information as to:
    a. Employment status: employed, unemployed, or underemployed _____
    b. Field of employment: related or unrelated to field of preparation _____
    c. Job retention, promotions, and level _____
    d. Continued education since leaving school, and whether related to field of preparation _____
    e. Satisfaction with occupational preparation provided by the school _____
    f. Satisfaction with placement services provided by the school _____
    g. Satisfaction with the institution's continuing interest in the occupational preparation and welfare of former students _____

18. Follow-up efforts include surveys of employers of former students to determine their satisfaction with the preparation of the school provided. _____

19. Satisfactory school-employer relations are evidenced by the expressed satisfaction of both the graduates and the employers. _____

20. Feedback from employers and other data from follow-up studies are used in institutional planning, in improving instruction, and in modifying programs and services. _____

21. Efforts are made in follow-up and follow-through evaluation to improve data collection methods; to reduce the number of former students whose status and whereabouts are unknown; and to increase the use made of follow-up studies in improving instruction, practices, and services. _____

Pilot Test Edition 12-71
Program Form

OCCUPATIONAL ADVISORY COMMITTEE
Characteristic

Evaluation:

> *An Occupational Advisory Committee assists in developing curriculum content, in keeping the curriculum current, and in maintaining contact with the occupational community.*

_____

Guidelines

1. An Occupational Advisory Committee has been appointed for the program and exists as a formal organization.

   _____

2. The membership of the Occupational Advisory Committee represents the clientele, students, and the occupation, including both employers and practitioners.

   _____

3. The Committee functions well, is used effectively, and meets with sufficient regularity to carry out its functions.

   _____

4. Program personnel are actively involved in Committee activities.

   _____

5. Minutes of Committee meetings are available for examination and reference by the institutional community.

   _____

6. Occupational Advisory Committee activities are analyzed, delineating major recommendations and actions taken to implement them.

   _____

7. The program head assures that preparation for meetings is adequate.

   _____

8. The work of the Committee and of its members is given public recognition and appreciation.

   _____

9. The Committee advises or assists in such matters as:

   _____

   a. Providing accurate, current occupational information
   b. Finding qualified instructors
   c. Establishing standards for equipment, facilities, instructor qualifications, instructional materials
   d. Placing students and graduates
   e. Arranging for field trips, customer work, work experience, guest speakers, and other aids to learning
   f. Providing opportunities for instructors to up-date and improve their occupational skills

g. Setting occupation-based performance objectives for students

h. Evaluating student achievement and program effectiveness

i. Arranging for donated equipment, supplies and services

For Discussion Only

THREE-PHASE SYSTEM FOR STATEWIDE ASSESSMENT OF EVALUATION OF OCCUPATIONAL EDUCATION

The Division of Vocational and Technical Education, State of Illinois, has developed a total occupational education program evaluation system. The Three-Phase System effectively combines the planning and assessment functions.[7]

This is a statewide assessment procedure, which the local school teacher or administrator can use to design a total program assessment procedure at the local level.

Phase I is based on the development of the local program plan. The assumption is that local program planning automatically entails evaluation procedures. For example, if past efforts to obtain follow-up information have been unsuccessful, the local program planner will evaluate these efforts and plan for future studies accordingly.

Phase II requires the approval of the local plan by regional vocational directors. This is an evaluation procedure. But the regional directors may serve as consultants in Phase I so that Phase II is perfunctory for districts which comply with known principles of vocational-technical education.

Phase III is the final assessment procedure. It requires the use of a visitation team to determine if various activities described in the local program plan are indeed being implemented.

The Three-Phase System may serve as a model for locally directed, total program assessment (Fig. 11-1). The Three-Phase System is based on eight program elements (entitled "Areas of Concern"). They are:

1. Administrative Organization
2. Personnel
3. Objectives
4. Evaluation
5. Occupational Programs
6. Resources

---

[7] State of Illinois, Division of Vocational and Technical Education, Board of Vocational Education and Rehabilitation, *An Overview of the Three Phase System For Statewide Evaluation of Occupational Education Programs* (Springfield, Ill.: Division of Vocational Education, 1971), 14 pages.

THREE-PHASE SYSTEM (STATE OF ILLINOIS)

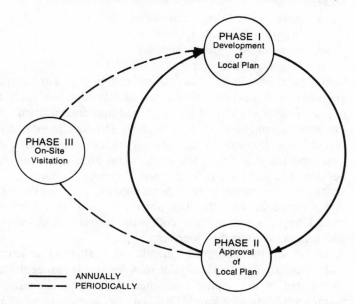

Courtesy Division of Vocational and Technical Education, Board of Vocational Education and Rehabilitation, State of Illinois.

Fig. 11-1

7. Guidance Services
8. Students Served

LOCALLY DIRECTED, TOTAL PROGRAM ASSESSMENT

The foregoing examples of total program assessment may serve as models for a locally directed system. Such a system requires close cooperation among general administrative staff, occupational program administrators, guidance personnel and instructors. Instructional effectiveness cannot be ascertained without such assessment techniques and is well worth the effort involved.

Procedure

The following detailed procedure is submitted as a guide to occupational education personnel interested in developing and implementing a total instructional assessment program.

1. Initial meetings should be planned to orientate fellow faculty members, administrators, and advisory committee personnel to the need for a total assessment procedure.

2. Committee assignments should be made regarding the following areas:
   a. Assessment Design Committee
   b. Program Planning Committee
   c. Element Analysis Committee
   d. Instrument Development Committee

   Every effort should be made to include faculty, administrative, guidance, and advisory committee membership on each committee. Timetables should be developed and agreed upon.
3. Program planning and element analysis activities should be completed simultaneously. Plans should be developed on a one-, five-, and ten-year basis. Major elements from the plans should be listed and defined by the Element Analysis Committee.
4. After program elements have been defined, the Assessment Design Committee and the Instrument Development Committee should begin work on data collection instrument development and general assessment procedures.

   A review of the previously mentioned evaluation instruments and others should provide guidelines for the Instrument Design Committee in developing assessment instrument formats. One major consideration should be that of economic evaluation. Course costs on a student credit hour basis should be established with an eye toward lowering the same. The old profit and loss statement is of increasing importance to occupational educators.
5. The major emphasis on a total program assessment procedure will most likely be keyed toward self-evaluation procedures. These techniques should be considered during assessment procedure design.
6. Development of a descriptive brochure should follow assessment design. This brochure should be made available to all participating school personnel, community leaders, advisory committee members, and other interested people.
7. Implement the assessment system. *It must be utilized to be effective.*
8. After a period of use, the assessment system should be revised to strengthen weak areas and account for new and emerging variables.

SUMMARY

Efficient program assessment requires close cooperation among all elements of the instructional community. Administration, faculty, students, and resource personnel must work together to assure effective occupational program operation.

This chapter also dealt with the following questions:

1. How does the process of assessment relate to the process of planning?

Planning and assessment go hand in hand. Program direction is based on various planning procedures. Assessment of the instructional program on a continuous basis assists in the development of realistic plans.

2. What is the difference between instructional assessment and instructional evaluation?

In this chapter, assessment has been differentiated from evaluation on the premise that assessment is a continuous and systematic *process* for relating instructional program direction to stated, measurable goals. When so defined, the relationship between the program planning functions and the assessment functions is clear.

3. What is the value of a continuous and systematic process of program assessment?

Instructional program assessment must be of a continuum nature. Community resources, manpower needs, course costs, instructor strengths and weaknesses, administrative support, and many other elements must be periodically assessed. Since any instructional program is dynamic in nature, so must be its assessment techniques. Thus, a continuous assessment procedure is paramount.

ACTIVITIES

1. Prepare information collection instruments that may be utilized by occupational education units at the secondary, post-secondary, and university levels to assess program effectiveness and efficiency.
2. Prepare an annotated review of literature on such assessment procedures as (1) cost differential analysis, (2) cost benefit analysis, (3) faculty self-evaluation, (4) placement and follow-up procedures, and (5) various noneconomic assessment techniques.
3. Prepare a written position paper describing the individual faculty member's role in total program assessment.

DISCUSSION QUESTIONS

1. Differentiate between assessment and evaluation.
2. What areas of concern should serve as the basis for a program assessment system?

3. What are the responsibilities of the various people in the school community with regard to program assessment?

4. What is the role of program element analysis in the assessment process?

5. How does program planning relate to program assessment?

BIBLIOGRAPHY

American Vocational Association. *Instruments and Procedures for the Evaluation of Vocational/Technical Education Institutions and Programs.* Project Director, Lane C. Ash. Washington, D.C.: American Vocational Association, 1971.

Bach, William J. "A Study of the North Central Association Re-evaluation Program in Twenty Illinois High Schools." Unpublished Ph.D. dissertation. Southern Illinois University, 1969.

Brennan, Robert L. and Stolurow, Lawrence M. "An Elementary Decision Process for the Formative Evaluation of an Instructional System." Washington, D.C.: Educational Resources Information Center, 1971.

Copa, George H. *Identifying Inputs Toward Production Function Application.* Minnesota Research Coordination Unit. (Mimeographed)

Du Bois, Philip H., ed., and Douglas, Mayo, G., ed. *Research Strategies for Evaluating Training.* Chicago: Rand, McNally, 1970.

Guba, Egon G. and Stufflebeam, Daniel L. *Evaluation: The Process of Stimulating, Aiding, and Abetting Insightful Action.* An address delivered at the Second National Symposium for Professors of Educational Research. Evaluation Center, Ohio State, 1968.

Harper, Aaron W. and Wittrock, Merlin C. *Guide for Planning Your Educational Program.* Danville, Ill.: Interstate, 1960.

Lortie, Dan. *The Cracked Cake of Education Customs and Emerging Issues in Evaluation.* EDO36875. September, 1968.

.... *Management Surveys for Schools:* Their Uses and Abuses. Washington, D.C.: American Association of School Administrators, 1964.

Moss, Jerome and Stromsdorfer, Ernest W. "Evaluating Vocational and Technical Education Programs," *Vocational Education: Today and Tomorrow,* edited by Gerald G. Somers and J. Kenneth Little. Center for Studies in Vocational and Technical Education, The University of Wisconsin, 1960.

National Education Association. *Profiles of Excellence.* Washington, D.C.: National Education Association, 1966.

National School Boards Association. *Quest for Quality.* Evanston, Ill.: National School Boards Association, 1960.

National Study of Secondary School Evaluation. *Evaluative Criteria.* Washington, D.C.: National Study of Secondary School Evaluation, 1969.

Provus, Malcolm. *Discrepancy Evaluation: For Educational Program Improvement and Assessment.* Berkeley, Calif.: McCutchan, 1971.

Rawlinson, Howard E. "Public Junior College and Community Needs: Development and Application of Evaluative Criteria." Unpublished Ph.D. dissertation, Southern Illinois University, 1963.

State of Illinois Board of Higher Education. *A Unit Cost Study Manual for Nonpublic Institutions of Higher Education in Illinois.* State of Illinois Board of Higher Education, 1969.

Western Interstate Commission for Higher Education. *Management Information Systems: Their Development and Use in the Administration of Higher Education,* edited by J. Minter and Ben Lawrence. Boulder, Colo.: Western Interstate Commission for Higher Education, 1969.

Chapter Twelve

Staff
Models
for
Occupational
Programs

INTRODUCTION

This chapter deals with one of the most important aspects of the educational enterprise—the instructional staff. The following questions are treated.

- How important is the instructional staff to the educational program?
- What is meant by the term "differentiated staffing"?
- What are some of the advantages and disadvantages of differentiated staffing?

Instructional staffing has been a topic of wide discussion in educational administration and management. A competent and cooperative staff is paramount to the success of any instructional endeavor. This chapter analyzes the roles of instructional staff members below the department chairman level.

SOCIAL ASPECTS OF THE EDUCATIONAL SYSTEM

The process of education is primarily social. It involves the interaction of various instructional personnel and learners. Depending in large part on the types of knowledge, skills, and attitudes to be acquired by learners, different competencies must be possessed by the instructional personnel. But all teachers must be able to perform in a variety of social settings. To be successful and effective, teachers must *get along with* many kinds of people. Thus staff selection, orientation, and interaction are prime considerations of program management.

Departmental activity is a social rather than a physical activity. The education department is a unit of the social rather than the physical world. This obvious statement appears, at first blush, to

361

be innocuous. But, in fact, it has great import. It implies that events in a university department follow the "normal distribution" of social events rather than the "normal distribution" of events in nature. They do not follow the Gaussian bell curve. Rather, they follow a curve under which the great bulk of results, say 80%, are produced by a quite small minority of the staff.[1]

Few if any functions performed by instructional personnel are carried out without interaction among various individuals. For example, the academic advisement staff works directly on one-to-one bases with students. They also work with curriculum committees and administrative personnel. Instructional materials technicians must discuss various aspects of specific teaching/learning situations with teachers to identify appropriate media, schedule presentations, etc.

TECHNICAL ASPECTS OF THE EDUCATIONAL SYSTEM

Whereas the educational process is in the main social, many of its components are extremely technical in nature. The several subsystems which must be combined to assure learning outcomes have technical features. English has likened the instructional enterprise to the modern business enterprise, based on Galbraith's analysis of the current organizational practice of multiple group decision making called the Technostructure. Analysis of the levels of activity involved in instruction makes this concept more understandable.

In the one-room school, the teacher was responsible for all duties involved with instruction—from carrying water or lighting the stove in the morning to sweeping the classroom at the end of the day. The teacher had to possess skills in areas such as instructional media development, record keeping, presentation, evaluation, first aid, curriculum development, etc. Hence, the teacher was responsible for all the decision making that occurred in the early instructional setting.

In many respects, contemporary teachers are not different from their earlier counterparts. Many technical functions must be performed in the day-to-day instructional setting. Attendance taking, instructional materials preparation, curriculum revision, individual counseling, examination giving, demonstration, and equipment and supply requisitioning are done in much the same manner in which they have always been done. However, in some instructional settings, many of these functions are carried on by *different* people at the instructional level. Many of these duties are better performed by student contact personnel with

---

[1] Ronald W. Stadt and Larry J. Kenneke, "Evaluating Teacher Education Departments," *Improving College and University Teaching*, xx (2) Spring, 1972, p. 125.

special abilities which they have learned through formal schooling and experience.

A beginning teacher, for example, will have little difficulty taking roll, preparing examinations, administering examinations, and completing various reports. An inexperienced instructor will no doubt find it difficult to present lesson materials to students via a variety of methods and techniques. Several years of professional experience are essential to meaningful analysis of student audiences and professional management of learning activities which truly *involve* students. The instructor with little training in audiovisual media will find it difficult and time consuming to develop instructional materials. Increasingly, educators come to the position that the ideal instructional staff is composed of individuals with outstanding abilities in different ones of the social and technical functions of instruction.

DIFFERENTIATED STAFFING

It is widely held that *ideal* instructional staffing may be realized through a technique called *differentiated staffing*. Differentiated staffing is an organizational scheme which is designed to make better use of educational personnel through systematic assignment of categories of responsibility. Through a formal analysis of instructional tasks, specific teaching functions are identified and classed according to horizontal and vertical responsibility groupings. These groupings become the specialties which are integrated into a functioning instructional system. Differentiated staffing in education is the same in form (if not function) as it is in durable goods manufacturing. Tasks are *specialized,* so that people who can perform them well may integrate along an evident or not-so-evident production line. Specialization and integration are the principles at the base of organizing people (and machines) for efficiency. The major consideration is: How specialized shall the respective responsibilities, the individual jobs be? If specialization is overdone, integration is difficult to achieve. Put another way, too many pieces are difficult to put together in meaningful ways.

Several approaches to differentiated staffing have been variously successful in education. In occupational education, there has not been sufficient research re differentiated staffing. In all manner of educational enterprises there has not been enough practice testing of various schemes.

Temple City Schools have developed the following categories and general position descriptions:[2]

[2] J. L. Olivero and Edward Buffie, *New Careers in Teaching: The Temple City Story* (Temple City, California: Temple City Unified School District, 1969), 10 pages.

Master Teacher	Doctorate or equivalent; 2/5's staff teaching
Senior Teacher	M.S. or equivalent; 3/5's staff teaching
Staff Teacher	B.A. and state credential; 100% teaching
Associate Teacher	A.B. or intern; 100% teaching
Academic Assistants	(A.A. Degree or equivalent)
Educational Technicians	
Clerks	

Obviously, these are vertical categories. Horizontally, specialization would be by subject matter, perhaps to the associate teacher level.

James L. Olivero further defines the functions of the various categories as:

> . . . the Associate Teacher, a novice, has a "learning schedule" and less-demanding responsibilities; the Staff Teacher has a full teaching load and is aided by clerks, technicians, and paraprofessionals; the Senior Teacher, a "learning engineer" or methodological expert in a subject discipline, or skill area teaches three-fifths of his time; the Master Teacher is a scholar and research specialist who teaches two-fifths time but also has curriculum expertise enabling him to translate learning research theory into workable classroom practices.[3]

It is important to note that differentiated staffing not only entails several levels of responsibility but also requires adjustments in fiscal policies so that salaries and wages may vary according to level of responsibility and formal training. As might be expected, the fiscal aspect of differentiated staffing is causing the greatest concern among teachers, administrators, and boards of education.

The following definition illustrates the relationship of human and dollar considerations in differentiated staffing.

> Differentiated staffing is a plan for recruitment, preparation, induction, and continuing education of staff personnel for the schools that would bring a much broader range of manpower to

---

[3] James L. Olivero, "The Meaning and Application of Differentiated Staffing in Teaching," *Phi Delta Kappan*, LII (1), Sptember, 1970, p. 37.

education than is now available. Such arrangements might facilitate individual professional development to prepare for increased expertise and responsibility as teachers, which would lead to increased satisfaction, status, and material reward.[4]

Differentiated staffing is a system for increasing the effectiveness of instructional manpower utilization and more. It is a system which facilitates the utilization of alternative instructional techniques by various levels of instructional personnel. It enhances the teaching profession, since it provides growth potential for people. It rests on the principle that rewards will be commensurate with levels of instructional responsibilities.[5]

DIFFERENTIATED STAFFING FOR OCCUPATIONAL PROGRAMS

Differentiated staffing has great potential in occupational education. By nature, the various functions in occupational teaching require varied types of expertise and regular upgrading. Occupational instructors must stay abreast of technological change. Teachers must also stay abreast of the hardware and software of instructional technology. Instruction related activities, such as managing cooperative work activities and advisory committee efforts, also require (and foster) staff competencies updating. A differentiated staff is better able to cope with these varying demands.

Because of the divergence of occupational education offerings, most models of differentiated staffing are not directly applicable. A differentiated staffing model that may be useful in occupational education programs is diagrammed in Fig. 12-1. Whereas this differentiated staffing model is not significantly different in appearance from many others proposed by various school systems throughout the country, the specific functions performed by each level of personnel lend themselves to occupational education.

The Master Teacher

The role of the master teacher in a differentiated occupational education staff is primarily one of coordination. This differs somewhat from the traditional description of master teacher as defined in academic differentiated staff models. This is in keeping with the major contrasts of occupational education and nonoccupational programs.

---

[4] Roy A. Edelfelt, "Differentiated Staffing: Is It Worth the Risk?" *New York State Education*, 57 (6), March, 1970, p. 23.
[5] *Ibid.*

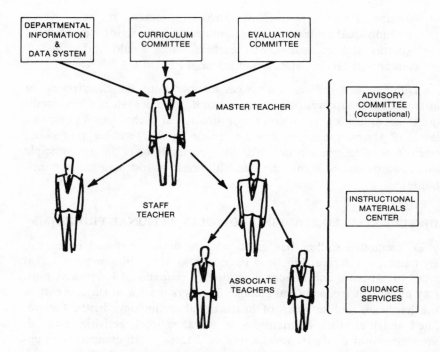

THE DIFFERENTIATED OCCUPATIONAL STAFF

Fig. 12-1

One of the unique features of occupational education is the utilization of a lay advisory committee to assist decision making at the instructional level. One of the major responsibilities of the master teacher is maintaining relationships with the advisory committee designated for the respective occupational area. One problem which has long been associated with advisory committees is lack of utilization of committee input by instructional personnel. Differentiated staffing can assume that the master teacher is assigned the liaison function and that advisory personnel can enhance the master teacher's contribution to program and school curriculum and evaluation committees.

The master teacher should also be responsible for maintenance of an occupational area or departmental instructional information system (see Chapter 8.) In this function, the master teacher should coordinate all instructional decision making in the occupational program. The master teacher must assure that the advisory committee, evaluation committee, curriculum committee, and instructional information system interact effectively. He must serve as the formal and informal link among these groups. Other responsibilities of the master teacher are listed in Table 12-1.

Table 12-1. Differentiated Staff Job Descriptions

POSITION	DUTIES
1. MASTER TEACHER	1. Liaison with program and school-wide committees 2. Curriculum research and development 3. Coordinate departmental instructional information system 4. Coordinate with occupational advisory committee 5. Serve on departmental or program evaluation committee 6. Assist staff teachers in decision making
2. STAFF TEACHER	1. 75% time to classroom or related instruction 2. Laboratory instruction 3. Work with occupational advisory committee 4. Establish and visit cooperative work stations
3. ASSOCIATE TEACHER	1. 100% time to direct laboratory & classroom instruction
4. TECHNICAL PARAPROFESSIONAL	1. Instructional materials preparation 2. Laboratory equipment maintenance 3. Equipment purchase recommendations 4. Special technical instruction

Staff Teacher

Whereas 75 percent of the staff teacher's time is devoted to instruction, some of his responsibilities also fall in the realm of coordination. Differentiated staffing facilitates articulation within the occupational education agency. The staff teacher coordinates the formal instructional aspects of the occupational education unit with specific individuals on the occupational advisory committee(s), in the instructional materials center, and in student personnel services. A full schedule of classroom and laboratory teaching would present interagency cooperation which is essential at the firing-line level of instruction/learning.

Another important function of the staff teacher is establishment of and visitations to cooperative education work stations. This function is important for two distinct but related reasons. (1) If cooperative education programs are to be effective, work stations must be chosen and developed very carefully by knowledgeable professionals. (2) The role of the cooperative education coordinator in public relations has great influence on the total occupational program. Much of what the local community thinks about the school is learned by participation in cooperative education programs.

The staff teacher's primary responsibility is that of instruction. His academic background and wealth of work experience in both teaching and business make him a valuable asset to the instructional process.

Associate Teacher

On the differentiated occupational education staff, the role of the associate teacher is very important. This is usually a beginning teacher who possesses minimum qualifications for teacher certification. The sole responsibility of the associate teacher is that of classroom/laboratory instruction and supervision.

Working with the staff teacher to perfect his skills as an instructor, the associate teacher is free of administrative and coordination responsibilities. This permits total concentration on the perfection of teaching abilities. The associate teacher position provides for natural progression from university training and teaching internship to full-time teaching.

The Paraprofessional

This function on the differentiated staff has been of great concern to all manner of professionals. So long as job duties are carefully defined in keeping with real, local needs, the paraprofessional is a very necessary and productive part of the occupational education staff. In most instances in occupational education there should be two distinct categories of paraprofessionals:

1. Technical Assistant and
2. Instructional Assistant.

The technical assistant should be well prepared by virtue of work experience in the technical aspect(s) of the program(s) which he will serve. His primary responsibility should be to assist associate teachers and staff teachers with the technical aspects of the instructional offerings. Recent work experience and familiarity with the instructional information system should assure that he can provide up-to-date technical information to students. In the main, technical assistants may be expected to remain in their jobs or go to universities for teacher training.

The instructional assistant should be a student intern, preparing for advancement on the differentiated staff to associate teacher. The responsibility of the instructional assistant is to assist associate, staff, and master teachers with classroom and laboratory instruction. The instructional assistant and the associate teacher functions are the major additions of differentiated staffing to conventional staffing.

ADVANTAGES OF DIFFERENTIATED STAFFING

Several advantages of differentiated staffing over the traditional omni-teacher approach to satisfying instructional personnel needs are:

1. Better learning situation for developing professionals,
2. Improved community relations,
3. Improved departmental articulation,
4. Improved teaching/learning situation,
5. Improved working relations with advisory groups,
6. Incentive for teaching excellence,
7. Performance centered, and
8. Well-defined job descriptions.

A closer look at each of the advantages is warranted.

Improved Teaching/Learning Situation

All of the instructional aspects of the educational enterprise are enhanced through the differentiated staffing approach. Learning is enhanced by situations wherein various individuals have the opportunity to devote the major portion of their time to such activities as laboratory preparation, audiovisual media development, lesson preparation and delivery, and other instructional activities.

Improved Departmental Articulation

If individual staff members are responsible for respective aspects of the occupational program and if the master teacher is responsible for the function, articulation of all student services is certain to be substantially better than in conventional situations.

Improved Working Relations With Advisory Groups

As was indicated previously, one of the roles of the master teacher is coordination of advisory committee work. Teachers in conventional settings do poorly at this task to the detriment of public relations. In the traditional occupational education department, little time is spent in working with advisory groups. In most cases, the administrative officer of the department assumes this responsibility and thereby prevents development of working relationships between instructional personnel and employer and employee groups. In the differentiated staff, instructional personnel have direct contact with all manner of advisory groups, through the master teacher.

Improved Community Relations

Again, the opportunity for people at the several instructional levels to work with various members of the community enhances community relations. Differentiated instructional staff have a variety of opportunities for direct contact with community agencies. Thus, community agencies realize more fully the problems of the firing-line instructional staff.

Better Learning Situation for Developing Professionals

Via experience in the entry-level role of instructional assistant and progression to the master teacher function, professionals learn more efficiently than they learn in conventional preparatory programs. Instructional assistant and associate teacher roles provide opportunities for beginning teachers to develop teaching skills in a live setting, relatively free of coordination and administrative responsibilities.

Clear Job Descriptions

A written job description for an occupational education teacher in a conventional situation requires several typewritten pages if it enumerates the various functions which must be performed. Because of specialization, job descriptions are much more concise and meaningful.

Performance Centered

Because job descriptions and responsibilities are clearly defined, differentiated staff members become much more performance centered. There is little question re specific responsibilities of the various categories of people on a differentiated staff. The paraprofessional knows his responsibilities and so on. Thus, people can be held accountable for what they are supposed to do. Knowing what is expected of them and that they can be assessed, they are encouraged to perform.

Incentive for Teaching Excellence

In traditional staffing patterns, outstanding teachers are often "promoted" out of the teaching ranks to administrative or research functions. Advantages of this procedure are more than offset by two disadvantages. (1) This procedure takes outstanding teachers from teaching. (2) It relies on the tenuous principle that outstanding teachers make good administrators. Features of differentiated staffing such as salary policies and the opportunity to supervise others tend to assure longer-range satisfactions for master teachers.

Good teachers should be provided opportunity to progress within the teaching ranks. The master teacher function in the differentiated staff makes this possible.

Potential Disadvantages of Differentiated Staffing

It would be remiss to discuss differentiated staffing without describing its major disadvantages. It must be noted, however, that these disadvantages are not inherent characteristics or weaknesses of the concept of the differentiated staffing. Rather, they are possible results of the reluctance of people who implement all or some of the features of differentiated staffing.

Revamping Traditional Pay Systems

Because of the additional levels of instructional personnel, traditional salary schedules must be revised. This presents problems in existing organizations. Practicing faculty must be categorized on the hierarchy and assigned pay scales accordingly. All existing faculty cannot be classified as master teachers. Thus, some will be displeased.

Promotion Systems and Attitudes

Promotion systems and attitudes must be changed. Length of tenure cannot be the basis for promotion and salary increases. The quality of performance of assigned duties must become the basis for rank and pay increases. This procedure conflicts with the points of view of many administrators and is opposed by many teacher associations.

Philosophical View of the Teacher's Role

The fundamental view of the teacher's role held by many professionals is in opposition to the concepts underlying differentiated staffing.

Many professionals feel that the teacher must be a man of many hats. They allege that interaction with all facets of the educational enterprise increases instructional effectiveness. The responsibilities of master teachers in differentiated settings are somewhat narrowed. In the authors' view the narrowing is in keeping with major desires of teachers in conventional settings. Teachers want to be responsible for instruction and not bothered with minutia. Giving up peripheral responsibilities permits teachers to focus on professional tasks.

SUMMARY

The instructional staff is the most important element of the instructional system. A strong, efficient staff is essential to program quality and productivity. Regardless of the type of instructional staffing systems to be utilized, personnel who have direct contact with students are the most important personnel in the educational enterprise.

Differentiated staffing is an organizational scheme which makes better use of educational personnel through a system of formal responsibility assignments. Through a formal analysis of instructional procedure, specific teaching functions are identified and classed according to levels. These categories are utilized as job descriptions for teaching and related instructional roles. The advantages of differentiated staffing are:

1. Improved teaching/learning situation,
2. Improved departmental articulation,
3. Improved working relationships with advisory groups,
4. Improved community relations,
5. Better learning situation for developing professionals,
6. Clearer job descriptions,
7. Performance centered, and
8. Incentive for teaching excellence.

ACTIVITIES

1. Conduct a local survey to determine how local teachers view differentiated staffing. Repeat the survey with local administrators. List and chart your findings.
2. Prepare an organizational plan for differentiated staffs in industrial-oriented occupational education programs at secondary, community college, and teacher training institutions.
3. Prepare job descriptions for personnel in the above programs.
4. Develop a plan for introducing local faculty, administrators, and community personnel to differentiated staffing.

DISCUSSION QUESTIONS

1. What is differentiated staffing?
2. What are the responsibilities of the various members of a differentiated staff?
3. What are some of the advantages of differentiated staffing? Disadvantages?
4. Why is differentiated staffing a "natural" for occupational education programs?
5. Why is education a social function?

BIBLIOGRAPHY

Allen, Dwight W., and Bush, Robert. *A New Design for High School Education.* New York: McGraw-Hill, 1964.

Bowman, Garda W., and Klopf, Gordon J. "Auxiliary School Personnel: Their Roles, Training, and Institutionalization," New York: Bank Street College of Education, 1968.

Cockerill, Clara E. "Differentiated Staffing: A Way to Individualize Instruction," *Pennsylvania Education* (November-December, 1969).

Committee for Economic Development. "Innovation in Education: New Directions for the American School." New York: The Committee, July, 1968.

Earl, S. A. "Differentiated Staffing." Paper Presented at The Western Canada Administrators' Conference, Banff, Alberta, October, 1969, ED 036 885.

Edelfelt, Roy A. "Differentiated Staffing: Is It Worth the Risk?" *New York State Education,* Vol. 57, No. 6 (March, 1970).

English, Fenwick. "The Differentiated Staff: Education's Technostructure." Educational Technology, Vol. 10, No. 2 (February, 1970).

English, Fenwick. "Teacher May I? Take Three Giant Steps! The Differentiated Staff," *Phi Delta Kappan,* Vol. 51, No. 3 (December, 1969).

Firester, Lee, and Firester, Joan. "Some Reflections," *New York State Education,* Vol. 57, No. 6 (March, 1970).

Lown, Donald E. "Proceed with Deliberation on Differentiated Staffing," *New York State Education,* Vol. 57, No. 6 (March, 1970).

McKenna, Bernard H., compiler. *A Selected Annotated Bibliography on Differentiated Staffing.* Washington, D.C.: National Commission on Teacher Education and Professional Standards, National Education Association, and ERIC Clearinghouse on Teacher Education, October, 1969.

National Education Association, National Commission on Teacher Education and Professional Standards. *The Teacher and His Staff: Selected Demonstration Centers.* St. Paul, Minn.: 3M Education Press, 1967.

Olivero, James L. "The Meaning and Application of Differentiated Staffing in Teaching." *Phi Delta Kappan,* Vol. 52, No. 1 (September, 1970).

Schaefer, Carl J. "Differentiated Staffing—An Approach Leading Nowhere." *Industrial Arts and Vocational Education,* Vol. 59, No. 1 (January, 1970), Te 10-11.

Selden, David, and Bhaerman, Robert. "Instructional Technology and the Teaching Profession," *The Record,* (February, 1970).

Chapter Thirteen

Establishing
Classroom
and
Laboratory
Managerial
Policy

INTRODUCTION

To maximize career education at several levels, educators must develop written policies concerning the many variables which relate to instructional effort. Understanding development of managerial policy will be facilitated by answers to the following questions.

- What elements should be considered in the design of an instructional data collection, storage, and retrieval system?
- How should student personnel services be described within a total managerial policy?
- How should policies regarding safety and safety education be described within a total managerial policy?
- How should material and facility management procedures be described within a total managerial plan?

Instruction can be facilitated (or hindered) by written policies regarding (a) data collection, storage and retrieval, (b) pupil personnel services, (c) safety, and (d) material and facility management. Preparation and implementation of written managerial procedures can foster good relationships at several levels of control, safe and optimal learning conditions, and efficient use of materials and facilities. Policies can serve to eliminate confusion and misunderstanding. Human and technological resources can be conserved in the interest of efficient movement toward career education goals only if policies and procedures are businesslike.

INFORMATION COLLECTION, STORAGE, AND RETRIEVAL

Collection, collation, and reporting of more and more detailed information about career education programs are required by sponsoring agencies. Specific data about learner and institutional characteristics must be submitted to one or more funding sources who, in turn, synthesize the data for reporting to subsequent levels of government. Information such as average daily attendance is important in funding formulae and the planning process.

Because the teacher has daily contact with learners, he is expected to gather much of the raw data for the institution. Data on learners include: name, address, age, sex, race, social security number, handicap, grade level, occupational code, disadvantage, and work experience. Data on institution and programs include: name and number of career-related classes, number of pupils enrolled in each class, instructor's name, instructor qualifications, learning experience descriptions, and attendance. Collecting such data is a mundane chore, but is nonetheless an integral and important part of professionals' jobs.

Data collection and record-keeping chores may be minimized by judicious development and implementation of information collection, storage, and retrieval systems. This can best be accomplished through four steps:

A. Determine institutional policy.
B. Prepare a written plan.
C. Have supervisor evaluate the plan.
D. Provide for data storage and retrieval.

A teacher must know the overall institutional policy regarding data systems before formulating a plan for his part of it. He needs to determine what kinds of pupil, program, and staff data are needed, how often it must be reported, and the manner in which it is to be submitted. Small organizations normally gather, store, and synthesize all information manually, whereas large agencies utilize electronic data processing technology. Note the sample Student Information Sheet (Fig. 13-1).

No form will serve the needs of all programs and courses. In addition to fulfilling institutional information needs, such sheets provide classroom teachers with necessary data about individual learner interests and subsequent motivations.

Knowledge of institutional policy will enable the teacher to prepare or secure the kinds of forms most appropriate for the task at hand. Teacher-prepared forms should be approved by the immediate supervisor. Critical data collection dates and report submission dates should appear on teaching plans or a special events schedule. Such items cannot be trusted to memory.

Efficient teachers provide for organized storage and rapid retrieval of records. Nothing is so frustrating as being unable to find records which were painstakingly prepared. One of the easiest and most common meth-

STUDENT INFORMATION SHEET

1. Name_____ Grade_____ Date of Birth_____

2. Address_____ Telephone Number_____

3. Homeroom_____ Study Hall Periods_____

4. Father's Name_____ Occupation_____

5. Mother's Name_____ Occupation_____

6. Number of and ages of brothers and sisters_____

7. Schools attended _____

8. Do you have a part-time job? _____

9. If so, what type of work do you do? _____

10. Please list your hobbies _____

11. List the clubs or organizations to which you belong_____

12. Work experience _____
    When? (summers, after school, both) _____

13. List extracurricular activities you have and/or are partici-
    pating in _____

14. Name projects you have made.
    At home _____

    At school _____

15. List equipment and tools with which you have worked_____

Fig. 13-1

ods of storing records is to use manila folders and a cabinet with several file chambers. Each folder should be clearly and concisely labeled and placed in an appropriate section of the file. Each file drawer and each section within a drawer should be clearly marked. The organization may be alphabetical by major area, e.g., instructional, pupil, or administrative. Other organizations can serve as well. The teacher should choose a *workable* system.

In short, efficient management of learner and institutional data requires a procedure which utilizes acceptable information sheets, assures that collection and reporting dates will be honored, and provides for efficient and effective storage and retrieval of desired information.

ESTABLISHING A STUDENT PERSONNEL SERVICES SYSTEM

Development of written policy pertaining to the organization, direction, and control of learner activity and progress is essential to the efficiency of career-education programs. Written policy should define procedures for matters such as (a) pupil progress, (b) classroom, laboratory, and cooperative work experiences, (c) tool and equipment utilization, (d) clean-up practices, (e) fees, and (f) safety. With the exception of safety, these will be discussed in turn in this section. Safety is treated in a separate section.

Central to any successful managerial policy is the establishment of a student personnel system wherein learners assume appropriate responsibility for the conduct of learning experiences. Student personnel systems are especially important in laboratories, shops, and field experiences. Organization and implementation of a framework for learner participation and cooperation is important to the development of desirable work habits and attitudes.

Numerous student personnel systems have been developed by teachers and supervisors; no one system is best for all situations. The local situation dictates which plan is best suited for unique needs. Note the student personnel organizational plan in the sample Pupil Personnel System form (Fig. 13-2). In this plan, the instructor has ultimate responsibility and authority in the organizational hierarchy. To lighten his administrative load, the teacher delegates appropriate responsibility to a competent general foreman. The general foreman (elected or appointed) oversees the conduct of nonprofessional activities. He is charged with the responsibility of coordinating the efforts of his foremen and classmates for efficient operation of the facility. Students assume responsibilities as area, safety, tool, record, and clean-up foremen, and thus learn myriad leadership roles.

Of course, authority for final decisions rests with the teacher. The extent to which students are involved in decision making should depend

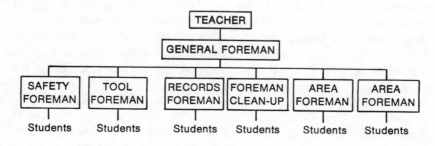

PUPIL PERSONNEL SYSTEM

Duties

GENERAL FOREMAN	RECORDS FOREMAN
A. Starts each class	A. Take attendance
B. Oversees all work	B. Record daily attendance
C. Supervises foremen	C. Report absentees
D. Appoints replacements	D. Assist with progress charts
E. Dismisses class	E. Maintain project security

SAFETY FOREMAN	CLEAN-UP FOREMAN
A. Reports unsafe conditions	A. Signal clean-up time
B. Reports poor work habits	B. Supervise clean-up activity
C. Assist with inspections	C. Rotate clean-up jobs
D. Promote safety	D. Inspects clean-up activity
E. Make recommendations	E. Signals satisfactory clean-up

TOOL FOREMAN	AREA FOREMAN
A. Check for missing tools	A. Supervises activity in said area
B. Maintain tool crib or panels	B. Reports machine malfunctions
C. Check-out tools	C. Reports pupil behavior
D. Check-in tools	D. Keeps pupils supplied with materials
E. Keep tool inventory	E. Checks on pupil progress-questions
F. Report missing tools	F. Assists teacher when needed

Fig. 13-2

upon the individual teacher's managerial philosophy. With increased student activism and interest in goal setting, it is well to weigh carefully the benefits of a democratic versus an autocratic personnel system. In many situations, student participation in decision making will promote understanding and cooperation.

Provisions should be made for rotation of pupils through different supervisory roles. Whereas it is tempting to let a "good man" remain in a critical supervisory job indefinitely, many of the purposes of personnel systems are lost through such inaction. The responsibility and prestige of leadership positions is powerful incentive for some learners. Each student should be afforded opportunity to exhibit leadership skills before his peers. This should be done, if for no other reason than to help an individual to discover that supervisory responsibilities are not to his liking.

It is good practice to develop a student personnel board, chart, or similar device that clearly illustrates which students must perform what duties. The personnel chart should be displayed in a prominent place. It should also facilitate changing assignments with a minimum of effort and confusion. The interval at which assignments should be changed should be governed by student characteristics, the course, the facility, and the duration of marking periods or terms.

Several personnel charts are illustrated in Fig. 13-3. The first chart utilizes a rotating wheel with letters and pointers. Each letter corresponds to a foreman, e.g., general foreman, safety foreman. The stationary portion of the chart has numbers, which correspond to students. When a change of supervisory personnel is required, the center wheel is simply rotated.

The second personnel chart utilizes numbered cards. Each card represents a student. Specific responsibilities are listed on the right-hand side of the chart. The numbered cards are held in place behind a clear plastic plate. When a change of personnel is desired the numbered card at the bottom of the chart is removed. The remaining cards drop down and the card just removed is reinserted at the top of the chart. The student merely checks his assigned number and determines his new responsibility.

The third personnel chart utilizes cup or "L" hooks and numbered tags. The numbered tags correspond to students. When responsibilities are changed, tags are placed on appropriate hooks. These and other assignment systems have advantages and disadvantages which the teacher must weigh. One technique will not serve all situations. Each should be weighed for its merits and shortcomings. The system selected should (a) facilitate development of pupil leadership potential, (b) improve pupil-teacher rapport, and (c) relieve the instructor of routine duties.

A written plan for recording and displaying individual progress is an integral part of a total managerial policy. The teacher may make

STUDENT PERSONNEL CHARTS

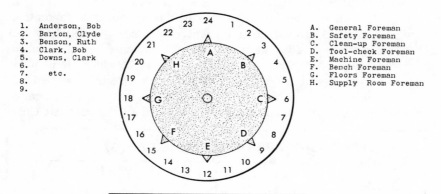

1. Anderson, Bob
2. Barton, Clyde
3. Benson, Ruth
4. Clark, Bob
5. Downs, Clark
6.
7.   etc.
8.
9.

A. General Foreman
B. Safety Foreman
C. Clean-up Foreman
D. Tool-check Foreman
E. Machine Foreman
F. Bench Foreman
G. Floors Foreman
H. Supply Room Foreman

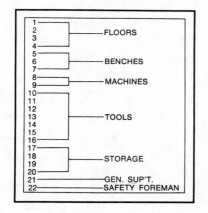

NO.	STUDENT NAMES
1	Andrews, Mary
2	Burton, Mark
3	Clinton, Ruth
4	Dutton, Bill
5	Edwards, Stuart
6	
7	etc.

NO.	STUDENT NAMES
1	Benton, Helen
2	Cane, Herb
3	Ellis, Herman
4	Fearal, Milton
5	Henric, Liz.
6	Menlo, Barb.
7	Tenneson, Rob.

	PERIODS					
	1	2	3	4	5	6
SUP'T.	3	10	2		20	8
SAFETY	4	11	7		9	4
TOOLS	18	1	3		12	3
CLEAN-UP	20	7	19		17	15
BENCHES	5	9	24		22	10
FLOORS	9	20	13		19	6

Fig. 13-3

provisions for a student records foreman to assist with recording and updating student progress charts. Charts which illustrate the progression of learners through career education sequences can aid and abet motivation. Displayed in a well-traveled area of the classroom or laboratory, progress charts focus attention on where students are and how fast they are mastering skills and knowledges. The manner in which student progress is recorded is dependent upon the way in which learning experiences are organized. Program and objectives determining the kinds of concepts, topics, projects, activities, operations, tasks, or competencies which should appear on progress charts appear in the Progress Chart

PROGRESS CHART (CONCEPTS)												
COURSE: Material-Process UNIT: Material Removal	Concepts	Turning	Shaping	Planing	Drilling	Boring	Etching	Shearing	Milling	Mechanical Cutting	Heat Cutting	Separating	
Learner Names													Comments
Abbott, Ralph		B	C	B	C	C	C	B					
Bennet, Ruth		C	C	C	D	C	C	D	D				
Carter, Wayne		A	B	A	A	A	B	B	B	B			
Dear, Wm.		D	D	E	E								DROP
Ferger, Helen		C	C	C	B	C	C	C	C				
Herns, Don		C	C	B	B	C	B						
Munson, Carol		B	B	B	B	A	B	A	A	A			
Potter, Stan		C	C	C	C	B	B	B	A				
Zane, Bob		C	C	C	C	B	C	C	C	C	C	C	Re-doing work

Fig. 13-4

(Concepts), Progress Chart (Projects), and Progress Chart (Tasks). See Figs. 13-4, 13-5, and 13-6.

The Progress Chart (Concepts) reflects mastery of concepts concerning materials and processes (see Fig. 13-4). It employs the traditional means of evaluation, i.e., assignment of letter grades or levels of

PROGRESS CHART (PROJECTS)

COURSE: Creative Cooking

UNIT: Appetizers & Canapes

Learner Names	Projects	Bacon Wraps	Cocktail Ham Biscuits	Cucumber Canape	Shrimp & Onion	Cheese Balls	Cheese Puffs	Pecan Canape	Stuffed Celery	Cheese Toast	Mexican Appetizer	Crabmeat Pattie	Comments
		5	10	10	5	5	5	5	5	10	10	10	
Aherns, John		4	8	8	4	4	5	4	3	8	8		
Collins, Jeff		3	8	7	3	4	4	3	3				
Dees, Joe		3	7	7	4	3							
Esner, Mary		3	7	6	3	3	3						
Hewlitt, Nancy		3	8	7	4	3	5	3					
Kerns, Bob		4	9	8	4	4	4	5	5	9	10	10	Extra work
Liget, Helen		2	7	7	2	3	3	3					
Peron, Bill		3	7	7	3	4	3	3					
Smith, Carol		3	7	7	4	4	4	5	3				

Fig. 13-5

competence. As the learner masters subsequent concepts, the letter grade is entered in the appropriate row and column of the chart. Posting of letter grades (A, B, C, D, E) has a decided drawback in that a cumulative total of earned points is difficult to determine. Pupils and teacher

PROGRESS CHART (TASKS)

COURSE: Secretarial Science

UNIT: Performing Mailroom Duties

Learner Names	Calculate Postal Rate 10	Log Incoming Mail 15	Operate Automatic Letter Opener 10	Operate Postage Meter 10	Operate Mailing Sealer 10	Sort Mail 15	Stamp Envelopes (Manual) 10	Label Bulk Mail 10	Uze Zip Code Directory 10	Weigh Items 10	Wrap & Tie Packages 10	Comments
Billings, Sharon	9/9	13/22	9/31	10/41	8/49	14/63	10/73	8/81	9/90	9/99	8/107	Extra credit 10/10, 9/10
Collet, Sally	10/10	14/24	7/31	10/41	10/51	13/64	9/73	9/82	8/90			
Downs, Bill	8/8	12/20	8/28	8/36	9/45	12/57	9/66					
Esin, Ralph	9/9	13/22	10/32	8/40	9/49	14/63	10/73	10/83	9/92	8/100		
Ferns, Henry	6/6	12/18	7/25	5/30	7/37	13/50	8/58	7/65				
Gerig, Sue	5/5	10/15	5/20	6/26								
Klopp, Mary	10/10	13/23	10/33	9/42	8/50	12/62	10/72	9/81	10/91	8/99	10/109	Extra credit 9/10
Newton, John	10/10	15/25	9/34	7/44	7/43	15/63	10/73	10/88				
Opper, Connie	6/6	8/14	6/20									Illness— withdrawl

Fig. 13-6

alike must convert the letter grades into points before statistics such as averages or class standings can be ascertained.

Learners can readily view the class achievement record. Some maintain that such practices do not foster wholesome pupil attitudes toward mastery of requirements. They contend that such charts discourage slow learners who might otherwise try to keep pace with faster learners. On the contrary, evidence suggests that visual evidence of pupil achievement helps teachers and students to understand where they are with respect to required learning activities. Such charts help teachers identify those who need assistance with learning difficulties. They help pupils identify their own shortcomings and prompt them to seek appropriate aid.

An alternate charting method reports learner progress according to projects completed and earned points for each project. In the Progress Chart (Projects), the projects to be completed are listed across the top of the chart (see Fig. 13-5). The maximum allowable points which may be earned for each project are listed directly beneath each project title. As the pupil completes a project, he submits it to the instructor for evaluation. The earned points are entered in appropriate rows and columns of the chart. Earned points may be compared to the maximum possible points which appear at the head of each column to establish class standing and individual progress.

The instructor should (1) keep duplicate charts in his own record book to guard against loss, theft, or alteration of the progress chart, and (2) let it be known that the posted chart is only a copy of the official record.

At the end of a learning experience, the teacher or his designated aide may merely add earned points for each pupil and enter the sum in the proper space. The space for comments at the far right may prove helpful in recording outstanding work, extra-credit assignments, or similar significant items.

A third reporting format describes learner progress in terms of tasks completed. In the Progress Chart (Tasks), the maximum points possible earned for successful performance of tasks appear directly beneath each task title (see Fig. 13-6). Note that this chart employs a cumulative method of recording actual earned points. The upper-left area of each square shows the earned points for the task and the lower-right area shows the sum of all earned points to that date. Thus, a running total of each student's earned points is displayed as each succeeding task is completed. Whereas this technique is more time consuming than the two previous methods, it does make for easy interpretation of where each learner stands upon completion of any given task.

A teacher must decide upon a reporting technique which will clearly and concisely describe student progress to learners, teachers, supervisors, administrators, and parents. The chart should be placed in a well-traveled place in the learning environment. Needless to say, the chart should be updated at least daily. A dependable student records aide can assure good maintenance of such a reporting system. Readily accessible and current records of learner progress do much to create student interest and motivation.

BEHAVIORAL POLICY

Another part of the total managerial policy concerns student behavior. A typical conduct code is provided in Student Rules and Regulations (see Fig. 13-7). Students deserve to know acceptable behavior

---

STUDENT RULES AND REGULATIONS

Be in your assigned seat by the time the tardy bell sounds.
Secure an admit slip if late.
Bring an excuse slip if you have been absent.
Listen carefully for Important announcements.
The general shop foreman will give you the signal to commence working.
Do not leave class without the instructor's permission.
Keep your talking to a minimum.
Do not use abusive language.
There will be no running or horseplay tolerated.
Treat members of the opposite sex with courtesy and respect.
Abide by all safety rules and regulations.
Clean-up your own work station when done with a job.
Contribute your part to the total laboratory clean-up effort.
Take your assigned seat at the end of the class period and wait for the general shop foreman to dismiss you.

*Carefully consider your behavior, remembering that failure to adhere to rules will result in appropriate action by your instructor.

Fig. 13-7

---

limits. These must be clear, concise, and written. Much student and teacher confusion and anxiety can be alleviated by a carefully prepared behavior policy. It is essential that such policy be simply worded, duplicated, and placed in student hands as early as possible. For maximum effectiveness the teacher should take class time to discuss and orient pupils to each expectation and regulation.

Conduct codes can be prepared in several ways. They may be prepared by a single instructor, a faculty committee, a student-faculty group, a pupil standards committee, or other kinds of groups. Whoever is responsible for developing behavior policies should consider five sources of information before drafting rules and regulations. These are:

A. Existing institutional behavioral policies and regulations.
B. Existing division or departmental policies and regulations.

    C. Student governing body codes.
    D. Unique characteristics of facilities and learning experiences.
    E. Prevailing behavior philosophy.

In many, but not all, educational agencies, institutional policy establishes behavior parameters. The teacher should familiarize himself with institutional regulations. Knowing the overall rules and regulations, teachers can determine division or departmental regulations by which he must abide. In many situations, favorable response and cooperation can be obtained if policy is developed in concert with student organizations. It is often practical to enlist their aid and counsel.

Careful consideration must be given to the unique characteristics of career education classrooms, laboratories, shops, or field centers. Characteristics of some career education learning sequences may require variance from standard operating procedures. For example, there may have to be stringent regulations regarding smoking, clothing, talking, or other variables which might be hazardous to health and safety. In such cases, the purpose of special rules must be explained to pupils, fellow teachers, supervisors, parents, and administrators.

Finally, behavior policy should reflect the emotional and personal temperament of the instructor. If a teacher is to maximize opportunity for learning career skills and knowledges, he must operate in an environment which is compatible with his personality. For example, an instructor whose emotional composition requires that he work in a loosely structured learning environment may well encounter difficulties in an institution which fosters highly structured situations. The teacher should develop a written behavioral policy which is in keeping with his own temperament *and* compatible with the larger demands and regulations of the educational enterprise.

Development of behavioral policy is dependent upon formulation of answers to the following questions:

    A. How will learning experiences be begun in an orderly manner?
    B. What rules will assure safe and meaningful learning experiences?
    C. How will learning activities be culminated in an orderly manner?

It is imperative that the teacher answer each of these questions in writing prior to taking charge of a learning situation. The manner in which one chooses to begin learning experiences is very critical. It sets the stage, i.e., the precedent, for subsequent student activities. For example, if a learning experience is begun in a slovenly manner with little regard for behavior standards, subsequent student behavior will reflect disorganization and indecision.

Policies which are important to the beginning of learning sequences include regulations relating to punctuality and attendance. The teacher must determine how he will take roll and what will constitute being in class on time. The following should be considered:

A. Will students take seats first, and then go to work?
B. What constitutes tardiness? Must pupils be in seats when the bell rings?
C. Who will take attendance?
D. Who will read announcements?
E. Who will send students to work stations?

The individual career learning situation will, in many instances, suggest answers to these questions. For example, a laboratory or work station which requires frequent pupil movement presents barriers to accurate attendance measures. Likewise, high machine or student noise levels prohibit effective announcements. Such matters must be weighed carefully before procedures are determined for starting learning units.

It is also essential that work rules for activities in classrooms, laboratories, shops, or cooperative work stations be written and disseminated. Adherence to clearly written work regulations is especially important to the success of cooperative work experience because pupils are not under constant supervision of a teacher. Teachers, students, and others should consider the following matters:

A. Pupil dress, hair style, jewelry, shoes, etc.
B. Horseplay, fun, and games.
C. Abusive language.
D. Eating, drinking, and gum chewing.
E. Leaving the learning environment (excused-unexcused).
F. Boy-girl relationships.
G. Tool and machine utilization.
H. Tool check-out.
I. Collection of laboratory fee.
J. Others which are suggested by the local situation.

Written policy regarding these items will vary widely from one career education level to another and from one local education agency to another. For example, check-out procedures for tool utilization may vary from a tightly secured tool crib with an assigned student foreman to an open tool panel. Collection of fees may range from payment of a lump sum at the beginning of the term in the central business office to an instructor-controlled, punched laboratory fee card, as displayed in the Laboratory Fee Ticket (Fig. 13-8). The specific way in which these matters are treated is not important. But it is important to take a course of action which is in keeping with institutional policy, local conditions and unique laboratory situations, safety considerations, and personal traits.

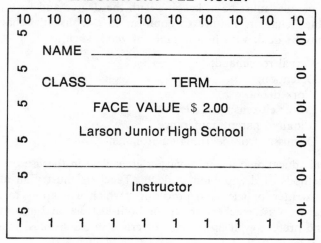

LABORATORY FEE TICKET

NAME _____

CLASS_____ TERM_____

FACE VALUE $ 2.00

Larson Junior High School

_____

Instructor

Fig. 13-8

Finally, the teacher must develop policy regarding clean-up and dismissal practices. If there is no planned system, the teacher will do many of the mundane clean-up chores. Prior thought and consideration need be given the following:

A. When will clean-up occur?
B. How often will clean-up occur?
C. Who will clean up?
D. When will dismissal occur?
E. Where will dismissal occur?
F. Who will dismiss students?

Again, the specific learning environment should, in large part, define the plan.

Preparation of written procedures for starting, controlling, and terminating daily career learning experiences must also include provisions for enforcement of regulations. A specific course of action must be prepared. It should spell out in certain terms what will occur if pupil behavior fails to meet set standards. It is usually beneficial to involve student representatives in formulation of such procedures. Students respect guidelines and can lend support to enforcement programs if they have had a part in the design stage.

Plans for enforcement of regulations must be practical and in keeping with institutional policies and professional ethics. Action taken to reprimand a student for infraction of regulations must be carried out in a consistent manner for all learners. Likewise, punishment for infraction of rules must be in keeping with the degree and severity of unacceptable behavior. Failure to conform to established behavior standards may be dealt with in a number of ways, such as:

A. Verbal reprimand.
B. Detention.
C. Work detail.
D. Lower citizenship grade.
E. Required parent conference.
F. Dismissal from learning environment.

Local educational agencies vary a great deal in the use of these and other methods of disciplining students. Teachers must plan ahead, developing written policies and procedures which will apply to situations as they arise. Wise teachers anticipate both instructional and managerial needs and prepare well in advance of crises in classrooms, laboratories, or workplaces.

ACCIDENT AND FIRE PREVENTION PROGRAM

There is growing concern in many segments of society regarding the improvement of safety and health standards for America's work force. Passage of the Occupational Safety and Health Act (OSHA)* in December of 1970 forced continued interest in accident prevention among all segments of the economy. The act grants certain powers to the Federal government to specify and enforce detailed occupational safety and health standards. All occupations in enterprises dealing in interstate commerce come under the jurisdiction of OSHA. Public educational institutions and agencies are not covered in the provisions of this act. Nevertheless, career educators must be concerned with accident prevention. Now, more than ever, educational agencies have a moral and ethical responsibility to assume leadership in developing safe work habits. Because schools are preparing youth and adults for gainful employment, they must create safe and healthful learning environments which surpass minimum standards which have been stipulated for American enterprise.

---

* See Public Law 91-596, 91st Congress, S2193, Dec. 29, 1970.

A further incentive for improvement of educational safety and health standards is the growing number of pupil injury cases which end up in the courts. Such litigation not only poses serious economic problems to school districts and teachers but presents embarrassing challenges to the competence and professionalism of affected teachers. Increasingly, educational managers and teachers are recognizing the best line of defense against damage claims is a well-organized, comprehensive, and ongoing accident prevention program.

An effective accident prevention program must have widespread support and complete participation of all institutional administrative units, instructional units, student groups, and the community at large. Without total cooperation, the thrust and direction of a safety program can be greatly impaired. Development and initiation of a total safety program is best achieved through the following procedures:

A. Secure top management support.
B. Identify key personnel.
C. Formulate program objectives.
D. Develop safety instruction.
E. Inspect facilities.
F. Analyze job safety practices.
G. Devise a system for investigation, reporting, and recording of accidents.

The most effective manner of eliciting widespread institutional support for safety programs is through the "boss." A firm commitment from the board of education, regents, chancellor, president, or superintendent will do much to bring about cooperation. A clear and concise statement of management's support for an accident prevention program should be secured and distributed to all concerned. A sample safety statement follows:

The board of education has authorized the formation of an executive safety committee and the appointment of a part-time safety and fire prevention coordinator. This action is taken with a firm commitment to support the recommendations of both the executive committee and coordinator. This will result in safer learning and working conditions for learners and teachers; greater protection of district property; and a primary means of reducing accidents.

We are now initiating a high-priority program which has been carefully planned with full administrative support. We urge all persons to cooperate in every manner possible at all levels and in all learning situations. Support for the safety program will be considered along with other contributions to institutional goals at times when rank and pay increases are determined.

Statements of this sort inform everyone that management places high priority on development and successful implementation of accident prevention programs.

The next step in program development is identification of personnel who will plan, develop, and eventually implement and control activity. Program success depends upon involvement of learners, teachers, supervisors, administrators, industrialists, businessmen, and parents. Each should be represented on the executive safety committee. This body should be charged with overall program planning and organization. The committee should appoint a safety program coordinator. The criteria should be (a) knowledge of accident prevention and safety methods, and (b) qualities which will command the respect and cooperation of all personnel.

After the coordinator has been selected, he and the executive committee determine accident prevention program objectives. A sample of program objectives follows:

A. To minimize and eliminate accidents.
B. To create a healthy and safe learning environment.
C. To establish preventative and emergency controls.
D. To identify unsafe conditions and practices and take action to eliminate them.
E. To facilitate learning of safe work habits.

All personnel should be apprised of overall program objectives and involved in development and implementation of the program. Personnel should be organized to assist in the administration and conduct of safety program activities. A sample organization chart is diagrammed in Fig. 13-9. The chart illustrates one method by which executive safety policy and objectives may be disseminated and implemented throughout a given district. Each building in the district is required to set up its own accident control group. As indicated above, these bodies include district and community representatives. These groups provide specific guidelines for the conduct of their own building accident prevention plan.

Each building accident control group acts independently of other groups, but attempts to coordinate effort with the overall district safety program. Effort in each building is scrutinized by an executive safety committee. Each building is divided into logical categories called division control groups. A division includes instructional departments with activities which require similar facilities, materials, and equipment, e.g., physical science, industrial orientation, business practices, creative arts,

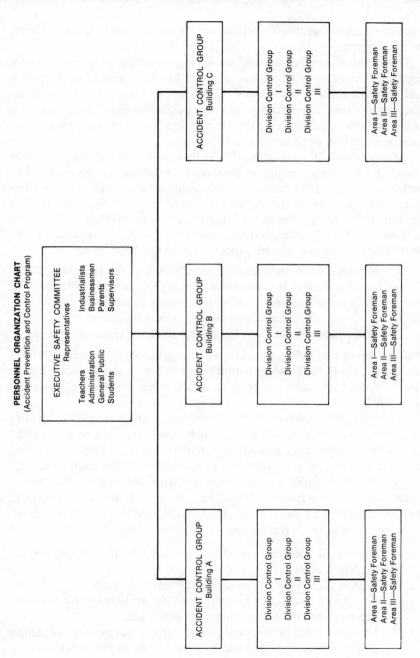

PERSONNEL ORGANIZATION CHART
(Accident Prevention and Control Program)

EXECUTIVE SAFETY COMMITTEE
Representatives

Teachers   Industrialists
Administration   Businessmen
General Public   Parents
Students   Supervisors

ACCIDENT CONTROL GROUP
Building A

Division Control Group
I
Division Control Group
II
Division Control Group
III

Area I—Safety Foreman
Area II—Safety Foreman
Area III—Safety Foreman

ACCIDENT CONTROL GROUP
Building B

Division Control Group
I
Division Control Group
II
Division Control Group
III

Area I—Safety Foreman
Area II—Safety Foreman
Area III—Safety Foreman

ACCIDENT CONTROL GROUP
Building C

Division Control Group
I
Division Control Group
II
Division Control Group
III

Area I—Safety Foreman
Area II—Safety Foreman
Area III—Safety Foreman

Fig. 13-9

etc. Instructors in each division assume frontline responsibility for accident prevention plans.

Each instructor develops an accident prevention program in keeping with the unique needs of his area and the district-wide safety policy and objectives. Each instructor's written safety plan is carefully scrutinized by the division control group, the building control group, and the executive safety committee. This evaluation and approval process assures articulation of accident control efforts.

Students will be receptive of accident prevention if they assist in planning and implementing a classroom or laboratory program. The judicious teacher will appoint or have pupils elect a student safety foreman. This position should relate the safety effort to the total student personnel system. The necessary number of student safety helpers will be determined by learning activities and features of the facilities. A student safety foreman might be expected to do the following:

A. Report unsafe conditions or work habits to the teacher.
B. Aid the teacher in orientation of new and transfer students.
C. Help the teacher perform periodic safety inspections.
D. Promote safety conscientiousness among his peers.
E. Make recommendations for improvement of learning conditions.

It is important that action be taken when suggestions are made. Students are quick to note times when action is not taken to remedy unsafe conditions which they report. If positive action is not forthcoming, they act accordingly.

Every teacher must study his instructional environment to identify situations which require safety instruction. Learners must be given clear and concise instruction regarding potential hazards. Such instruction must be an integral part of daily presentations. Instructions must be clearly understood prior to learner involvement with potentially dangerous machines and materials. Before learners are allowed to begin work, they should be told what they must do and not do to prevent accidents. Some representative directives are:

A. Report all accidents and near accidents to the teacher or the student foreman.
B. Report all unsafe situations and potential hazards.
C. Pass respective safety tests with 100% accuracy before operating machine and using dangerous materials.
D. Do not operate mechanical equipment without proper instruction and authorization. (See the Release Forms in Fig. 13-10).
E. Wear appropriate personal protective equipment. (See state safety regulations for specific requirements.)

RELEASE FORM

This card is evidence that

_____
(student name)

has successfully completed both operating and safety examinations for the items listed below. Instructor's Initial _____

DATE	ITEM	DATE	ITEM

PARENTAL APPROVAL FORM

_____
(student's name)

has permission to operate equipment in the career learning laboratories for the period beginning_____
and ending on_____.

In the event of an injury please secure medical assistance from Dr. _____.

Signed

Date_____   _____

_____
(parents or legal guardian)

Fig. 13-10

SAFETY EDUCATION

Every effort must be made to communicate rules and regulations to learners. Evidence suggests that the multimedia approach is the most effective means of reaching students. These include safety posters, printed

COURTESY: NATIONAL SAFETY COUNCIL   (CHICAGO · THE COUNCIL)

Fig. 13-11

handouts, verbal messages, motion pictures, filmstrips and slides, video-tapes and similar media. Fig. 13-11, the Handout Sheet—General Safety Rules (Fig. 13-12), and the Motion Picture Reference List (Fig. 13-13) illustrate some of these.

Frequent and thorough safety and fire prevention inspections are another essential element of a total accident prevention program. The responsibility for regular inspection of an instructional area lies with the teacher in charge. He may enlist the aid of the student safety foreman,

---

HANDOUT SHEET — GENERAL SAFETY RULES

GREELY MIDDLE-SCHOOL CAREER LEARNING LABORATORY

———

Guidelines for Safety

———

1. Always obtain proper instruction before using any power equipment.

2. Always use the machine guards as directed.

3. Always wear proper personal protective devices.

4. Always pay attention to what you are doing.

5. Never distract a fellow student when he is operating machinery.

6. Always clean up your work station and machine when finished with a job.

7. Do not wear loose clothing. Roll up your sleeves.

8. Remove all jewelry and rings.

9. Wear a hair net If there is a possibility of catching hair in a machine.

10. Keep the floor areas clear of rubbish and scrap.

11. Report any unsafe conditions to the instructor.

12. Be alert and use good judgment in your actions.

Fig. 13-12

---

but responsibility cannot be delegated to the student. Ultimate responsibility for inspection and adherence to standards rests with the instructor. Inspections should occur as frequently as is possible and practical. Local and state regulations may stipulate mandatory intervals at which inspections of educational facilities must occur.

MOTION PICTURE REFERENCE LIST
(Accident Prevention)

FIRE

ABC & D's of Portable Fire Extinguishers

Shows how fire extinguishers function. Demonstrates their use in suppressing small fires. Demonstrates the proper use of the right kinds of extinguisher for the type of fire.

28 minutes   1970 Color

GENERAL

Confined Space Hazards

Defines confined spaces and shows the dangerous gasses that lurk inside, or escape from them. Shows how to test for dangerous atmospheres. Demonstrates use of protective equipment, and procedures for safely entering confined spaces. Stresses teamwork.

15½ minutes   1970 Color

Way to Live, A

An agricultural crop duster shows the harmful properties of dangerous dusts and gasses. Demonstrates protective breathing equipment for a variety of dangerous atmospheres.

18½ minutes   1970 Color

Zero in on Safety

Discusses methods for improving safety records through zeroing in on one safety problem at a time. Shows use of accident analysis to isolate causes and prevent repetition. Applies the same concern to analyzing near misses.

10 minutes   1970 Color

HOUSEKEEPING AND FALLS

Down and Out

An athlete demonstrates falls. Shows many traps—on the floor and above floor level.

10 minutes   1970 Color

Fig. 13-13 cont'd on next page

PERSONAL PROTECTIVE EQUIPMENT

Eyes, Hands and Feet Series

Series of three short films. No commentary. The impact is pleasantly visual.
"Wear Eye Protection"—Demonstrates common eye hazards.
"Beware of Hand Traps"—Dramatizes a variety of hazards to workers' hands.
"Wear Safety Shoes"—Dramatizes the variety of hazards to unprotected feet.

9½ minutes   1970 Color

Hear—It Takes Two

Workmen in a variety of noisy working environments talk about their exposure to noise and the ways in which hearing loss affects their lives. Describes hearing mechanism. Shows ear plugs and hearing aids in use. Emphasizes that ear protection has no value unless it is used.

20 minutes   1970 Color

Hearing—The Forgotten Sense

For general audiences. Shows the ill effects of impaired hearing on people's lives. Describes the hearing mechanism. Lists causes of hearing loss. Emphasizes noise damage. Shows control of noise at source. Shows use of ear protection and hearing aids. Shows simple test for recognizing hearing loss.

16 minutes   1970 Color

The Shield

Plain spoken, unrehearsed statements from many men who escaped blindness because they wore eye protection on the job. Shows variety of eye protection devices. Evokes a new appreciation of the gift of sight. Excellent kick-off film for use in setting up an eye protection program.

15 minutes   1970 Color

Sound of Sound

Directed at people who work in moderate to high noise areas. Designed to motivate them to wear proper ear protection.

16 minutes   1970 Color

Fig. 13-13

NATIONAL STANDARD SCHOOL SHOP SAFETY INSPECTION CHECK LIST

Prepared by the Joint Safety Committee of the
AMERICAN VOCATIONAL ASSOCIATION—NATIONAL SAFETY COUNCIL

_____ Date_____

INTRODUCTION

A safe environment is an essential part of the school shop safety education program. The safe environment will exist only if hazards are discovered and corrected through regular and frequent inspections by school personnel—administrators, teachers and students. Safety inspections are to determine if everything is satisfactory.

Inspections may be made at the request of the board of education, the school administration or upon the initiative of the teacher. Some communities have drawn upon the cooperative service of professional safety engineers, inspectors of state labor departments, insurance companies and local safety councils to supplement and confirm inspections by school personnel.

The National Standard School Shop Safety Inspection Check List, recommended by the President's Conference on Industrial Safety is an objective inspection procedure for the school shop.

DIRECTIONS

WHO INSPECTS?
This will depend upon local policies. It is recommended, however, that shop teachers, and students—the student safety engineer and/or student safety committee—participate in making regular inspections. This not only tends to share responsibility but stimulates a broader interest in the maintenance of a safe school shop.

WHEN TO INSPECT?
As a minimum, a safety inspection should be made at the beginning of every school term or semester. More frequent inspections may be advisable.

HOW TO INSPECT?
Inspections should be well planned in advance.

Inspections should be systematic and thorough. No location that may contain a hazard should be overlooked.

Inspection reports should be clear and concise, but with sufficient explanation to make each recommendation for improvement understandable.

FOLLOW-UP
The current report should be compared with previous records to determine progress. The report should be studied in terms of the accident situation so that special attention can be given to those conditions and locations which are accident producers.

Fig. 13-14 cont'd on next page

Each unsafe condition should be corrected as soon as possible In accordance with accepted local procedures.

A definite policy should be established in regard to taking materials and equipment out of service because of unsafe conditions.

The inspection report can be used to advantage as the subject for staff and class discussion.

CHECKING PROCEDURE

Draw a circle around the appropriate letter, using the following letter scheme:

S—Satisfactory (needs no attention)
A—Acceptable (needs some attention)
U—Unsatisfactory (needs immediate attention)

Recommendations should be made in all cases where a "U" is circled. Space is provided at the end of the form for such comments. Designate the items covered by the recommendations, using the code number applicable (as B-2). In most categories, space is provided for listing of standards, requirements or regulations which have local application only.

A. GENERAL PHYSICAL CONDITION

1. Machines, benches, and other equipment are arranged so as to conform to good safety practice ..S A U

2. Condition of stairways ....S A U

3. Condition of aisles ....S A U

4. Condition of floors ....S A U

5. Condition of walls, windows, and ceiling ....S A U

6. Illumination is safe, sufficient, and well placed ....S A U

7. Ventilation is adequate and proper for conditions ....S A U

8. Temperature control ....S A U

9. Fire extinguishers are of proper type, adequately supplied, properly located and maintained ....S A U

10. Teacher and pupils know location of and how to use proper type for various fires ....S A U

11. Number and location of exits is adequate and properly identified
S A U

12. Proper procedures have been formulated for emptying the room of pupils and taking adequate precautions in case of emergencies ....S A U

13. Lockers are inspected regularly for cleanliness and fire hazards. ..S A U

14. Locker doors are kept closed.
S A U

15. Walls are clear of objects that might fall....................S A U

16. Utility lines are properly identified
S A U

17. Teachers know the procedure in the event of fire including notification of the fire department and the evacuation of the building ....S A U

18. Air in shop is free from excessive dust, smoke, etc. ....S A U

19. _____ S A U

20. _____ S A U

21 _____ S A U

22. _____ S A U

23. Evaluation for the total rating of A. GENERAL PHYSICAL CONDITION
S A U

Courtesy—Natl. Safety Council (Chicago, The Council)

Fig. 13-14

FACILITIES INSPECTION

Inspections of educational facilities or cooperative education work stations can be done well only with the aid of detailed inspection lists. Several sample inspection checklists are shown here. The first National Standard School Shop Safety Inspection List (Fig. 13-14) was prepared by the "Joint Safety Committee" of the American Vocational Association and the National Safety Council. The following areas of concern are treated:

A. General Physical Conditions
B. Housekeeping
C. Equipment
D. Electrical Installation
E. Gas
F. Personal Protection
G. Instruction
H. Accident Records
I. First Aid

The State of Oregon Fire Prevention Inspection List (Fig. 13-15) is utilized by a state fire prevention inspector. This inspection assesses three general categories which are grouped according to flammable liquids, housekeeping, and fire extinguishers. The State of Oregon General Safety Inspection List (Fig. 13-16) is a guideline for evaluating general industrial safety practices. Emphasis is placed upon evaluation of the categories; fire protection, housekeeping, hand power tools, and unsafe practices.

The inspection checklist which is used in a given situation should be compatible with overall safety program policy. The foremost concern is that an appropriate checklist is actually (and not perfunctorily) used in inspections. The teacher should not attempt an inspection without the aid of written guidelines. It is impossible to commit to memory all the many facets of an accident prevention program. Action to remedy observed unsafe or hazardous conditions must be taken immediately. Infraction should be reported up the organizational hierarchy, accompanied by completed, planned, or proposed corrections.

STUDENT OBSERVATION

Regular observation of learner work methods in laboratory or cooperative education work stations is as important as facilities inspection. The instructor and the safety foreman should make frequent, scheduled

STATE OF OREGON FIRE PREVENTION INSPECTION LIST		
Location	Agency	Date of Inspection
Inspected By	Page 1	No. Items Requiring Correction
Names of Persons Responsible for Follow-up	2	
	3	
	4	

	Item	ok	not ok	Action Required
Flammable Liquid	Approved safety container for storage & dispens.			
	Pressure relief dev.			
	Bung vents			
	Approved faucets			
	Approved pumps			
	Drip pans in place			
	Extinguisher nearby			
	Safety solvent considered			
	Minimum supply stored inside			
	Approved storage by fire department			
	No gasoline in print shops			
	No gasoline used in cleaning			
	Not stored In sun			
	Drums grounded			
	No smoking signs			
	Bond straps			
	Chemical compatibility			
	Dip tank safety devices			
	Paint spray operations			
	Approved storage by fire department			
	Properly labeled			
House-keeping	Oil rags—storage			
	Solvent contaminated paper in approved containers			
	Rags in approved container			
Fire Extinguishers	Clear access			
	Inspection tag—current			
	Properly mounted & secure			
	Proper type			
	Safety pin intact			

Courtesy—State of Oregon (Salem, State Accident Insurance Fund)

Fig. 13-15

STATE OF OREGON GENERAL SAFETY INSPECTION LIST		
Location	Agency	Date of Inspection
Inspected By	Page 1	No. Items Requiring Correction
Names of Persons Responsible for Follow-up	2	
	3	
	4	

	Item	ok	not ok	Action Required
Fire Protection	Exits			
	Doors—escape hardware			
	Hoses			
	Extinguishers—charged			
	Fire drills—date last held			
	Alarms			
	Smoke detectors			
	Storage of flammables			
	Approved wiring			
	Emergency lights			
	Emergency power systems			
Housekeeping	Storage—stacking of material			
	Stairways—halls			
	Basements			
	Attics-closets			
	Under stairways			
	Waste disposal			
	General cleanliness			
	Outside storage areas			
	Parking lots			
	Shops-laboratories			
Hand Power Tools	Mechanical condition			
	Properly grounded			
	Safe storage			
	Condition of wires-plugs			
	Proper tools for job			
	Proper guards			
	Powder activated-approved			
Unsafe Practices	Smoking in prohibited areas			
	Horseplay			
	Running in buildings			
	Failure to use protective equipment			
	Operating at unsafe speed			
	Removing warning notice			
	Removing a machine guard			

Courtesy—State of Oregon (Salem, State Accident Insurance Fund)

Fig. 13-16

tours, looking for unsafe work habits. The majority of accidents occur as a result of one or a combination of the following:[1]

A. Operating without authority.
B. Willful disregard of or failure to follow instructions.
C. Working without proper instruction.
D. Inattention to job.
E. Working in a hazardous position.
F. Failure to wear recommended protective equipment.
G. Unsafe handling or placing of materials.
H. Operating vehicles in an unsafe manner.
I. Using improper or defective tools or equipment.
J. Working or operating at an unsafe speed.
K. Working with safety devices made inoperable.
L. Failure to secure work.
M. Repairing equipment while it is in operation.
N. Distracting co-workers or engaging in "horseplay."
O. Running in buildings and shops.
P. Failure to report unsafe conditions.

ACCIDENT REPORTING

The last phase of a safety program is planning a system for investigating and reporting accidents. Written policy for accident investigation serves the dual purpose of determining cause and assisting in prevention of similar occurrences. A representative accident investigation scheme follows:

A. Go directly to accident victim.
B. Assure that proper medical treatment is afforded the injured.
C. Gather information from the injured and from witnesses.
D. Complete an accident report form. See the Supervisor's Accident Investigation Report (Fig. 13-17).
E. Investigate probable cause.
F. Take action to correct unsafe conditions.

The system by which accident reports are stored for future use is essential to effective analysis and control of accidents. All instructional areas should utilize the same forms for reporting and the same system for storing accident information. Meaningful reports help the safety organization to (a) identify areas of high accident occurrence, (b) determine

---

[1] George Wolnez, *Occupational Accident & Fire Prevention Program For Oregon State Agencies* (Salem, Ore.: Executive Dept. 1972), p. 14.

SUPERVISOR'S ACCIDENT INVESTIGATION REPORT

State Agency_____ Division or Unit_____ Date Reported To Supervisor_____

Name of Injured Employee_____Occupation_____
Date of Injury_____Hour___a.m.___p.m. Exact Location_____
Witnesses (1)_____ (2)_____

Body Part Injured		Nature of Injury		Action
Face or head	Fingers	Wounds	Amputation	First Aid
Eyes	Legs	Strain or sprain	Burns	Doctor's Care
Trunk	Toes or foot	Hernia	Foreign body	Lost Time
Arms	Internal	Fracture	Skin (occ)	
Back	Lungs			
Knee	Hands			

Remarks:_____ Remarks:_____ Remarks:_____

ACCIDENT:
Describe accident; include the machine, object or substance involved, all details—use back of form if necessary.

_____

_____

CAUSE:

UNSAFE ACTS
1. ☐ Operating without authority
2. ☐ Operating at unsafe speed
3. ☐ Making safety devices inoperative
4. ☐ Using unsafe equipment or equipment unsafely
5. ☐ Unsafe loading, placing, or mixing
6. ☐ Taking unsafe position
7. ☐ Working on moving or dangerous equipment
8. ☐ Distraction, teasing, horseplay
9. ☐ Failure to use personal protective devices
10. ☐ Other:_____

UNSAFE CONDITIONS
1. ☐ Inadequately guarded
2. ☐ Defective tools, equipment or substance
3. ☐ Hazardous arrangement
4. ☐ Improper illumination
5. ☐ Improper ventilation
6. ☐ Unsafe clothing
7. ☐ Unguarded
8. ☐ Unsafe design or construction
9. ☐ Other: _____

Fill Out Claim Form (WCR Form 801)
if medical or time loss is involved.

Why was the unsafe act committed?_____

Why did the unsafe condition exist?_____

PERSONAL DEFECTS:
General observations (attitude, lack of knowledge or skill, physical deficiency)

BACKGROUND:
Are there any contributing factors other than job related?_____

Immediate Supervisor:_____Employee:_____
Safety Supervisor:_____

Courtesy—State of Oregon (Salem, State Accident Insurance Fund)

Fig. 13-17

causes of accidents, and (c) improve the several levels of the safety system.

Establishment of a comprehensive accident prevention program is a main step toward fulfillment of moral and ethical responsibilities regarding pupil safety. A safety program is also the first line of defense against litigation resulting from injuries in the educational environment.

MATERIALS AND FACILITIES MANAGEMENT

A sound resource management plan is essential to good education. Learning environments cannot continue to be suited to changing career education needs unless they are managed according to plan. An orderly procedure for management of materials and facilities requires:

A. Assessment of current and predicted material needs.
B. Sound fiscal planning.
C. Simplification of practices.
D. Maximum facility utilization.

A materials and facilities management policy can be determined by analysis of guidelines set forth by various controlling bodies. Federal, state, district, and building policies suggest procedures for managing materials and facilities. Characteristics of the career program also suggest procedures. The features which have most to do with facilities management are: (a) long-term career program goals, (b) the level of career programs, and (c) specific learning experience objectives.

Clear and concise understanding of goals and activities at respective career education levels in the total program enable the planner to develop the following:

A. Ongoing and accurate inventory systems.
B. Preventive maintenance programs.
C. Budget systems.
D. Requisition and purchase policies.
E. Facility arrangement and utilization plans.

INVENTORY SYSTEMS

Development and implementation of a continuous system for accurate inventory of material resources must be carried out within the established framework of the institution. Many large school districts have sophisticated and in some cases computerized inventory systems. Small districts may have no system at all. Regardless, it is good practice to establish an inventory procedure. Only if some system is given to supply and material inventories can the teacher be certain of having the wherewithal for instructional units.

An inventory plan can also aid and abet operation of a preventive maintenance program and support requests for new resources. In order to lighten his record-keeping load, the wise teacher will enlist the aid of a reliable student or students to assist in inventory activities. Such help is especially valuable where policy requires frequent and detailed inventory of all resources.

Appropriate record forms for machines, tools, supplies, and instructional materials need to be secured or developed by the instructor. Note the typical Machine Inventory Form (Fig. 13-18). Also, note that a single form is used for each piece of equipment. The form describes many features of the machine, such as model and serial number, horse-

MACHINE INVENTORY FORM

Career Level_____
Career Lab._____ Machine Inventory   Instructor_____

Description:_____   Motor_____HP._____Volts_____
Model #_____Serial #_____   RPM_____Belt size_____
Installation Date_____19____   MFG._____
Vendor:_____   Serial #_____
Address:_____
                                    REMARKS
Phone:_____
Cost $_____

Machine Inventory			Accessories & Maintenance			
Date	Condition	Instructor	Date	Description	Cat. No.	Mfg.

Fig. 13-18

power, supplier, and belt sizes. It also provides for description of accessories and accounts for repairs. Whereas it requires a great deal of detail, the form does provide a ready reference for assistance in getting service, parts, or justifying replacement. Note the Simplified Machine Inventory Form (Fig. 13-19). Although quicker and easier to maintain,

SIMPLIFIED MACHINE INVENTORY FORM

Machine Inventory

Career Level_____

Career Laboratory_____   Instructor_____

Machine Description	Vendor	Cost	Date:	Condition	Date:	Condition	Date:	Condition	Date:	Condition

Condition Code   G—Good   F—Fair   P—Poor

Fig. 13-19

it lacks much specific information which may be needed when malfunctions or breakages occur.

Note the sample Tool Inventory Form (Fig. 13-20), Supply Inventory Form (Fig. 13-21), and Instructional Material Inventory Form

TOOL INVENTORY FORM										
Tool Inventory										
Career Level_____ Career Laboratory_____ Instructor_____										
Tool Description	Vendor	Cost	Inventory Dates							
			Date:	Condition	Date:	Condition	Date:	Condition	Date:	Condition
Condition Code G—Good F—Fair P—Poor										

Fig. 13-20

(Fig. 13-22). The extent to which each form should be modified is subject to individual district policy.

PREVENTIVE MAINTENANCE PROGRAMS

Closely allied to inventory practices is preventive maintenance. Information from inventory record forms can be applied to a general maintenance chart (Preventative Maintenance Chart). The maintenance schedule illustrates graphically when each machine and specific components are due to be serviced (Fig. 13-23). Students can assist in the

SUPPLY INVENTORY FORM										
Supply Inventory										
Career Level_____										
Career Laboratory_____			Instructor_____							
			Inventory Dates							
Description	Vendor	Cost	Date:	Condition	Date:	Condition	Date:	Condition	Date:	Condition
Condition Code G—Good F—Fair P—Poor										

Fig. 13-21

conduct of a maintenance program. Maintenance can facilitate pupil interest and motivation in the care and use of all resources.

BUDGET SYSTEMS

Teachers are more and more involved in the preparation of budgets. The two major features of a budget are capital expenditures and operating expenses. Decisions regarding each of these require examination of current and predicted career program needs. Much necessary information can be derived from the five-year career education plan described

INSTRUCTIONAL MATERIAL INVENTORY FORM										
Inventory										

Career Level_____
Career Laboratory_____   Instructor_____

Description	Vendor	Cost	Inventory Dates							
			Date:	Condition	Date:	Condition	Date:	Condition	Date:	Condition
Condition Code G—Good F—Fair P—Poor										

Fig. 13-22

in Chapter 3. Resource requirements can be readily identified through analysis of the population to be served, overall career program goals, objectives at several career education levels, and objectives of specific learning options. Preparation of a long-range budget involves projecting needs for equipment, tools, instructional materials, supplies, and services.

The Five-Year Projected Program Budget (Fig. 13-24) is a form which will assist in fiscal planning activities. Based upon requirements of current and projected career education experiences, it provides a picture of resource needs and estimated costs over an extended period

PREVENTATIVE MAINTENANCE CHART												
MACHINE	jan.	feb.	mar.	apr.	may	june	july	aug.	sept.	oct.	nov.	dec.
completed												
completed												
completed												
completed												
completed												
completed												
completed												

Fig. 13-23

FIVE-YEAR PROJECTED PROGRAM BUDGET

CAREER LEVEL _____

LEARNING OPTION _____ INSTRUCTOR _____

(title)

YEAR	EQUIPMENT	Cost	TOOLS	Cost	INSTRUCTIONAL MATERIALS	Cost	SUPPLIES	Cost	SERVICES	Cost
1										
total										
2										
total										
3										
total										
4										
total										
5										
total										

Fig. 13-24

of time. Such planning facilitates orderly development of career programs, addition of new resources, and replacement of outdated and worn equipment. It also facilitates additions and deletions as requirements change. A well-prepared long-range budget will do much to impress supervisors and program administrators with the necessity to improve learning experiences at all levels of the career continuum.

REQUISITION AND PURCHASE POLICIES

Policies for procurement of material resources is a logical extension of a well-prepared, long-term budget. The teacher or educational manager who follows a long-range plan will be better able to determine:

A. When to purchase.
B. What to purchase.
C. Where to purchase.

Timing is a critical aspect of the procurement process. If needs can be anticipated well enough in advance of utilization, much human energy and substantial sums can be saved. When material and supply needs are projected over a period of time, great savings can be effected through purchase of sales merchandise. This is especially applicable to large districts or institutions where savings are realized through purchase of large lots.

Determining exactly what to purchase is a critical phase of the entire procurement process. Specifications for machines and other items should be written with knowledge of:

A. Career program goals.
B. Career program level.
C. Learner characteristics.
D. Available monies.

Before any piece of equipment or tool is considered for purchase, it should be criticized for appropriateness to the career learning option for which it is intended. It must likewise be appropriate to the specific career level at which it will be used. Equipment and materials should be appropriate to both the physical and mental maturity level of the range of learners who will utilize them.

Equipment which is under consideration for a given career level should be carefully analyzed in terms of the following:

A. Program requirements
B. Capabilities
C. Life-expectancy

D. Accuracy range
E. Required operator characteristics
F. Safety features
G. Maintenance, reliability, and servicing
H. Setup requirements
I. Cost of operation
J. Comparative cost of owning, leasing, or renting
K. Total worth

These must be weighed, one against the others, before selection.

Materials to be purchased for use at a specific career level and in a given learning option should be analyzed according to:

A. Program objective and requisites
B. Workability
C. Waste
D. Cost

There are many suppliers of educational equipment and instructional supplies. It is often difficult to select a vendor. Obviously, it is desirable to deal with dependable and reputable vendors who provide quality merchandise, prompt and courteous service, reasonable delivery, and competitive prices.

Surplus items made available by Federal and state agencies are an alternate source of instructional hardware and software. Sometimes bargains can be found in the surplus yards. However, such material deserves especially careful examination. A low-priced surplus item may require so many repairs that it is not really a bargain. Surplus gear may also be incompatible with the existing facility. For example, such features as thread sizes, voltage ratings, and overall size may prohibit use of inexpensive equipment and materials. To acquire the kind of equipment and tools needed, the teacher must provide the business officer with detailed specifications. This is ordinarily accomplished through use of an equipment or tool requisition form. See Purchase Requisition Form (Fig. 13-25). A request for educational hardware or software should include specifications of the number of items needed, unit price, item description, total costs, and alternate vendors. Exact specifications are essential. They assure that an inferior product cannot be substituted. Note the completed Equipment Request Form (Fig. 13-26).

FACILITY ARRANGEMENT AND UTILIZATION PLANS

Arranging and scheduling career learning facilities is essential to maximizing pupil mastery of objectives at rates commensurate with in-

PURCHASE REQUISITION FORM

Requisition Form

Career Level_____   Date_____

Career Laboratory_____   Instructor_____

Alternate Vendors   Justification

_____
_____
_____
_____

QUANTITY	DESCRIPTION	UNIT PRICE	AMOUNT

Requested by_____ Approved by_____

_____

Fig. 13-25

dividual interests and abilities. Efficient arrangement of workplaces and adequate control of environmental conditions do much to maximize any educational experience. Learners and workers function more effectively and enthusiastically in pleasant and healthful surroundings. Everyone likes to learn and work in a facility which is well organized, safe, and cheerful. Effort to provide such environmental conditions will be rewarded with improved student morale and more efficient learning experiences.

EQUIPMENT REQUEST FORM

TO:　　Harold Robbins, Career Education Director

From:　Sharon Little

Topic:　Year two of five year projected equipment
　　　　requirements
　　　　Purchase of 12 adjustable typing stations

Justification:

> These tables will replace 12 - 20 year old
> wooden typing stations which are no longer
> sturdy enough to support typewriters.
> Replacement of this furniture was unanimously
> recommended by the steno-secretarial advisory
> committee.
> Through purchase of this furniture the steno-
> secretarial staff will be better able to offer
> first-rate career learning experiences for
> the youngsters of this district.

Specifications:

> Tops:
> > 5/8 inch thick, Birch plywood and plastic
> > laminate finish
>
> Frames:
> > 16 gauge welded steel - Beige
>
> Glides:
> > 1 inch diameter rubber, all adjustable
>
> Adjustment range:
> > Platforms adjustable from 26" to 30" high
>
> Accessories:
> > Heavy-duty outlet box containing three-
> > wire receptacles - 10 amp. 120 volt
> > capacity @ $12.00 per station

Price:　　　　　　　　　　　　Vendors:

　$ 95.00 each　　　　　　　　Hometown Office Supply
　$ 12.00 each accessories　　Sears
　$107.00 each　　　　　　　　Clayton Brothers
　　　　　　　　　　　　　　　Barkley, Inc.

Fig. 13-26

The following determine a facility's appropriateness to the conduct of career education activities:

A. General safety conditions.
B. Cleanliness and housekeeping.
C. Placement of work stations and machines.
D. Size of work areas.
E. Human and material flow patterns.
F. Adequacy and security of storage areas.
G. Clean-up facilities.
H. Heating, lighting, ventilation, and other utilities.
I. Color conditioning.

Safety is a foremost consideration in determining suitability of any facility. The general physical condition of the facility, housekeeping practices, equipment, and electrical installations must conform to accepted local and state safety and fire prevention standards. Machines, equipment, benches, and other work stations should be arranged in a manner which facilitates safe and orderly flow of people and materials. Work areas should be large enough to allow learners freedom of movement without endangering fellow students. Work stations and equipment should be of the kind, size, and quantity appropriate for use at given career education levels. Sufficient storage and warehousing areas should be provided to assure safety to projects, experiments, and the entire facility.

Even in the most modern facility, the teachers must be aware of heating, cooling, lighting, and other facilities. Instructors and students need to work in a climate which is comfortable and free of dust, fumes, and noise. Proper illumination throughout the facility and especially in selected areas is essential to safety and learning. Excessive noise must be minimized and/or eliminated. In some cases, special utilities such as gas, compressed air, electricity, etc., are necessary to career learning activities. Learners and teachers also require convenient washroom and sanitary facilities which enable them to prepare for, as well as clean up after learning activities.

The interior of the facility should create an atmosphere conducive to learning and work. Attention to color conditioning of walls, ceilings, work areas, machines, and tool storage racks can add to the attractiveness of the facility. Likewise, bright and cheery bulletin boards, planning areas, and display cases can encourage learning and work.

Publications which provide valuable information for facilities planning and design include *A Guide for Planning Facilities for Occupational Preparation Programs for:*

Dental Laboratory Technicians
Dental Assistants
Laboratory Animal Science Technology
Dental Hygienists
Data Processing
Automotive Service
Home Economics*

A final concern is scheduling facilities for maximum utilization. Career education facilities are most efficient when they are used on a continuous basis from morning to night, six days a week, and twelve months of the year. Maximum utilization involves judicious concerns, which include:

A. Scheduling
B. Supervision
C. Maintenance
D. Cleanup

A comprehensive facility use plan is essential. The plan will include provisions for scheduling the facility for individuals and groups. It must also assign qualified staff authority for supervision of learning activities. Specific responsibility must be delegated for facility upkeep and maintenance and regular cleanup. Provision must be made for the coordination of many and varied activities. Whereas continuous facility use poses many problems, it is a necessary part of a totally articulated program of career education.

SUMMARY

This chapter has answered the following questions:

1. What elements should be considered in the design of an instructional data collection, storage and retrieval system?

A plan for collecting learner and institutional data must provide for efficient assessment techniques, meeting of critical target dates, and efficient and effective information storage and retrieval methods.

2. How should student personnel services be described within a total managerial policy?

Written policy must clearly and concisely define procedures for administration of plans dealing with (a) student progress, (b) classroom,

---

* All available from the Center for Vocational & Technical Education, Ohio State University, Columbus, Ohio.

laboratory, and cooperative work experiences, (c) tool and equipment utilization, (d) cleanup practices, (e) fees collection, and (f) safety procedures.

3. How should policies regarding safety and safety education be described within a total managerial policy?

A comprehensive accident and fire prevention program for all levels of career program should have administrative support, an assigned director or coordinator, objectives, and a thorough program of safety instruction. It will also include provisions for periodic safety inspections, analysis of job safety practices, and a system for investigation, reporting, and recording of accidents.

4. How should material and facility management procedures be described within a total managerial plan?

A comprehensive managerial plan will provide for (a) assessment of current and predicted material needs, (b) sound fiscal planning, (c) simplification of procurement, and (d) maximum facility utilization.

ACTIVITIES

1. Obtain several different kinds of forms used by school districts to gather information about their students. In writing, compare/contrast each of the forms.
2. Observe alternate personnel systems currently operating within several school districts. Write out your own pupil personnel system. Use what you think is the best material from each of the observed systems.
3. Study several methods of handling pupil behavior and write out alternate techniques which you feel will work for you.
4. Review various sources dealing with pupil behavior and write out those aspects which are in opposition to those illustrated in this chapter.
5. Observe various learning situations which employ different pupil progress reporting techniques. Analyze each method and write out a progress reporting plan which you would like to use. Be prepared to defend your selection.
6. Observe a teacher who conducts a highly structured career learning activity. Then observe one who utilizes an unstructured organizational format. In writing, compare/contrast the observed effects of each method.
7. Investigate alternate laboratory fee collection techniques and report your findings in writing.

8. Carefully read Public Law 91-596, "The Occupational Safety and Health Act" and write out what you see to be the implication this act holds for career education.

9. Invite the safety director from a local industry to speak to your class on accident and fire prevention. Take notes on his presentation and summarize what you feel to be the most important message in his speech.

10. Observe an in-plant industrial safety program. Write out those aspects which you feel could be applied to career learning activities.

11. Visit a career education laboratory which has an on going comprehensive safety program in operation. Analyze its many characteristics and incorporate the best points into a safety program of your own design.

12. Write to the National Safety Council for literature pertaining to your teaching specialty.

13. Prepare a collection of inventory, maintenance, requisition, and budget record forms. Review each and select those which you feel will best enable you to manage both material and facility resources. Be prepared to defend your choice.

14. Prepare a set of written guidelines which you feel will enable you to make maximum use of available instructional materials, equipment, and physical facilities.

15. Invite a school administrator to speak to your class on the topic of "fiscal planning." Take notes on the presentation and summarize the most important aspects of his speech.

DISCUSSION QUESTIONS

1. In what ways can a comprehensive, written managerial policy serve to enhance achievement of career education goals at every continuum level? Be specific in your responses.

2. Of what importance is a system for efficient and accurate collection of learner and institutional data?

3. Discuss the major barriers to effective collection, analysis, storage, and retrieval of educational information.

4. Of what consequence is an effective pupil personnel system to achievement of selected career goals?

5. Discuss the pros and cons of displaying pupil progress charts in a well-traveled portion of the career laboratory.

6. Discuss the advantages and disadvantages of using a detailed personnel organization and chart versus an individual self-regulating plan.

7. Compare/contrast the merits of a teacher-prepared and -enforced set of behavioral regulations versus student-initiated and -regulated guidelines.
8. What factors must be considered when initiating behavioral guidelines?
9. Discuss the pros and cons of the alternate disciplinary actions listed within this chapter.
10. What are the foremost barriers to establishment of a comprehensive accident and fire prevention program? How do you propose to overcome them?
11. How can you best enlist the aid and cooperation of learners in your quest for implementation of a total career education safety program?
12. Discuss the relationships existing between inventory practices, fiscal planning, procurement procedures, and maximum facility utilization.
13. What do you see as being the greatest barriers to achieving full facility utilization? How can these hurdles be overcome?

BIBLIOGRAPHY

American Association of School Administrators, *Planning America's School Buildings*. Washington, D.C.: The Association, 1960.
American Industrial Arts Association. *A Guide for Equipping Industrial Arts Facilities*. 1201 - 16th Street, Northwest, Washington, D.C. 20036, 1967.
Chase, Brown, Russo. *Basic Planning Guide for Vocational and Technical Education Facilities*. Washington, D.C.: Department of Health, Education, and Welfare, United States Government Printing Office, 1965.
Conrad, M. J., Wohlers, E. E., and Griggs, Norman. *School Plant Planning: An Annotated Bibliography*. Columbus, Ohio: The Administration and Facilities Unit, School of Education, The Ohio State University, 1968.
Finchum, R. N. *Extended Use of School Facilities*. Washington, D.C.: United States Department of Health, Education, and Welfare, 1967.
Heinrich, Herbert William. *Industrial Accident Prevention*. New York: McGraw-Hill, 1959.
Larson, John C. *The Human Element in Industrial Accident Prevention*. New York: New York University, 1955.
Leaf, Monro. *Safety Can Be Fun*. Philadelphia: Lippincott, 1961.
McMahon, Gordon G. *Planning Facilities for Occupational Education Programs*. Columbus, Ohio: Merrill, 1972.
National Council on School House Construction. *N.C.S.C. Guide for Planning Plants*. East Lansing, Michigan: The Council, 1964.
National Safety Council. *Accident Prevention Manual for Industrial Operations,* Sixth Edition. Chicago, Ill.: The Council.
"Occupational Safety and Health Standards," *Federal Register*, Volume 36, number 105, May 29, 1971, p. 10466-10714.

Stevell, Wallace H., and Burke, Arvid J. *Administration of the School Building Program*. New York: McGraw-Hill, 1959.

Stratemeyer, Clara Georgeanna. *Accident Research for Better Safety Teaching*. Washington, D.C.: National Education Association, 1964.

United States Department of Health, Education, and Welfare. *A Guide to Improving Safety Education Programs in School Shops*. Washington, D.C.: Office of Education, Circular Number 616, 1960.

Williams, Wm. A., ed. *Accident Prevention Manual For Shop Teachers*. Chicago: American Technical Society, 1963.

Wilson, Russell E. *Flexible Classrooms—Practical Ideas for Modern Schoolroom*. Detroit, Mich.: Carter Company, 1953.

Index